To the memory of my Mum & Dad.

William Cooper:

'I were a socialist. We socialists wanted to make a city of brotherhood, a city of light on a hill for all to see, free from poverty and crime and meanness. Is there such a city yet?'

From the film *Men of Rochdale* 1944.

A City of Light

Socialism, Chartism and Co-operation – Nottingham 1844

Christopher Richardson

Loaf On A Stick Press
Nottingham

A City of Light

Socialism, Chartism and Co-operation – Nottingham 1844

Christopher Richardson

www.acityoflight.wordpress.com
acityoflight@phonecoop.coop

Published by

www.peopleshistreh.wordpress.com
peopleshistreh@riseup.net

Published Nottingham May 2013
1st reprint October 2013
2nd reprint June 2014
3rd reprint December 2014

Printed by Russell Press Ltd

Russell House
Bulwell Lane
Basford
Nottingham
NG6 0BT
www.russellpress.com

Generously supported by the
Nottinghamshire Local History Association

ISBN 978-0-9569139-4-4

Contents

Illustrations

Acknowledgements

I should like to thank Stephen Yeo for his constant support and encouragement and for the Foreword; Philipp K. for his encouragement, support, and for the many hours of dedicated and meticulous work on editing, layout and design; Robert Howard for constructing the street map; Anthony Blane, Ange Taggart, Anthony Gariff, Susan Griffiths and Roger Clayton-Pearce for their helpful advice along the way; Trevor Foulds for leading me to Blidworth; Peter Hoare for exchanging information on Operatives' Libraries; Pam Hupner for exchanging information on her great grandfather Henry Knight.

Thanks are also due to the staff at Nottinghamshire Archives and Nottingham Local Studies Library, and libraries and archives at Nottingham University, the Co-operative College, London School of Economics, Salford Museum and Local Studies Library, Working Class Movement Library in Salford, People's History Museum in Manchester, Bishopsgate Institute, British Library and National Archives.

For coping with the 'eureka moments' of joyful discoveries and the periodic miseries that have accompanied this book over the past three years special thanks go to my partner Richard.

Christopher Richardson
Nottingham
May 2013

Christopher Richardson has lived in the Lenton area of Nottingham for more than forty years and been an active member of the Co-operative movement for almost as many. He has a B.A. (Hons) degree in History and Politics from the University of Warwick.

Foreword

There are many ways of marginalising a first-class work of history of the kind that Chris Richardson has produced for us, whether we work for a new moral world, live in Nottingham, are interested in what they call History at school, or not.

Merely 'local' history? But all history is located. It is just that some professional historians pretend to a detached, as-if-universal voice. Chris is scrupulously fair, celebrates the fact that his book comes from a famous Midlands town (just like The Making of the English Working Class by E P Thompson came from the West Riding of Yorkshire) and identifies with the struggle for a co-operative politics in which the word 'social' is strong enough to include and challenge the word 'economic'. We need work like this now, more than ever before in human history. We need the movements given new life in this book, against any idea that 'there is no alternative' to the values which rule our lives now.

I was going to write that Chris has 'dug up', rather than produced this book for us, but it is not like that. His book is an excellent example of self-publishing, with necessary help from friends. He has indeed dug deep into every available source to put this story together: local and national newspapers; correspondence like the Robert Owen letters and the G J Holyoake papers which are held in Manchester by the Co-operative College for the Co-operative Heritage Trust; archive collections, academic and public; the work of historians of Nottingham regardless of their particular interests; and the rich body of labour and social history on radical and working-class ideas and movements which the last sixty years of committed work by historians, professional and otherwise, has made available.

The material in this book on Church Rates; on the many Operatives' Libraries, Halls and reading rooms in Nottingham; on the struggle for a 'free press' measured by how many people and what opinions have access to print rather than by the twenty-first century 'free' license for global corporations to make giant profits; on the Democratic Chapel; and on what inclusive social and political education can mean... all this is fresh and invaluable. So is Chris's recovery of local Chartism and Owenite socialism. Above all else it is the intricate overlaps between all this cultural creativity that this book uncovers.

Chris follows trails of evidence wherever they lead, cleverly discovering local Owenite emigrants to the Ridott community in Illinois. He has also built the book well, taking great care to make the structure, radiating out from 1844, clear and coherent. He listens carefully to socialists and to those who tried to put them down as infidels. He quotes Co-operators, Radicals, Feminists and Land Planners, followers as well as leaders, and gives space to those who were terrified of people thinking and acting for themselves, as well as to those who believed that a new moral world could be constructed step by step from an ugly, competitive, displacing capitalism. Twenty-first century Co-operators are still working for the same cause.

Hopefully schools and colleges will use this book, taking students back to the sources to follow their own enthusiasms. As was said in the Nottingham Review in October 1847, citing the Fourth Annual Report of the Radford Operatives' Library, 'this proves that where the working classes take their affairs into their own hands, they and they alone know how best to manage them'. One day we WILL have a global (Owenites preferred the word 'universal') 'Social Festival', when we celebrate the Association of All Classes and All Nations for which Chris's Nottingham citizens worked.

Stephen Yeo

Oxford

May 2013

Since leaving Ruskin College as Principal in 1997 Stephen has worked mainly with the Co-operative College in Manchester. He chaired the Board of Management during the move back to Holyoake House alongside Co-ops UK, and now chairs the Co-operative Heritage Trust which is busy giving new life to the Pioneers' Museum in Rochdale and to the National Co-operative Archive. He continues to write about the past and present of co-operation and mutuality among other things.

Introduction

Why has this book been written, was Nottingham really a 'City of Light', and what has 1844 got to do with it? You have read this far so you must at least be curious. A few explanations would be as a good place as any to begin.

Three years ago I read that a People's Histreh group would be holding a meeting on Feargus O'Connor and Chartism. Although I had lived in the city for many years this was the first I had heard of the group and, having a long-standing interest in working class history, I set off on a cold February evening to find out more. From time to time I had idly wondered where the Chartist 'Democratic Chapel' had been and the event prompted me to stop wondering and do some research. From there the project developed, and this book is the result.

The structure of this book – taking issues that were to the fore in a particular year and tracing their sources and outcomes – I owe to a suggestion by Professor Stephen Yeo. The choice of 1844 as the reference point was mine. It was a year of change and transition as Owenite socialism went into decline and Chartism changed character and direction with the Land Plan. These trends were particularly noticeable in Nottingham. In that year all of the important struggles described in these chapters were being played out in the town and the surrounding areas.

Nottingham in 1844 was a town of some 53,000 people, more than 40,000 of them crowded together in the narrow streets and yards around the Market Place and in the parish of St Mary. Houses, inns and gin shops, brothels and workshops, were packed together in scarcely more than half a square mile. Framework knitting and lace making were the most numerous occupations, around 25% of the town's population being dependent upon framework knitting alone[1].

Outside the town boundaries were other settlements which would one day form part of the present day City, and towns and villages of Nottinghamshire beyond, where framework knitters and lace workers frequently formed common cause with their brothers and sisters in the town, creating trade union branches, co-operative societies, opened meeting rooms and libraries, organised schools, held festivals and

---

[1] *Some Organisational and Cultural Aspects of the Chartist Movement in Nottingham,* James Epstein, 1982.

anniversary dinners, talked, marched, argued, and sometimes even bore arms.

The biggest political movement of the time was Chartism and the town and county of Nottingham are well known for having been one of the main centres of the movement for the six points of the People's Charter.[2] The town has the distinction of having been represented by Feargus O'Connor, the only Chartist MP ever to be elected to Parliament. Chartism has held a fascination for historians of the labour movement ever since, as the first mass, organised working class movement in Britain during a period of revolutionary ferment in Europe. Accordingly most aspects of Chartism have been scrutinised in great detail. There are several published accounts of local Chartism and I have made no attempt to cover the same ground as these.[3] This is not a book about Chartism. Chartists and Chartism do, however, occupy central roles in most of the stories here.

Campaigns against the New Poor Law and against compulsory Church rates were, in many towns, the prelude to the forming of Working Mens' Associations and branches of the National Charter Association. Other activities and campaigns, such as the friendly societies, temperance and freethought, had fewer, if any, formal links with the Chartist movement. Nevertheless, they had common origins in the life of the working class in the city, and were taken up at a time when the people's right to representation in the political life of the country was disputed by the ruling class of the country. They shared hopes of a better future, in which the material conditions of life would improve, education and enlightenment would be free from political and religious restraints, and the stifling patronage of middle class reformers that appears frequently in these chapters would be overcome by a growing independence of thought and action by working class men and women themselves.

'A City of Light' is a term I borrowed to represent those aspirations but is one that, I hope, evokes some of the ideas and idealism of their time.

With 1844 as the reference point, there are struggles here which began

---

[2]   Universal manhood suffrage, secret ballot, abolition of property qualification for MPs, payment of MPs, equal sized constituencies, annually elected Parliaments.

[3]   In particular I would cite *Nottingham Chartism*, Peter Wyncoll, 1966; and *Some Organisational and Cultural Aspects of the Chartist Movement in Nottingham*, James Epstein, 1982.

long before. The resistance to the 'taxes on knowledge' has been taken back to 1819, the origins of Co-operation to 1771, the search for community living to 1827. Associated campaigns and events have been woven into the story, so that the cholera which came to the town in 1832 becomes part of the intertwined stories of underlying ambivalence towards the medical profession, the resistance to the Poor Law and the movement for the People's Charter which are at centre stage for much of 1844 and the years immediately before and after.

And as Nottingham was not an island, local events have often been placed in the context of other events in neighbouring counties, and in London, Salford, Newcastle in particular. And as the resolution of many of the campaigns, such as those against the newspaper tax and the compulsory Church rates, did not take place until many years later, the narrative has been taken forward to conclude the tale.

My particular interest in working class history is the Co-operative Movement, much neglected even among historians of the labour movement. It was inevitable that research into Chartism would lead to links with Co-operation, and so it proved, though not in ways that I had expected. The year 1844 was the year that the Rochdale Society of Equitable Pioneers was founded, considered a landmark in the history of the movement, and that was a further reason for choosing 1844 as the point of reference.

The co-operative model which traces its origins to Rochdale did not appear in Nottingham until 1863, in the suburb of Lenton, but the progress of that society has been used in the Conclusion to trace an ongoing relationship with many of the stories and themes in the chapters of this book. By chance, 1863 was also the year when the Co-operative Wholesale Society was established, in which the Lenton co-operative has long been absorbed.[4] So that's two sesquicentennials to celebrate in 2013. And a new baby too: the Blueprint for a Co-operative Decade, born of the UN International Year of Co-operatives in 2012. May this book be a part of the celebrations and contribute to the work that is still to be done, for that 'city of light upon a hill for all to see' remains beyond our grasp.

This book begins with the visit of a Social Missionary to Nottingham in August 1844. Seek reference to it in the town's newspapers, or in historical

---

[4]   Now known as the Co-operative Group.

accounts of the period, and it will not be found.[5] Were it not for extensive reports in the *New Moral World* it would have all but disappeared from recorded history, and along with it part of that movement which challenged basic tenets of Christianity and Victorian moral doctrines of the time. In recognition of her ideas and her courage it is with Emma Martin that this book will begin.

So, now you know why the book was written, why the 'A City of Light' and why 1844. Perhaps you've also learned a new word as I did (thank you *google*). And did I discover the whereabouts of the Democratic Chapel? Well, you'll just have to read on and find out for yourself. Thank you, dear reader, for travelling with me this far. I hope you enjoy the rest of the trip.

---

[5] Brief mentions of her visit have been inaccurately credited to Leicester. See Edward Royle, *Victorian Infidels*, 1974 and Barbara Taylor, *Eve and the New Jerusalem*, 1993.

Chapter 1: Emma Martin Comes to Nottingham

In the summer of 1844 William Saville, a twenty nine year old labourer from Arnold, was convicted of the murder of his wife and three children in Colwick Woods, on the testimony of a boy who had been collecting birds' eggs in a tree, beneath which Saville slit their throats.

On the 8th of August the hangman's noose was set up on the steps of Shire Hall in High Pavement, in the midst of the most populous part of the town. 'As far as the eye could reach from the scaffold in front of the County Hall, nothing could be seen but a sea of heads.'[6] There being a shortage of spectacles to rival that of a public hanging, the narrow street was thronged:

> 'When the bolt was removed and the body fell, the immense crowd of many thousands of men, woman and children began to move away, and in their hurry, there being no barricades, many were at the top of Garners Hill, and were thrown down, and the rush being uncontrollable, those who fell were trampled on, and at the foot of the steps lay in a great heap, piled one upon another, crushed and lamed or suffocated.'[7]

Scores of people were taken to the General Hospital in carts and wagons, twelve were killed at the spot and five died afterwards, and more than a hundred suffered major or minor injuries.

A week later on Wednesday 14th August 1844 Emma Martin arrived in the town. Emma was one of more than twelve Social Missionaries and her visit was part of a well organised national programme of debates and lectures by the 'Rational Society' to spread the word about the new moral world of socialism.[8] But on her arrival she soon decided to abandon the lecture she had prepared and spoke instead on another controversial and topical theme. Her first address was inspired by the trial of William Saville and the circumstances surrounding his crime and punishment.

At the time of Emma Martin's visit to the town it was the tragedy of the spectators' deaths after William Saville's execution that dominated local

---

[6] *Nottingham Date Book 1750-1850*, R Sutton, 1852.
[7] Ibid.; *History of Colwick*, Alan Cook, 1970.
[8] The Rational Society: Owenite socialists had a predilection for long names. For the sake of brevity their last and shortest has been used in this chapter.

conversation, but Emma Martin chose to make the subject of capital punishment the theme of her lecture. Her audience would have included people who were present at the execution, their eyes and ears still filled with the sight and screams of the crowd and of people falling to their deaths from Garners Hill. Her subject could have been a risky choice, just a week after the execution, with the capacity to generate resentment, anger and violence among the crowd. But Emma Martin 'had wit and the courage of several men, and delivered lectures in the stormiest times and to the most dangerously disposed audiences'[9] and she was not to be diverted by the prospect of a hostile crowd. In the event the lecture passed off without any disorder and was deemed a tremendous success by the socialists present:

> 'She delivered her sermon in the Market Place, where she had the satisfaction of addressing five thousand people, and the mayor, who was present, and who we believe is a liberal man, had the gratification of seeing that although the brutal exhibition of a *public murder*, attended by priestly teachers, may bring together a multitude, that there are other and better who for wiser purposes can gather the people together, and turn their thoughts into nobler channels.'[10]

The socialist weekly journal the *New Moral World* reported the occasion. 'Nature smiled on her efforts to disseminate the glorious truths of rationality, for never did the sun shine with greater refulgence ... and never did the assembled thousands drink in with greater eagerness the knowledge she endeavoured to impart'.[11] Speaking eloquently, and challenging the crowd with her uncommon views, she argued that Saville's crime could be attributed to lack of education and proper training, that crime could not be extinguished by capital punishment. 'Criminals should be kept apart from society, surrounded with good circumstances, instructed, and made useful', she said. 'A great deal of money had been spent in the building of new churches, which were appropriated to no useful purpose whatsoever', she told the crowd, and she trusted the time would soon arrive 'when the people would take possession of them and

---

9   *The History of Co-operation*, G J Holyoake, 1908.
10 *The Movement*, No 38, August 1844 (original emphasis). In the evening she spoke again to another crowd of 5,000 on the subject of bible societies.
11 *New Moral World*, 31st August 1844.

turn them to their own advantage'. Religionists, she told her audience 'taught their dogmas in order to enslave them ... If the people would seek after knowledge ... if they would surround themselves with good circumstance and acquire knowledge, crime and poverty would soon cease'.[12]

An attempt had been made in Parliament in 1841 to ban public executions but it was laughed out of the chamber. After the Saville débacle the Mayor of Nottingham proposed that local executions be moved away from the constricted environment of the County Gaol in High Pavement to a more remote location, but the Home Secretary rejected the proposal. 'The principal objective of capital punishment' he said 'is the terror of example.'[13]

Neither the abolition of public executions nor the abolition of capital punishment were central planks in the socialist programme, but they were a natural outcome of the belief that people were conditioned by their circumstances and that, in the new society which socialism would introduce, the causes of crime would be eradicated. There would be no need for executions, public or otherwise, and maintaining control of the populace by terror would be irrelevant when the people were made intelligent and rational beings. Whilst not all opponents of capital punishment would extend their argument this far, there were others in Nottingham who had, individually, already taken up the cause of abolishing capital punishment. Three had done so publicly and none were socialists: the William Linwood, R T Morrison and William Small.

Mr Linwood, a Unitarian Minister in Mansfield, and a member of the middle class Complete Suffrage Union, often spoke at local meetings with Chartists. The socialists also thought highly of him. 'Mr Linwood is one who speaks out himself, regardless of the consequence, so much so that he has aroused all the holy thunder of both Mansfield and the surrounding neighbourhood about his ears', reported the New Moral World.[14] In June 1844, after the murders by Saville, but before the trial and hanging, speaking to a large audience in the Guildhall, Mr Linwood was 'prepared to show that crime might be prevented by removing the evils which cause

---

[12]   Ibid.
[13]   Hanging in the Balance: A History of the Abolition of Capital Punishment in Britain, B Block and J Hostettler, 1997.
[14]   New Moral World, 1st June 1844.

it' insisting that it was 'the duty of every individual to aim at prevention, rather than the vindictive punishment of crime ... and that crime might be prevented by education ... which would lead to the development of the whole man, and the necessity of clothing, feeding, and lodging the body in comfort.'[15]

The vote of thanks to Mr Linwood was moved by R T Morrison. He had raised the subject of capital punishment in a letter to the *Nottingham Review* two years earlier, remarking on the hypocrisy of 'those who call on the Almighty to have mercy on the deceased *soul* after they have mutilated the body'.[16] A middle class Chartist, though one who did not have the vote, Morrison was critical of those Christians who put the rights of property before natural rights and who, by their opposition to Parliamentary reform, 'deprive one part of the community of a share in making laws ... they cannot be Christians; and oppose the precepts of Christianity'.[17] Despite being a Christian himself he shared with the socialists a belief that character was determined by environment and therefore 'Where is the justice of punishing any party for transgression, unless they are conscious they are acting wrong.'

William Small was another speaker at the Guildhall meeting. He was the Medical Officer for Radford and Lenton who, two years later, would be dismissed from his post for 'rudeness to a patient', a spurious accusation which followed an earlier unsuccessful attempt by the Guardians to remove him. At a public meeting to avert his dismissal it was reported that the grounds were 'ordering beef, wine, and other necessary support for his patients.'[18] James Saunders, by profession a druggist of Denman Street, Radford, and by conviction a Chartist, who had been elected to chair the meeting, had visited all of the Parish Guardians 'and the only reason he had got out of them for removing Mr Small was that he had been "too good to the poor" '.[19] R T Morrison had been present at that meeting too and spoke in support of Small.

In many ways this convergence of views on crime and punishment by socialists and Chartists, dissenting Christians and infidels, middle and

---

15   *Nottingham and Newark Mercury*, 28th June 1844.
16   *Nottingham Review*, 8th July 1842.
17   *Class Legislation Exposed: or Practical Atheism identified with the advocates of Property Qualification for Legislative Enfranchisement*, R T Morrison, 1841.
18   *Nottingham Review*, 11th September 1846.
19   Ibid.

working class men and women, was typical of the ways in which campaigns advanced at this time, participants appearing and reappearing, at times converging or colliding. Religion was frequently at the centre of the collisions.

Although the William Linwood and Emma Martin shared similar views on the causes of crime and the ineffectiveness of capital punishment, they held very different opinions on the role of religion. For one, religion contributed to the solution to criminal behaviour, for the other religion was a contributory cause.

Emma's reputation had spread in recent years throughout Britain and her infidel views were well known among the devout and for that reason she was regarded in some quarters as an unwelcome visitor to the town. Another account of her visit was given in the *New Moral World* by Horace Roche, a socialist from Derby:

> 'During the past week this town [Nottingham] has been disgraced by one of the most flagrant acts of injustice that could be conceived ... Mrs Martin arrived here on Wednesday last, and thinking the excitement caused by the unfortunate accident at the late execution, a good reason why she should endeavour to enlighten the people on the subject of capital punishment, the assembly room was engaged for that purpose; an announcement was immediately issued that Mrs Martin would preach a funeral sermon on Thursday the 15th. We had forgotten that priests had been trained to preach sermons, and that they would consider this an encroachment on their privileges. Priests, however, are not so forgetful; they are ever on the alert to maintain the position of their order, and are peculiarly sensitive when anything of a popular nature occupies public attention. Such was the case in the present instance. A priest entering the building in which the sermon was to be delivered, observed the board announcing the same at the door, he seized the board and carried it into the house, declaring that nothing of the kind should take place there, and that if the landlord did not stop the meeting, he would send the police to do so ... The landlord, frightened almost out of his wits, complied with the demand of the priest, and thus disappointed many hundreds of people. Mrs M was not to be beaten, but immediately intimated her

intention of preaching her sermon in the Market Place, on Sunday afternoon, at three o'clock.[20]

Illustration 1: Assembly Rooms, Low Pavement.
Scene of Emma Martin's banishment in 1844.
All that remains in 2013 is the frontage.

The Assembly Rooms on Low Pavement had long been a place of 'gaiety and refined amusement' but had physically deteriorated to the point where it had been put up for sale in 1800. Wesleyan Methodists had made an attempt to buy it but had been thwarted by 'disciples of the *merry* God' who 'thereby saved the temple from being *polluted* with preaching, exhortations, and prayers'.[21] In 1836 the old building was demolished and 'a splendid new suite of rooms erected on the site, in Grecian style, with pilasters'.[22]

It was not saved, however, from the presumption of the Anglican Vicar at St Mary's, Joshua Brooks, recently appointed to the post at the age of 54,

20 *New Moral World*, 24th August 1844.
21 *The History of Nottingham*, John Blackner, 1815 (original emphasis).
22 *Directory of Nottingham*, White, 1844.

and keen to waste no time in the pursuit of infidels. Seeing an advertisement for Emma's lecture at the Assembly Rooms he had written to the proprietors urging the cancellation of the booking, on the grounds that the proposed low admission charge of 1d would encourage 'all the scum of the town, the sweepings of the streets' to attend.[23]

Illustration 2: Joshua Brooks, Vicar of St. Mary's 1843–1864.
Scourge of Emma Martin.

Emma's choice of subjects – capital punishment and religion – reflected two of her particular concerns, but both were integral to the message of socialism that she brought to Nottingham. It is probably no accident that her visit, attracting one of the largest crowds since Feargus O'Connor's triumphal arrival in the town in February 1842, was not reported by any of the town's newspapers, not even by the *Nottingham Review*, the middle class radical paper which gave regular prominence to Chartist meetings with verbatim reports of speakers' contributions. Chartism, when it was respectable, was regarded as an important ally by the middle class radicals, but socialism and religious infidelity were not.

The only reference to 'the several thousands assembled in the Market Place to hear Mrs Martin expound her infidel tenets' was incidental, in a report by the *Nottingham and Newark Mercury* about a petition presented

---

[23] *Freethought in Nineteenth Century Nottingham*, Robert Morrell, 2010; *Nottingham Review*, 31st August 1844.

to the Mayor and Magistrates to ban public meetings in the Market Place on Sundays:

> 'We are no advocates for the interference with the civil or religious liberties of the people; on the contrary we respect them to the fullest extent; but when we find the preachers of politics, Mormonism, and infidelity, availing themselves of the facilities thus afforded, for giving publicity to their dangerous doctrines, we are sure that the religious and moral portion of the community will unite with us in the opinion, that it would be far better to do away with all "outdoor" preaching than to inflict so great an evil as must follow the propagation of these principles to which we have alluded.'[24]

The petition to the Mayor and magistrates failed, but the limits to freedom of speech that would be countenanced by the Whig elite, for whom the *Mercury* spoke, had been clearly marked. The next intending speaker, the Chartist lecturer from Leicester, Jonathan Bairstow, was banned from lecturing in the Market Place. He had to move his lecture to the Forest, an open space more than half a mile away over the brow of the hill on the Mansfield Road.

---

[24] *Nottingham and Newark Mercury*, 23rd August 1844.

Chapter 2: Owenite Socialism

Socialism as it was understood at that time was associated with the name of Robert Owen, and frequently referred to as Owenism. Its ultimate goal was that people should live harmoniously in a state of community in the pursuit of universal happiness. Of the seven communities established by Owenites, or influenced by Owenite ideas, in the second quarter of the century, only Queenwood at East Tytherley in Hampshire between 1839 and 1846 was the product of Robert Owen and the Universal Community Society of Rational Religionists, or the Rational Society as it was later known, at the head of which Owen had placed himself. This experiment of 'socialism in one county' heralded the beginning of the 'new moral world' and was expected to become so successful that in no time at all it would become the chosen way of working and living for millions of people.

What has disparagingly been called Owen's 'one big idea' was that 'the character of man is without a single exception, always formed for him'.[25] Robert Owen was not one to put names to past influences on his thinking, but the spirit of the Enlightenment was evident in his belief that environmental circumstances determined human behaviour, and that rational human intellect was capable of dealing with irrational inherited influences and reconstructing the world. The greatest obstacles to the achieving the new moral world were seen to be the lack of education and the pattern of family life among the working classes – and religion. But Owen was the perennial optimist and had asserted as early as 1813 that 'Any general character, from the best to the worst, from the most ignorant to the most enlightened, may be given to any community, even to the world at large, by the application of proper means.'[26]

Owenism sought to prepare adults for living in the new moral world through lectures, educational classes, publications, branch meetings, and social activities, by building Social Institutions and Halls of Science where these activities would take place, and by generating funds for the establishment of communities. The *New Moral World* stressed the importance of re-forming the characters of the future inhabitants of the new moral world through social and educational activity: 'Social Festivals

---

[25] *A New View of Society*, Robert Owen, 1813.
[26] Ibid.

to improve the Habits and manners of the Working Classes, and cultivate kind feeling and social fellowship among all classes.'[27] Social Festivals were held every fortnight:

> 'attended by many of superior education and rank in society, who desire to promote an improved conduct among the industrious classes, and who wish them to enjoy a fair share of happiness, believing that to be the easiest and most effectual mode of inducing them to become good and useful members of society'.[28]

Illustration 3: Hall of Science, Manchester.
Meeting place of the Salford and Manchester socialists, including Henry Knight and other Social Missionaries who lectured in Nottingham.

At a price of 1s 6d per ticket the festivals in London were not cheap, but clearly low enough to be open to those uninstructed in the behaviour expected of them. 'Any parties deviating from the rules of propriety, or rational politeness', the article continued, 'have notice given them by the Master of Ceremonies; and, if not attended to, the offending parties are required to withdraw and remain absent until they discover the necessity of "doing to others as they would desire others to do to them".'

What may now appear to be a patronising approach towards working people should be viewed in the context of Owen's belief (not necessarily shared by most of his working class supporters) in uniting all social classes, and socialising a new industrial class in the ways of effective self-

---

[27] *New Moral World*, 20th December 1834.
[28] *New Moral World*, 28th February 1835.

government. This is made clear in an advertisement for Social Festivals in another edition of the *New Moral World*: 'The improvement of the habits and manners of the industrious classes is thus gradually promoted, while the feelings, commonly so prevalent, of envy and ill-will on the one hand, and of contempt and disgust on the other, promise soon to have no place in the assemblies of The Association of All Classes of All Nations.'[29]

Referring to the socialists' educational arrangements for lectures and discussions in London in 1835, the *New Moral World* explains that the lectures by Robert Owen on Sunday evenings are intended to lay 'a solid foundation for another and far superior state of society' and the discussions held on Wednesday and Friday evenings 'have been established to promote a more general knowledge of the principles, but more especially, the practice, of the new state of society which Mr Owen and his friends advocate, and which they believe is rapidly approaching.'[30]

A different approach was taken to the education of children. The declaration that 'Children have never yet been well educated by parents in single-family arrangements; nor is it possible that children should ever have a superior character formed by such parties under such arrangements' led of necessity to rearranging the ways that children lived and were taught.[31] Their education and socialisation would be provided outside of the family.

The child welfare and education regimes for children at the socialist community at Queenwood were first practised in Robert Owen's factory village of New Lanark, in the New Institution for the Formation of Character. It has been said that Owen's enthusiasm for admitting children into the school from the age of one was clearly connected with his wish to reduce parental influence and expose children to new experiences and opinions and, 'just as the private family had to be abolished in the new moral world, so a new and more appropriate concept of childhood was required.'[32] At Harmony Hall in Hampshire, which was built some thirty years later to precise specifications for community living, the children lived away from their parents in dormitories, and the corrupting influences of their families could be more effectively dealt with than at

---

[29] *New Moral World*, 21st February 1835.
[30] *New Moral World*, 28th February 1835.
[31] *New Moral World*, 17th January 1835.
[32] *Robert Owen and the Owenites in Britain and America*, J.F.C. Harrison, 1969.

New Lanark where opposition from parents, or the attentions of the priesthood, had been more difficult to deal with.

Illustration 4: The Theatre, St. Mary's Gate.
Scene of lectures by Robert Owen, socialists and Chartists.
All that remains is this entrance to an electricity sub-station.

The conditions in the community for the formation of character were described enthusiastically by Owen when he spoke at The Theatre in Nottingham in 1840:

> 'rooms for balls, concerts, libraries, and every source of amusement and pleasure, theatre, gardens, hall of science, houses without staircases (the nurses and children to be taken up and let down from the upper apartments with a machine, as at the Colosseum, in London)[33] and the inhabitants are to have gas, hot air, good ventilation, in their rooms and dwellings, and they are to be made by instruction rational and intelligent beings. The external circumstances are to be of such superior description, that they will have an effect upon infants at their birth, nay before they are born that has never yet been witnessed.'[34]

---

[33] *New Picture of London and Visitor's Guide to its Sights*, Edward Mogg, 1844: 'By the aid of machinery that carries a moveable room through the centre of the building, the visitor is raised to a level with the summit of the panorama, and thus spared the trouble of mounting a staircase'. The Colosseum was in Regents Park, London, 1823-1875.

[34] *Nottingham Review*, 3rd July 1840.

The effects of Owen's words among his listeners can only be guessed. Here was a vision of a new world almost beyond imagination, with well-ventilated homes with gas lighting and hot air central heating, the upper floors reached by a lift, the buildings surrounded by parkland. This was not mere wishful thinking. A visitor to Harmony Hall at Queenwood in 1842 found a machine 'which through a tunnel, conveyed the dishes from the kitchen to the door of the dining hall,' while socialist lavatorial arrangements left Friedrich Engels flushed with wonderment: 'In the communist colony at Harmony in England not merely are the water closets, which are so conveniently fitted out in the English fashion, cleaned automatically, but they are also provided with pipes which take the waste directly to the great dung-pit.'[35]

In community living the roles of parents in the lives of their children was being diminished, and hence the need for conventional marriage bonds was being eroded, divorce became a possibility, the rituals surrounding births, marriages and deaths could be rationalised. This was an era when late Victorian standards of family life were only beginning to take shape and such ideas could still be articulated, but the challenge which the Owenite socialist ideas represented did not go unnoticed by their critics.

Emma Martin's conversion had begun when she attended a lecture on the means by which poverty and crime could be entirely removed by the establishment of the co-operative state of society, given by the Social Missionary, Alexander Campbell. 'I listened with riveted attention to so clear an exposition of the evils I had so lamented ... the next evening ... a second lecture ... raised my expectations as to the establishment of human happiness to something like a certainty'.[36] Thenceforth her conversion to socialism was complete and she was soon welcomed into the socialist ranks to spread the gospel of the new moral world.

For her religious opponents, living in community was tantamount to living in sin. 'Oh, the delights of promiscuous intercourse! What an elevation of our "common sense" to live in one universal brothel' cried James Brindley, one of the most persistent of the itinerant Christian

---

[35] *Description of Recently Founded Communist Colonies Still in Existence*, Friedrich Engels, 1845.
[36] *A Few Reasons for Renouncing Christianity and Disseminating Infidel Opinions*, Emma Martin, 1850.

debaters. 'What a pure enjoyment to revel in filthy communication without any restraint'.[37] The fount of all morality was Christianity and the socialists were claiming to create a new morality of their own. This was an intolerable affront to the established Church and the Christian religion. Her message was all the more unwelcome as she had herself been a Baptist preacher, a collector for the Bible Society, proprietor of a Ladies' Seminary, and one who had pitted herself against the socialists in public debate, who had learned all the arts of effective public speaking on behalf of Christianity which she was now using against it.

George Jacob Holyoake described her as 'a small lady, of attractive expression, with dark luminous eyes, a pleasant, far-reaching voice, and a womanly woman'.[38] The strength of her personality and the power of her rhetoric is suggested by a report on her appearance before a church congregation in Salford: 'up rose Mrs Martin, the Socialist lecturer (a woman of rather corpulent dimensions) who has never compressed her chest and waist to the destruction of the viscera within, nor sought to cut off the communication between her head and her heart, since she wants lungs for use not a waist for admiration'.[39] Maybe it was Emma who was responsible for the unattributed article in the *New Moral World* that same year entitled 'The Injurious Effects of Corsets and Tight Lacing' but maybe not.[40] It was after all a subject one would expect from a movement committed to rational ideas and which had been experimenting too with rational dress.[41]

Of all the Social Missionaries and lecturers employed by the Rational Society, Emma Martin was the most fervent in communicating the socialist ideas of reforming marriage and 'single family arrangements', challenging the role played by religion in maintaining outdated and pernicious customs and morals, poisoning the relations between men and women and maintaining women in a state of subjection. 'Who could have

---

[37] *The Marriage System of Socialism*, James Brindley, 1840.

[38] *The History of Co-operation*, G J Holyoake, 1908.

[39] *The Missionary Jubilee Panic and the Hypocrites Prayer addressed to the Supporters of Christian Missions*, Emma Martin, 1844.

[40] *New Moral World*, 3rd August 1844.

[41] Robert Owen had long ago established unisex clothing at the school in New Lanark to establish an equality between the boys and the girls, all of whom wore 'a beautiful dress of tartan cloth, fashioned in its make after the form of a Roman toga'. See *Concept of Popular Education*, Harold Silver, 1965. See illustration in Chapter 10 (p. 144).

palmed such an immense imposture upon mankind?'[42] she asked. 'The object of human existence, in this world, is the production of pleasurable emotions. The test of the morality of an act is in its utility, its tendency to the creation of pleasurable emotions.'[43]

Emma ceased to be a Social Missionary in 1846 after the financial crisis which accompanied the demise of the Queenwood community and which led to the abandonment of paid missionaries and lecturers. She 'dedicated the final years of her life, not simply to women, but to their wombs', reversing the Christian doctrine of creation by personally assisting in the 'fundamental act of creation in childbirth'.[44] After being refused membership of the Royal Maternity Charity on the grounds that she was an atheist, which would have precluded her from offering prayers at the bedside before and after delivery, and unable to find employment as a midwife elsewhere, she practised privately, dying of tuberculosis in October 1851 at the age of 39.[45]

Emma had continued to speak regularly at the Social Institution in Fitzroy Square, London, on subjects as diverse as the religions and laws of the ancient Mexicans and the characters of Robespierre and Marat; and she maintained her campaign against capital punishment to the end of her short life. In 1849 she spoke out against the hanging of a London couple, 'a weak husband and an avaricious wife' (the wife had also been wrongly accused by the press of being an atheist).[46] Her message remained unchanged, conveying the same utilitarianism, humanism and optimism of her missionary past:

> 'We object to the punishment of death because it PREVENTS ALL HOPE OF FUTURE REFORMATION; yet few criminals are so wholly lost as to preclude the expectation that full employment and strict discipline may not mend them. There must be no return to the barbarism of past centuries. No, no, the civilization of the 19th century cannot return to the savage brutality of retributive justice. The principle on which its laws

---

[42] *A Few Reasons for Renouncing Christianity and Disseminating Infidel Opinions*, Emma Martin, 1850.

[43] *Religion Superseded*, Emma Martin, 1850.

[44] *Emma Martin and the manhandled womb in early Victorian England*, D Janes in The Female Body in Medicine and Literature, A Mangham and G Depledge, 2011.

[45] *The Reasoner*, 23rd February 1848.

[46] *The Punishment of Death*, Emma Martin, 1849.

must be modified and continually improved is utility and prevention of crime, not vindictive punishment.'[47]

Illustration 5: Emma Martin.

A moving tribute to Emma Martin was rendered by George Jacob Holyoake, socialist and personal friend. Visiting her two weeks before her death at her home in Finchley:

> 'I never saw her look so beautiful. Her large black eyes were radiant with fire, and the hectic vermilion which suffused her cheeks imparted a superhuman beauty to [her] expression ... as she wished me to speak at the grave I did so. Her desire in this respect was intended to being indicative of her unchanged opinions. ... We have lost the most important woman that stood on our side ... The story we have to tell is brief and sad. A life so useful, closed at 39 years, is dead; yet the sadness has a joy with it. For life is a drama, and, as Mrs Martin herself used to repeat, "it matters not how *long* it has been acted, but how *well*." How well she performed her part we know, and, on that ground, rejoice.'[48]

---

[47] Ibid. (original emphasis). Public executions were abolished in 1868.
[48] *The Last Days of Mrs Emma Martin, Advocate of Freethought*, G J Holyoake, 1851 (original emphasis).

Chapter 3: Nottingham Socialists

Emma Martin's visit to Nottinghamshire in 1844 was not the first by a Social Missionary nor was it the first by a female socialist lecturer. The business of organising the socialist cause in the county had begun in earnest in 1838. From the outset of the central Owenite socialist organisation[49] in 1834 there were moves by supporters to set up branches in other towns. Three years later the *New Moral World* published the first of its regular columns headed 'Progress of Social Reform' with news from the growing number of branches, mainly in the old heartland of the earlier co-operative movement, in Yorkshire and Lancashire. In May 1838 the Congress at Manchester appointed six Social Missionaries to spread the branch network further afield. William Throsby reported tentative moves had already been made to set up a branch in Leicester a few months earlier and Robert Owen gave a series of lectures there in April.

Nottingham was no stranger to the community schemes of Robert Owen. There had been a society in the town in 1827 inspired by the ideas of the 'Co-operative System', nurtured perhaps by the regular reports of the first community in Britain created from Owen's ideas (though not a creation of Owen himself) at Orbiston near Motherwell between 1825 and 1827. Reports from Orbiston had somehow found their way into the *Nottingham Mercury* during the first two years of its publication, when it alone of the three Nottingham weekly newspapers gave space to the progress of Owenite socialism. The society was small in number but functioned as a forum for discussion and for the collection of subscriptions that would one day enable the members to join a community, as a letter from 'J.S.' of Nottingham explained in June 1827. The correspondent – who may have been the same J.S. who reported a secular discussion group at the Rancliffe's Head in a letter to the *Republican* in 1825 – was clearly an Owenite. 'From individual acquisition and private accumulation' he said 'flow nearly all that variety of crime which we behold daily.' From the 'superior advantages of the Co-operative and Communal System of Society' would spring a new society: 'In short, I

---

[49] *Robert Owen and the Owenites in Britain and America*, J F C Harrison, 1969: The British and Foreign Consolidated Association of Industry, Humanity and Knowledge, 1834; Association of All Classes of All Nations, 1835; Missionary and Tract Society, 1837; National Community Friendly Society 1837; Universal Community Society of Rational Religionists, 1839; the Rational Society, 1842.

support the System as a political, moral and religious regenerator.'[50]

Despite the accumulation of problems at Orbiston, largely arising from the haste with which the community had been launched, one of the Superintendents at Orbiston, John Lambe, was able to find the time to travel to Nottingham in October 1827 to meet the members of the society. By this time the Orbiston community was in difficulties from which it was unable to extricate itself, although there is no hint of this in the *Nottingham Mercury*. 'The compact party he met in Nottingham excited feelings of satisfaction ... if no other good has been done, it has enabled several individuals to lay a small proportion of their hard earnings with the intent to make a trial of the system' it reported.[51] By December the community at Orbiston had come to an end, and there were no further mentions of Owen, co-operative communities or the society in Nottingham in the pages of the *Nottingham Mercury*. It was to be another ten years before socialism was organised again in the town.

At the end of July 1838 there was news in the *New Moral World* of a new socialist branch in Nottingham:

> 'I beg to inform you that on Sunday last, we formed a society here, on the views advocated by Owen. Not having a private room, we met at the Stag and Hounds, Count Street, where we shall be compelled to meet until we increase in numbers, which we feel no doubt we shall soon do. We had three friends from Arnold ... who have joined us. Our number is ten ... we should be glad if someone would come to Nottingham to lecture (Mr Owen if possible) ... Yours etc, William Smith, Cross Street, Secretary.'[52]

In late September Robert Buchanan, one of the newly appointed Social Missionaries, set out on a lecture tour including Nottinghamshire and south Yorkshire. He reported to the *New Moral World*:

> 'On Thursday evening, the 6th, I set out for Nottingham ... lectured the same and the following evening, in a large room

---

50 *Nottingham and Newark Mercury*, 30th June 1827. For more on 'J.S.' See Chapter 7: The War of the Unstamped Press.
51 *Nottingham and Newark Mercury*, 27th October 1827; and *Orbiston: The First British Owenite Community 1825-29*, Ian Donnachie, in Spaces of Utopia: An Electronic Journal, No. 2, Summer 2006.
52 *New Moral World*, 11th August 1838.

in Pelham Street on our moral and economical views ... The lectures were rather thinly attended, from the shortness of notice, and the want of any kind of excitement ... about a dozen of our friends have formed themselves into a society, and meet once a week, to read the *NMW*, and discuss the principles, but as yet have not an efficient leader'.[53]

Buchanan's lectures, at the Durham Ox, were also reported by the *Northern Star*, one of the few reports it carried on matters not directly related to the struggle for the People's Charter.

Buchanan moved on to Mansfield from where, after speaking to 'the people of this poverty stricken place', he sent a gloomy report, no less pessimistic than that of George Sheppard who spoke in Newark, 'this stronghold of priestly domain', on the 16th and 24th September.[54] Sheppard persevered, however, and succeeded in bringing a small group together but his success was short lived, as a report in the *New Moral World* confirmed in June 1839: 'we have discontinued our weekly meetings, partly on account of the persecution experienced by some of our more zealous members, at the hands of the intolerant Christians' but more particularly on account of the (unexplained) departure of George Sheppard.[55] Meanwhile, perseverance had paid off in Mansfield and in October 1839 it was reported that a branch (No. 57) had been formed there, 'but the neighbourhood having been disturbed by the late political excitement and the attention of the people thus drawn away from a rational consideration of the means most likely to benefit them no great number have become members'.[56] Frederick Hollick, another Social Missionary, who had been a fellow student with George Jacob Holyoake in Birmingham, lectured in the town in support of the branch. 'Mr John Paulson who has superintended the formation of the branch ... has lectured at the Black Swann ... the only place that can at present be obtained for the purpose ... an effective branch will no doubt be formed ... S.P.'[57] A new name appears as the contact for the branch in January 1841, one Thomas Rivers, but no further reports are printed of branch activity and the final accounts of the Rational Society presented to the 1845 Congress show payments to the

[53]   *New Moral World*, 22nd September 1838.
[54]   *New Moral World*, 29th September 1838.
[55]   *New Moral World*, 22nd June 1839.
[56]   *New Moral World*, 5th October 1839.
[57]   Ibid.

Society for one year only, of £1 10s 6d for the year 1840.

In March 1840 a third Missionary, James Rigby, arrived in Nottingham. Rigby had been born in 1806 and had been active in the early co-operative movement in Salford, attending the Co-operative Congress in Huddersfield in 1833.[58] On this occasion a debate was arranged with a religious opponent of socialism, an arrangement which the socialists preferred to straight lectures as it offered opportunities for excitement and audience participation which invariably led to larger attendances:

> 'Mr Rigby spoke last Wednesday and Friday ... put up with a virulent opponent ... also debated with the man on Tuesday. On Wednesday Mr Rigby lectured on the marriage system ... the audience seemed reluctant to depart, so pleased were they. Mr R spoke nearly two hours. The results of this visit have been that a room has been engaged, which though not large enough for a Lecture Room, will be convenient for managing the business of the society ... met there and appointed a secretary, president, treasurer, and committee and declared themselves a class under the Leicester branch ... The prospect is very cheering. For the last two years it has been gloomy, but a bright day has arisen. William Smith, secretary.'[59]

Then 'at the request of some friends in Nottingham, Rigby lectured at Arnold, a small village in the vicinity ... The bellman was employed to announce the lecture ... someone told him that he would go to hell for doing so [and] he let drop the bell, and declined to finish his job.'[60]

An unsuccessful attempt was then made to spread the word in Retford, 'this hotbed of fanaticism'[61], but the success of the recent activity in Nottingham led the members of the Congress held in May to consider appointing a Missionary in the district 'which would include Derby, Nottingham, Northampton, and other important towns. At Nottingham he [James Rigby] had lectured recently, in the Concert room, to good audiences. A nucleus of friends had been formed ... previous to becoming

---

[58] *Pathfinders*, W H Brown, 1925.
[59] *New Moral World*, 4th April, 1840.
[60] *New Moral World*, 23rd May 1840.
[61] *New Moral World*, 6th June 1840.

an independent branch.'[62] Plans were being laid to meet the request made at the first meeting of the branch two years earlier for a visit by the 'Social Father' himself, Robert Owen.

In the months before Owen's visit the town was treated to a visit by Reverend Brindley, 'the well known and highly talented lecturer against socialism ... with a view of delivering a course of four lectures upon the abomination of socialism'. The indefatigable former toothbrush salesman and Christian lecturer at once distributed handbills, headed "Socialism Unmasked!" He was willing, he said:

> 'to enter into a discussion with any regularly authorised agent of Robert Owen or representative of the Socialists in Nottingham ... He would prove the existence of a personal; intelligent God, the impracticability of the Socialist schemes, and would show that this system of economists is a direct and atheistical fraud upon the working classes ... the system is very absurd, immoral, blasphemous, and atheistical ... Festivals and tea parties are constantly held on the Sabbath, where profane singing and music are introduced.'[63]

On the occasion of Brindley's third evening lecture the chairman read out a letter from William Smith, the socialist branch secretary, proposing a debate between the socialists and Brindley, each side to choose a chairman, each speaker to address the audience for half an hour, the admission charge to be as low as possible and the proceeds to go to the indigent poor. At the end of the meeting Luke Bartles from New Lenton accepted a challenge on behalf of Robert Owen to debate with Brindley in Nottingham within two months, each side depositing £5 as surety in case neither speaker appeared as arranged.

Owen's visit was one of the few socialist events reported by any of the local newspapers. Owen, despite his current association with infidelity had had a progressive record for the past thirty years, was a person of renown, and was now approaching his seventieth birthday. The radical *Nottingham Review* could scarcely ignore his coming, and reported each of the three lectures he gave in The Theatre, St Mary's Gate, in July 1840.[64] On the first night he spoke 'before a crowded house' on the old immoral

[62]   *New Moral World*, 23rd May 1840.
[63]   *Nottingham Review*, 8th May 1840.
[64]   *Nottingham Review*, 3rd July 1840.

world, condemning 'all the religions of the world ... they produce ignorance and all the vices (applause and hisses)'. He was asked to debate with the Reverend Brindley but replied that he 'only met with gentlemen, and Mr Brindley was not a gentleman'. On the second night he spoke on the socialist system for marriage and separation, and on the third evening answered a series of questions on religion, completing his lecture with details of the plans for communities, but religion and the proposed debate with Brindley remained the bone of contention and even Owen's stupendous powers of endurance were becoming exhausted. 'I will get shut of this rubbish before I proceed with the lecture' he declared, dismissing Mr Brindley now as 'an ignorant baboon.' His refusal to debate with Brindley cost the local socialists the loss of their £5 surety, which the chairman arranged to distribute to one hundred unemployed men of the town.

The sustained campaign of lectures and debates in Nottingham during 1839 and 1840 was paying off. By the beginning of 1841 the Nottingham socialists were no longer a 'class' of the Leicester branch but a branch in their own right, number 65, and received a charter to display in their meeting room. In April George Alexander Fleming, one of the second batch of Missionary appointments, lectured in the town 'on the prospects of the society; at the close of which he urged upon our friends the necessity of making vigorous exertions to establish a school [at the socialist community at Queenwood]'.[65] The collection raised £36. This was in addition to a sum previously subscribed by local members, making a total of £60. This was a very large sum for a small band of members to have raised, and of some fifty functioning branches only those in Edinburgh, Glasgow, Hyde and London contributed more. It does suggest that the socialists in Nottingham comprised a more middle class membership with access to more wealthy donors than most other branches.

At the end of April 1841 another socialist lecturer, Henry Knight, spent some time in the town. 'I have visited Nottingham frequently' he reported 'and may safely say that branch now promises well.'[66] During one of his visits he spoke at a public meeting of inhabitants, called by the Mayor, and held in the Town Hall 'to consider the propriety of giving cottage gardens

[65]   *New Moral World*, 17th April 1841.
[66]   *New Moral World*, 24th April 1841.

to the working people, to enable them to better their conditions by raising a portion of their food by their own direct industry'.[67] He listened for a while and then 'had an opportunity of introducing our views of politics, commerce, population, competition etc all of which were loudly applauded.' Arrangements were then made for himself and George Fleming to speak at The Theatre; Fleming, on Monday evening, on the "Practicability of the Social System"; and himself on Tuesday and Wednesday evenings on "political and moral reform". However:

> 'the saints, though invited to discussion, choose rather to open all their chapels every evening for prayer etc than to attend. We were consequently not overcrowded; and assuredly there was a good impression made on those who did attend. The first 3 nights being over, we continued on Thursday, Friday and Saturday, free to the gallery, one penny to the pit, and sixpence to the boxes: opponents free to all parts of the house. But it was of no use, they would not come. We were obliged to occupy each night with a lecture; after which, many written questions were put and replied to. On the whole, it has been a good stir for Nottingham.'[68]

Despite the optimistic conclusion to Knight's report, it is clear that Knight's intention had been to engage local Christians in debate, but they had chosen prayer in preference to disputation and some desperate measures had been taken to fill the seats of The Theatre, a building well situated at the heart of St Mary's parish near the Wesleyan Chapel.

The meeting in the Town Hall, referred to in his report, had provided another opportunity to contrast the position of the socialists with that of mere reformers: the 'cottage garden' question was, beside religion, another issue in which the socialist outlook differed from that of both the Chartists and middle class single-issue campaigners. Having given a cautious welcome to Feargus O'Connor's ideas on land ownership in March 1838 the *New Moral World* had made explicit its hostility in August 1840: 'Could the allotment system be generally adopted, it would in fact, be a national retrogression, in arts, science, and the distinguishing features of advanced civilisation.'[69]

---

[67] Ibid.
[68] Ibid.
[69] *New Moral World*, 15th August 1840.

Reports from Nottingham on the state of the branch continued to be published through 1841. In June Mr Knight addressed an assembly on the Forest and debated with Chartists in Arnold. In Nottingham he lectured in the socialists' room. 'We have a good many friends here, and all that is wanting to constitute a flourishing branch is, a good room in a central situation.'[70] Although the propaganda campaign was not unsuccessful in its own right, there were still problems in getting a branch permanently established. Always there was one more serious obstacle to be overcome; first it was the lack of a speaker, then the absence of an effective leader, then the lack of a room, then the need of a Missionary, and once again the lack of a room in a central location.

The next month a report assures the readers that the socialists of Nottingham 'associated in this town for the purpose of moral welfare, are not idle.'[71] Time would be needed to uproot old prejudices and disseminate truth but 'meantime we are glad to learn that a spirit of union and brotherly love is growing up amongst the members of the branch. Let them be united and strong within, and all external difficulties will vanish before them.'[72] The external difficulties are not specified but may refer to the opposition from priestly sources, from dissension within the socialist movement, or from rivalry for working class support from local Chartists. There is almost a sense of being under siege. There is no mention of William Smith ceasing to be the secretary, although his name has not been mentioned since May, and the next report comes from 'M.B.'

In August 'M.B.' assures the *New Moral World* that:

> 'the best feeling prevails amongst us: and by the exertions of our female friends, who exhibit an untiring energy, and zeal of a most exemplary character, the branch is fast arriving at a state of prosperity ... we don't increase much in numbers, yet those few we do receive are of the right material, as they are drawn to us not by any public excitement, but by the overpowering truth of our principles.'[73]

The report goes on to describe the 'amusement class' on Mondays, the 'mutual improvement class' on Tuesdays, an evening for 'free enquiry' on

---

[70] *New Moral World*, 12th June 1841.
[71] *New Moral World*, 10th July 1841.
[72] Ibid.
[73] *New Moral World*, 21st August 1841.

Wednesdays, a 'social convivial meeting' on Saturdays which 'gives our friends an opportunity to improve their language by delivering recitations of a moral tendency', and the Sunday lectures given by members. They have also accumulated a library of three hundred volumes, which they maintain by levying an entrance charge of 3d 'or the present of a book'. This is the first real evidence of a thriving, if small, branch and resembles some of the descriptions of the Nottingham Chartists at their meeting place, the Democratic Chapel.

In September 1841 it was announced that Mrs Margaret Chappellsmith had been engaged to lecture in Derby, Leicester and Nottingham. Described by Holyoake as 'an eloquent and accomplished lady'[74]; by *The Charter* newspaper as having a 'livid and impressive manner'; and by the (doubtless male) reporter from Leicester as 'a highly useful advocate of, and a great ornament to, our cause.'[75] She arrived in Nottingham in mid October. In a rapturous account James Nixon, now the reporter for the Nottingham branch, declared that 'the town has been visited by Mrs Chappellsmith, whose teachings have caused quite a sensation.' He claimed that a report:

> 'became current through the town that a woman to lecture was a hoax, it could not be; that it was a man dressed in woman's clothes: and this was the impression of many of the audience, on the first night up to the time of her appearance ... However, when she appeared doubt vanished, and delight and wonder seemed the more manifest "why, it is a woman" was the general exclamation. Yes, and a woman that has done more to arrest the attention of all parties here to the blessings derivable from an adoption in practice of the new views, than even its advocates calculated on. All are enquiring "When will the lady come again?" Our friends here are delighted. The whole affair has been replete with good effects.'[76]

It was still unusual for a woman to be giving any kind of lecture in a public place, even such as The Theatre, and this was taking place three years before Emma Martin's lectures in the Market Place. The *Nottingham*

---

[74] *The History of Co-operation*, G J Holyoake, 1908.
[75] *New Moral World*, 2nd October 1841.
[76] *New Moral World*, 16th October, 1841.

Review noted Margaret Chappellsmith's visit to the town with a brusque report: 'A female Lecturer: Mrs Chappellsmith, delivered in The Theatre, on the evenings of Wednesday and Thursday, on the corn laws, the national debt, and the present condition of the country. Discussion was invited.'[77] Curiosity among the members of the audience about the subject of her first lecture seemed to have been lacking, or perhaps they were still stunned by her gender, but any discussion on the Corn Laws would normally have attracted a vocal contingent of Chartists and sparked a lively discussion. The audience apparently found the National Debt to be of much greater interest the following evening, provoking 'a long and animated debate.' Her third lecture in the town was on '"The Present System of Marriage"'.[78]

Margaret Chappellsmith (nee Reynolds) had, like Emma Martin, started adult life as a convinced Baptist. Born in a working class family in 1806 in Aldgate, London, she was introduced to the ideas of Robert Owen in her early twenties. Her interests in the position of women in society, and in communitarianism were reflected in her writings, and by 1836 she was writing for the London *Weekly Dispatch.* In 1839 she was appointed by the Rational Society to become one of the socialist lecturers and, in common with Emma Martin, she chose to speak on controversial subjects such as the socialist policy on divorce, for which she was stoned by a group of women in Paisley and chased through the streets of South Shields by another group of women, who accused her of having seven husbands. In fact she had but one husband, John Chappellsmith, whom she had married in 1839, and who assisted at her lectures and supported her in her activities. After the demise of the Rational Society she and her husband emigrated in 1850 to the United States and took up residence at New Harmony, which Robert Owen had purchased in 1825 to found a socialist community, remaining there until her death in 1883.

Among the practices which Margaret Chappellsmith and other socialist lecturers engaged at the close of the lectures was the performing of secular naming ceremonies for babies.[79] This act of repudiation of priestly authority, and initiation into a new secular morality, was common among

---

[77] *Nottingham Review,* 17th September 1841.
[78] *New Moral World,* 16th October 1841.
[79] *Margaret Chappellsmith,* Kathryn Gleadle, Oxford Dictionary of National Biography, 2004.

both socialists and Chartists. One such naming had taken place in 1840 when a boy was named after the men who had led the columns of Chartist insurrectionists in Newport and been sentenced to death, becoming Zephanie Williams Frost Greensmith. Another took place in The Theatre after Robert Owen's lectures in Nottingham in June 1840 when a boy was taken into Owen's arms and named William Owen Millward Fairbairn.[80] In similar ceremonies the first baby to be born in the socialist community at Queenwood enjoyed the distinction of being named Primo Communist Flitcroft, and almost twenty years earlier Susannah and William Wright, of whom more will be said later, had named their third child Thomas Paine Carlile Wright.

In November 1841 Mr Knight intended to meet the Reverend Barker in debate in the Market Place. This 'restless Wesleyan preacher', as Holyoake described him, 'the best qualified adversary who occupied co-operative attention for a long period' was a popular opponent. 'The social advocates, who always had an appetite for an adversary, found Mr Barker much occupation. He excelled most men who as Christians destroyed respect for Christianity.'[81] The night in question was described as being dark and tempestuous, and Mr Knight was prevented by a previous engagement from taking part in the debate, but local socialists attempted to make up for his absence with a host of questions.

Henry Knight arrived the following week and spoke four times, during which time 'an opponent appeared in the person of Mr Grubb, the eloquent and persevering advocate of teetotalism.'[82] As the socialists themselves had a *penchant* for teetotalism ('in reality part of socialism, as only the sober can practice it')[83] the debate may have generated less excitement than they would have liked.

In January 1842 James Nixon reported to the *New Moral World* on the activities of the branch, which had now expanded beyond those of his report of the previous August:

> 'Sunday, lecture on Socialism; Monday dance class; Wednesday lecture on Science; Thursday public discussion in town, which we attend; Friday, meeting of members to read

---

80   *Nottingham Review*, 3rd July 1840.
81   *The History of Co-operation*, G J Holyoake, 1908.
82   *New Moral World*, 20th November 1841.
83   Ibid.

the *NMW*; ... coffee, lemonade, confectionery etc are all
provided; Sunday morning and afternoon school to teach
reading writing, geography etc ... Our meetings are more
numerous and more orderly than they have ever been before.
Our friends improve in intelligence and manners. Our funds
are in a prosperous state. ... We have engaged Mr Knight at a
weekly salary to be our lecturer, and we have every prospect
of renting or building a better room ... a good room would
enable us to reap a numerous harvest from the middle
class.[84]

Up to this point his report is a text book account of everything a socialist
branch should be: informing and educating, engaging in discussion and
debate, improving social skills and manners, enjoying teetotal
refreshment and creating pleasurable emotions by the score, while having
ample funds at their disposal too. A good meeting place still awaited, and
with the prospect of attracting more supporters from the middle class
when that elusive venue had been found. But not all was well: they had
had trouble from local youths and had sought the assistance of a
constable. The constable sent the youths packing but they returned in
greater number. 'The constable then got his head cut with a brick'.[85] The
socialists decided to pursue the perpetrator and 'On Monday we applied
for a warrant; he was examined and found guilty but let off with paying
the expenses, and promising to keep the peace in future'. Had he been
invited to join them to partake of lemonade and dance there might have
been no need to seek the 'retributive justice' that socialists scorned, but
Emma Martin's strictures on the subject in the Market Place were still
more than two years away in the future.

By mid-January Mr Knight, newly appointed by the branch as a local
lecturer on a weekly wage, had given fourteen lectures including a
discussion on the 'Relative Merits of Chartism and Socialism' with
Thomas Beggs, a bookbinder and lecturer who had arrived in Nottingham
from Leeds in 1840 and was to play an important role in radical activities.
Debates of this kind seem to have been lacking in Nottingham but this
one apparently gave the socialists hope that some of the Chartists were
beginning to see the superiority of the socialist case.

---

[84] *New Moral World*, 2nd January 1842.
[85] Ibid.

The female members of the socialist branch had meanwhile been fabricating a great variety of imitation flowers and, in a spirit of 'harmony and hilarity', the members had celebrated the 'Christmas festival'. This appears an odd thing for an organisation committed to rationalism to do, especially as Robert Buchanan, the man whose first lecture in Nottingham in 1838 had helped to launch the branch, had contributed to the movement a lengthy socialist song especially 'for the 25th December, commonly called Christmas Day.' Its first and last verses were:

'Socialists arise! But not to hail the day
(By faith and priestcraft's all pervading sway
Made great) when superstition's slaves come forth
To celebrate their man-god's WONDORUS birth ...

'Upraise the voice of gladness! That the dream
By priests invented is no more your theme;
That fiction's empire soon shall cease to be;
And truth alone be worshipped by the free;
When meagre want on man shall cease to frown.
Nor drones rob toil, and call fruits their own,
And peace her genial smiles on all bestow,
To realise a Paradise below.'[86]

As there is no accounting for the source of their harmony and hilarity, it may be too generous to suggest that Buchanan's verses were the cause, and some questions must remain about the extent to which the campaign against 'priestcraft', and the retaliation against 'infidels' by the Church of England in particular, ranked high among the priorities of the branch and its members.

In the same month, in January of 1842, Mr Knight reports the death of 'one of our aged, well tried, and staunch friends, Mr Pierce ... no sooner was he familiar with the new views, than they elicited his warmest approbation.'[87] Mr Pierce was a cotton spinner living in Mills Yard, Long Row, 64 years old at the time of his death and leaving behind a widow and several children. He had been a founder member of the Nottingham branch, which would seem to date his involvement to around 1838, unless he had been active in earlier socialist activity in the co-operative societies and trade unions of the early and mid 1830s. There is an early record of

---

[86] *New Moral World*, 19th January 1839 (original emphasis).
[87] *New Moral World*, 16th January 1842.

him in 1832 when he swore on oath to the magistrates that the long-standing organiser of the framework knitters' case for protection of the trade, Gravener Henson, 'did maliciously and contemptibly disquiet and disturb a Meeting assembly or congregation of Persons assembled for religious worship, in a licensed assembly room, in the Parish of St Mary ... and at the same time also disturb the Teacher officiating ...'[88] Pierce's complaint suggests that he was not, at that time at least, to be counted among the infidels, which raises some questions about what motivated him to become a socialist during the period of increasing hostility to organised religion among the socialists, and also what motivated the socialists in Nottingham at that time. It may be that the founders of the branch were still primarily attracted to the idea and practice of community, and that the religious debates thundering around them were of minor importance. The brief contents of other reports during 1842 suggests this was probably the case.

Illustration 6: Clifton Grove.
A 'foretaste of community life' (1807).

The year 1842 had begun with high hopes: 'This branch is at present marked by an unusual spirit of activity ... The sun of our hope, through its influence (Home Colonisation Society) shines now with an added lustre – community now seems a thing of *certainty*'.[89] Later that year, in

---

[88] *Borough Records*, Volume 8, 23rd April 1830.
[89] *New Moral World*, 16th January 1842 (original emphasis).

September 1842, the Nottingham branch members went walking in Clifton Grove. 'Our friends' reports James Nixon 'have but now emerged from a ramble amid its glades ... We are enjoying as it were a foretaste of community life!'[90]

The same report in September 1842 also mentions the loss of some of the members who had emigrated to America. The official socialist response to emigration was that it represented a spurious remedy for the ills of unemployment and poverty, and they were keen to point out the superiority of their own: 'We too recommend emigration-but it is not to "our outlying countries of Canada and Australia" ... No! The emigration we propose, is from the overcrowded hovels of our manufacturing hells, to the millions of cultivable waste lands at home'.[91] Home colonisation in socialist communities was their answer, and the Home Colonisation Society established in 1840 was the agency through which this would be achieved.

Lawrence Pitkethly, an early convert to socialism who had established the sixth branch of the Rational Society in Huddersfield in 1837, was unusual among socialists in favouring emigration. He was a founder member of the British Emigrants' Mutual Aid Society which was established in Halifax in September 1842, made a tour of the United States and Canada where he met emigrants from England, and developed a 'plan for Co-operative Emigration.'[92] In the summer of 1843 the *Northern Star* reported an enlargement in the aims of the Mutual Aid Society 'by fixing upon 20,840 acres of land, whereon to form a colony in one of the Western states of North America'[93] Pitkethly's allegiance to the socialist cause was irregular, being best known for his activities in support of Chartism and as a delegate to the 1839 Convention, for which he was well known among Nottingham Chartists, but it would seem that his plan was as much influenced by the setting up of communities as it was in assisting emigration.[94]

---

[90]   *New Moral World*, 17th September 1842.
[91]   *New Moral World*, 24th March 1838.
[92]   *Northern Star*, 23rd March 1844.
[93]   *Northern Star*, 27th May 1843.
[94]   A more recent source suggests that the land was to be divided into ten acre plots for individual farmers: *British Emigration to North America*, W S Shepperson, 1957.

Chapter 4: To the New World

The emigration of some of the Nottingham socialists was treated with circumspection by the reporters from the branch. Apart from the declaration in January 1842 that 'community now seems a thing of *certainty*' and the report in September that 'We are not so numerous as formerly, some of our friends having emigrated to America,'[95] there is no other English account of the emigration. Were it not for the accounts given in later years, preserved in the annals of American history, their story would have remained hidden from the history of English socialism.

William Smith, who had been secretary of the Nottingham branch since the early days in 1838, disappeared from branch reports after May 1841. It may have been around this time that the composition and views of branch members began to change and the idea of emigration to establish a socialist community in America began to take shape. In March 1842 the name of a new secretary appeared in the *New Moral World*: 'W Hopkins, care of Mr Hunt, confectioner, Pilcher Gate'.[96] Of Mr Hopkins there are no other accounts but it becomes clear that 24 year old Mr Hunt was also a socialist as he and his mother Eleanor were among the party who set sail for America in the summer of 1842.

It was on Wednesday 21st June 1842 that a party of seventeen adults and several children from Nottingham and Leicester left the port of Liverpool on the sailing vessel *Belmont*. Their departure at a time of great economic hardship, while motivated by hopes of a more prosperous and happy future, must have given rise to mixed emotions among themselves and their families, some of whom would never see them again. A member of the Salford socialists had witnessed a similar departure of friends in 1834. 'I saw them leave the pier head of Liverpool' he reported to *The Crisis*:

> 'without a murmur or sigh at leaving a country which had given them birth, and a circle of relations and friends which must ever be dear to them. Surely men thus determined must be actuated by strong feelings of disgust at society as it is at present instituted to forego such ties of nature, and resolve to seek a happy retreat in a foreign clime.'[97]

---

[95] *New Moral World*, 17th September 1842 (original emphasis).
[96] *New Moral World*, 5th March 1842.
[97] *The Crisis*, 10th May 1834.

The journey at sea in a sailing ship was long and arduous. The journey taken by the Nottingham socialists took more than two months.[98] 'Sixty five days on the ocean trip, they came directly West by an eight day journey on the Great Lakes to Chicago' and onward by the Fink and Walker stage coach to a timber tract at Silver Creek in Stephenson County, Illinois where they arrived on the 28th August.[99]

Lawrence Pitkethly's American tour did not begin until after the party had left England so their final destination must have been selected by some other person. Sometime in the previous twelve months a scout or agent had probably travelled through north America seeking suitable sites for settlement by English emigrants. One of these was at Silver Creek, in an area later named the township of Ridott, already partly occupied by some earlier East Friesian settlers. There they bought 40 acres of land close to the Silver Creek and built three log houses to accommodate themselves.

Their settlement did not survive and there is no evidence that they even chose a name for it. By the time that two years had passed the 'Owen colony', as it has been referred to, had broken up as a result of 'death, a division of sentiments and other causes'. Unlike the original Owenite community at New Harmony which inhabited buildings constructed by the Rappites before them, the colony at Ridott had arrived at a forest near a river and had to build their community from nothing. They were not alone in this. Many people left England in the depths of the severe economic recession of the 1840s, braved the long journey across the Atlantic, and arrived in a new land where they had no home to go to and little money to spend. Another Thomas Hunt (a London socialist) was among those who made a similar start in 1843 with a community they named Equality in Wisconsin. With no comfort, no food, no proper place to live, 'the community did not last long enough to get beyond the

---

[98] *Customs Bills of Entry, Port of Liverpool*, 1852. It is possible that they sailed on the *Olive and Eliza* to Boston or the *Echo* to New York and onwards to Chicago by stage coach, but the journey time for these Atlantic journeys was around 35 days, and these would not accord with the reference to their journey 'on the great Lakes'.

[99] *History of Stephenson County, Illinois*, A L Fulwider, 1910; *Portrait and Biographical Album of Stephenson County, Illinois*, 1888; C Aschenbrenner, *Please Don't Quote Me*; W Caudell, *Early Settlers* (Illinois). Information in some of these sources should be treated with caution, but most give the same dates of departure from Liverpool and arrival in Silver Creek, and the same names of emigrants. These sites are the main sources on the Ridott community.

struggle for survival that consumed most of everyone's daily time.'[100] This could probably have been said of the community at Ridott too.

After the break-up of the community some members moved elsewhere in Illinois, some travelled to Wisconsin, some have disappeared from the records or are as yet untraced, and others remained in Ridott to the end of their days.[101]

Illustration 7: Thomas Hunt, socialist, emigrant to Illinois in 1842. Pictured c. 1880.

Thomas Hunt has been described as the 'leader' of the 'colony', the man who the others entrusted with $1,200 in 'English gold' on their journey from England to Ridott, but that may be because he was one who remained in Ridott, became a pillar of Ridott society and was the last to die there in 1901. His accounts are probably the basis of most of the stories available today. Described in later life as 'of commanding appearance, the strong points of his character are marked in the lines of his countenance which beams kindly upon his friends while at the same time he frowns upon wrongdoing and has always made his simple love of justice one of his leading characteristics.' A man who could beam and frown simultaneously would have been an asset to any community. In all of the

[100] *Women in Utopia*, Carol A Kolmerton, 1990.
[101] Robert Knight, Charlotte Knight (nee Hurst), and George Barnes have been subsequently located in Mount Carroll, and Thomas Clay and his family in Orion, Fulton, Illinois; and Joseph Lester, former cabinet maker from Fisher Gate in Nottingham, in Wisconsin.

accounts he is described as a Democrat and credited with remaining a Freethinker to his death.

Another emigrant and long-time resident of Ridott was William Fairbairn. According to a reminiscence by Thomas Hunt, his friend William was 'the only one in the party who had had any training which would be considered to be agricultural' and he became a nurseryman in the nearby settlement of Winslow. Older than most members of the colony he was 36 when he emigrated with his wife Ellen and his 2 year old son, the boy who had been 'named' William Owen at The Theatre in Nottingham in 1840 by Robert Owen.[102] At that time William had been a framework knitter living in Poplar Street in the parish of St Mary. Although he too became a prosperous member of Stephenson County society, there are grounds for thinking that he also retained some of his Owenite beliefs after the Ridott community disbanded. Either that or he possessed an astonishing lack of originality in naming his second son Owen William.

The person most likely to have been the organiser of the emigration left Ridott soon after the dissolution of the community and by early 1845 was living in Missouri. No trace of his contribution to the community in Stephenson County appears to have survived in the history of that county but, with a background in Salford socialism, emigration and community building, he is the person most likely to have originated and planned the emigration to Ridott. This was Henry Layland Knight.

Henry was born in Manchester in late 1819 or January 1820, the son of Benjamin and Elizabeth Knight. His father was a silk warper who was said to have sent him to a Dickensian boarding school at Bowes Hall in Teesdale, a place so grim that a previous scholar, Richard Cobden, whom Henry was to know well in later years, suffered permanent injury from frostbite to his feet while a scholar there a decade earlier.[103] By his mid-teens, apparently having acquired no physical deformities in Teesdale, Henry was back in Manchester and first appears in the records of socialism in 1837 when, at the age of 17, on Sunday 10th December 'Mr Knight, of Salford, lectured at Stockport, to a zealous and full audience, and was well received.'[104]

---

[102] See Chapter 3.
[103] *Richard Cobden*, Gravelroots, 2006.
[104] *New Moral World*, 23rd December 1837.

Salford was at the centre of Owenite socialism, far enough removed from Owen and his supporters in London for an authentic working class version to become established and to thrive. In 1829 the First Salford Co-operative Society was founded. Their Principles reflected the writings of William Thompson, acknowledged that 'labour is the source of all wealth' and credited him accordingly. Their objects were to secure mutual protection for their members against poverty; to gain a greater share of the comforts of life; and the attainment of independence. To achieve these objects they would contribute to a common fund, used in trade, employing their own members, with the undivided profit accumulating to enable them to live in community 'on the principles of mutual co-operation, united possessions, equality of exertions, and of the means of enjoyments.'[105] They supported Thompson's belief that Co-operation and communities should not rely on the benevolence and organising ability of wealthy patrons or investors but on the self-organised efforts of the working classes.

Despite the preparations they made – their 'Principles, Objects and Laws' ran to 24 pages – the trading activities of the First Salford Co-operative Society were not successful and in 1831 the redundant shelves and counters at the store on Oldfield Road were turned to good use as schoolroom furniture. Led by Lloyd Jones, Charles Bury, James Rigby, Joseph Smith and Robert Cooper, they established a school which, when they published an appeal 'To The Friends of Education' in 1833, had 'upwards of 200 Adults and Children, of both sexes' aged between 12 and 40 being taught the 'rudiments of education.'[106] The school remained in being in Salford for at least six years.

It may be that after his term at Bowes Hall, Henry Knight continued his education at the Salford co-operative school as a scholar or as one of the unpaid lecturers. Robert Cooper did both. Having had some elementary education, Cooper was employed as a clerk and became an evening scholar at the co-operative school in 1831 at the age of 12, and two years later was appointed a teacher at the school, which by then had moved to larger premises in Great George Street, Salford. A few years later Cooper

---

[105] *Principles, Objects and Laws of the First Salford Co-operative Society*, in British Labour Struggles: Contemporary Pamphlets 1727-1850, 1972.
[106] *To The Friends of Education*, Salford Co-operative School, 1833; *Education in the Salford District 1780-1870*, A V Parsons, 1963.

became a Social Missionary, and along with James Rigby, Lloyd Jones and Henry Knight, he lectured in Leicester, Nottingham and Derby in the early 1840s.

Even if Henry Knight was not a scholar or teacher in the school, it would have been difficult to have been unaware of socialist activity in Salford where, with 440 members, the branch became the largest in Britain. Living in Scholefield Street, within sight of the cupola of St Philip's Church, close to the Social Institution in Great George Street, it was undoubtedly there that he became a socialist.

Salford socialists had discussed emigration on many occasions. Speaking at the 1833 Co-operative Congress 'Mr Rigby, from Manchester, made his report. He stated that he represented three interests, the first is schools, and the other two are social communities, the one for emigration, the other not.'[107] In May the following year *The Crisis* reported that 'the Manchester and Salford Community Company sent off a number of members, amounting to 23 of both sexes to Cincinatti, or its neighbourhood, in the United States, in order to purchase an eligible piece of land, whereon to try the principles of mutual co-operation, on something like the Owenian plan.'[108] Two years later another group left the port of Liverpool and the Salford branch wrote to the *New Moral World* that 'our friends destined for America have already proceeded thither a few weeks since; and it is hoped have nearly, if not quite, arrived. Our best wishes accompany them.'[109] Their precise destination and motives for emigrating are not clear, but there remains the possibility that connections with previous emigrants were maintained by Salford socialists and that they were utilised on future occasions when socialists left England to establish new communities.

After his first lecture in 1837, Henry Knight soon became a regular figure on the socialist lecture circuit, speaking in Rochdale, Oldham, Ashton under Lyne, Blackburn and Macclesfield in 1838. In 1839 the fourth socialist Congress in Birmingham appointed him an assistant lecturer for the Leeds District and there are reports of his speaking engagements in Bradford and Halifax.

In January 1841 Knight made his first report from Leicester where he had

---

[107]   *The Crisis*, 19th October 1833.
[108]   *The Crisis*, 10th May 1834.
[109]   *New Moral World*, 7th May 1836.

been appointed a Social Missionary, and he appears with his wife Margaret, whom he had married in 1839, and four month old daughter in the June 1841 census living in a shared house in Halford Street, Leicester, which George Jacob Holyoake later described as a 'vegetarian colony'. Also living there were William Holyoak and Josiah Gimson, also Owenite socialists, who later became founders of the Leicester Secular Society. A year later in 1842 the Nottingham branch was reporting that he had taken up an appointment as Social Missionary for the Nottingham District where he is 'most zealous in his exertions' and 'labours indefatigably.'[110] This is the last report from Henry Knight and six months later he was on his way to the United States.[111]

Illustration 8: Henry Knight, socialist, emigrant to Illinois in 1842. Pictured c. 1875.

In Nottingham, the branch members had continued to meet after the departure of the emigrants in June 1842, but those who had emigrated

---

[110] *New Moral World*, 16th January 1841; 17th April 1841; 24th April 1841; 12th June 1841; 20th November 1841; 8th January 1842.

[111] Henry Knight became a journalist and attorney, and secretary of the California Working Men's Party. For more on Henry Knight and the short-lived anti-Chinese CWM Party see *Frank Roney: Irish Rebel and Labour Leader*, Ira B Cross, 1931; *A History of the Labour Movement in California*, Ira B Cross, 1935; *The Indispensable Enemy: Labor and the anti-Chinese Movement in California*, Alexander Saxton, 1971.

'had adopted a line of policy in the management of the Branch ... which those who remained behind found they had not leisure at their command to properly attend to ... this management consulted more the agility of youth than the feelings of more matured years.'[112] The youthfulness of the emigrants has already been remarked upon and the branch which remained perhaps consisted of the more conservative and older members.

A year later the rifts appear not to have healed. A report following Robert Cooper's lecture in the town in July 1843 on the subject of 'Social Communities the only remedy for the Evils of Society', comments on the fears within the branch: 'some of the more advanced are afraid of some crude attempt being made to force the matter onwards faster than existing circumstances will warrant.'[113] The nature of this 'matter' must remain a subject for conjecture but the phraseology suggests it was related to community building, either in the manner of the emigration to the USA or to the affairs at the community at Queenwood in Hampshire. Robert Owen had recently been reappointed Governor at Queenwood following his forced removal the year before, and the indebtedness of the community, which eventually caused its demise, was becoming a matter of considerable concern.

During 1843 Robert Cooper, Salford colleague of Henry Knight, lectured on two more occasions, on 'Priestcraft a Moral Nuisance' and 'Socialism, Infidelity and the French Revolution'. Mr Linwood came to speak on the importance of the People's Charter 'but his expose of the social and religious, as well as political state of society, was such as would satisfy a Rationalist'.[114] William Hill, the editor of the *Northern Star,* gave a lecture 'far in advance of the generality of Chartist lectures, towards the views which we advocate.' In September Robert Owen arrived to speak in Derby followed by five evenings of lectures in Nottingham to audiences 'tolerably numerous, and exceedingly attentive.'[115]

It therefore comes as a surprise to find, only two weeks after Robert Owen's lectures in the town and a return visit to the sylvan glades of Clifton Grove with friends from Derby, a report from Nottingham in the *New Moral World* that 'the Branch formerly existing in this town, having

---

[112] *New Moral World,* 11th February 1843.
[113] *New Moral World,* 15th July 1843.
[114] *New Moral World,* 5th August 1843.
[115] *New Moral World,* 23rd September 1843.

ceased to maintain an official existence, no arrangements had been made for the delivery of a public lecture, by Mr Fleming, on the evening of Friday.'[116]

The branch appears to have suffered a rapid and terminal decline. Alexander Fleming and Robert Cooper arranged a private meeting with some supporters 'all of them occupying good positions in society', a fact substantiated by the magnitude of the collection (£155) but the expectations that the contributors would 'push the matter in their own rank, so that we may anticipate enlarged and substantial support from this town' were not fulfilled.[117] The branch was not revived and it is the last reference to any socialist activity in the town. Branch payments to the Rational Society funds for the whole of 1844 were a mere fifteen shillings and sixpence, one eighth of the amount paid in the previous year. When Emma Martin came to Nottingham in August 1844 she did so without the support of a local branch, reports of her visit were made by Horace Roche, a correspondent from Derby, and no new branch activity resulted from her lectures.

Socialism and community building by the pioneers in Ridott, Illinois, barely outlasted the socialist activity of their friends in Nottingham. Both had collapsed by the summer of 1844 and when socialism, co-operation and secular activity re-emerged in Nottingham they did so in forms different to those of the period described here. When a political banquet was held in March 1849 it was more in the nature of a wake. 'The Socialists and Republicans of Nottingham hailed the first anniversary of the Revolution of February 1848 on Saturday evening last at the house of Mr Smith, Low Pavement when a substantial supper was provided of roast beef, legs of mutton and plum pudding' reported the *Nottingham Review*. Toasts were drunk 'to the brave democrats of Paris, Mazzini, the brave Hungarians, Ernest Jones and the incarcerated victims of misrule, health and long life to Robert Owen, the philanthropist' and many more. This sounds like a gathering of old warriors looking back to past campaigns and, after the downing of some twenty toasts, watching silent tears dropping into their beer.[118]

---

[116] *New Moral World*, 30th September 1843.
[117] Ibid.
[118] *Nottingham Review*, 2nd March 1849.

Chapter 5: Defeat of the Church Rate Party

The charge of infidelity was usually levelled against the socialists, especially those such as Emma Martin and Robert Cooper who had been at the forefront of attacking the practices of organised religion and of the Church of England in particular. To be an 'infidel' implied a rejection of the 'one true religion'. Although Emma Martin possessed an intimate knowledge of all the finer points of theological disagreement between the numerous Christian sects, it was Christianity in its entirety that she rejected because it stood in the way of a new utilitarian morality. 'Morality is a science, and as such must be studied ... and not only is morality unassisted by religion, but it receives from it no light, no explanation, no enforcement', she wrote shortly before her death.[119]

Robert Owen was a Deist and explained his view on God in response to a question from the audience when he spoke in Nottingham in 1840: 'There is a power which pervades the universe, everywhere existing, and that this power directs the atom. Controls the aggregate of nature, and governs everything exactly as it is governed; and beyond that knowledge, all the learned men in the world that I have ever heard of, cannot proceed one step!'[120] This summarised the socialist position on the 'The Religion of the Millennium', which was spelt out succinctly in the second edition of the *New Moral World* in 1835.[121]

The charge of infidelity was levelled against Owen too by Christian zealots. It was one of the ultimate vilifications in the Christian wordbook, but had the dangerous capacity of being misapplied. It was a charge that needed to be handled carefully. It could be taken up as a badge of pride by those so named, become a rallying cry for those who denied the existence of any god. The radical printer, publisher and champion of freethought, Richard Carlile, said the description of him as an 'infidel', made at a time when he was still describing himself as a Deist and long before he became 'an exponent of philosophical atheism' was 'as agreeable as baron, baronet or squire', thus throwing an intended insult back at those who hurled it.[122] It could also be used to taint the reputation of a potential leader among

---

[119]   *Religion Superseded*, Emma Martin, 1850.
[120]   *Nottingham Review*, 3rd July 1840.
[121]   *New Moral World*, 14th November 1835.
[122]   *Popular Radicalism and Freethought in Early Nineteenth Century England*, Iain McCalman, 1996.

the more conservative working class. For this reason it was applied to Robert Owen from the late 1820s when his reputation amongst working class men and women was growing. One description of a nineteenth century 'infidel' was a person who 'did not necessarily deny the existence of God but one who had the temerity to convey to the lower orders the heresies of the respectable', a description which could be applied appropriately to Owen.[123]

The term of 'infidel' could also be used within the Christian churches themselves, not only against Catholics but against non-conformist Protestants, with the risk of creating dissension within the ranks of the devout. To describe them as Deists was scarcely less of an insult when Deists were being labelled as infidels. In 1833 a Unitarian, Benjamin Carpenter, complained bitterly in the *Nottingham Mercury* about its rival, the Tory *Journal*, which had accused Unitarians of being Deists. It was, he said, an 'offensive and calumnious charge'.[124] Archdeacon Wilkins repeated this error when he responded to the Quaker William Howitt's *History of Priestcraft* in 1834 by denouncing the Society of Friends and Unitarians as Deists rather than true Christians, which led to the Quakers going *en masse* to a vestry meeting at St Nicholas' Church and voting down a Church rate.[125]

Unitarians, Quakers, Methodists and members of other dissenting religions played an important role in the campaigns against Church rates. Why, they asked, should they have to pay for the upkeep of a Church which received numerous benefits from the state, when they themselves sought no subsidies for the upkeep of their own chapels. Those campaigns might have been led by middle class dissenters but the numbers attending vestry meetings, and the presence of participants known to be radical working men, suggests that they rallied a broad spectrum of people against the privileges of the established Church and against the imposition of local taxes. Ironically it was not socialists in Nottingham who were distinguished by campaigns against the Church, but Chartists, and they brought with them the capacity to rouse and organise a wide body of support from within the working class of the town and

---

[123] *Radical Politics 1790-1900:Religion and Unbelief*, Edward Royle, 1971.
[124] *Nottingham and Newark Mercury*, 10th August 1833.
[125] *The Anglican Church in the Industrialised Town, St Mary's Parish, Nottingham, 1779-1884*, Mary M Bowen, 1997.

surrounding villages. The campaigns took two forms, one against rates for the upkeep of Church buildings and rituals, and the other against the employment of Church men as chaplains in the workhouses.

On the 2nd of February 1844 the *Nottingham Review* reported the 'Defeat of the Church Rate Party at Bulwell.'[126] A meeting of parishioners had been called to approve a Church rate for repairs to the parish Church of St Mary. Vestry meetings had been uneventful here in the past, but on this occasion the parishioners did not wait for the arrival of the vicar but took control of the meeting themselves and elected someone of their own choice to chair it. When the Reverend Padley arrived he proceeded to take back the function of chair, which he regarded as his right, and proposed a 2d rate on parishioners for repairs to the Church buildings. Fearing adverse publicity for this proposal, the reporter from the *Nottingham Review* was asked to leave but refused to do so. He would leave, he said, if the meeting wanted him to. Cries of 'No, No' erupted from the meeting. The reporter remained in his seat. The Reverend then put his proposal for a 2d rate to the vote and twenty hands were raised in support. He did not ask for votes against. Calls were made from the parishioners for a show of hands on the proposal and 'A majority of at least five to one were held up against it'. The Reverend then swept out of the meeting 'declaring he would have nothing further to do with it'. The attempt to raise a Church rate had failed.

No names of the participants are mentioned in this report, but the meeting followed the style of many others that had taken place during the previous six years.

The campaigns against Church rates in Nottingham had begun in 1830 when Richard Sutton, editor of the *Nottingham Review* urged parishioners to attend vestry meetings and vote against the Church rates. His appeals at first met with little success but in 1833 the government abolished compulsory Church rates in Ireland where the majority Catholic population had been required to contribute to the upkeep of the hated Protestant Church of Ireland. This gave encouragement to English dissenters. In 1833 the vestry at St Mary's, the parish Church for the most populous part of the town, voted a Church rate to buy six acres of land for a new burial ground, made necessary by the large number of deaths from the cholera epidemic. The proposal was approved, but from 1834 onwards

---

[126] *Nottingham Review*, 2nd February 1844.

Church rates at St Mary's became a battleground where the Church of England fought to maintain its privileges against a burgeoning tide of non-conformist dissent and secular opposition to the growing burden of local taxation.

In the same year William Howitt, a Quaker, and a group of other dissenters hosted a public rally, said by Howitt's wife Mary to have been the first time that calls for the disestablishment of the Church of England had been made in public in the town.[127] A vestry meeting at St Mary's attracted so many people that when the Archdeacon, George Wilkins, barred access to the main body of the church, the meeting had to move elsewhere and eventually ended up in the Market Place. At a second unsuccessful attempt at gaining a Church rate an uproarious vestry meeting took place in the churchyard. Even the churchwardens had by now abandoned him and, their funds depleted, refused to supply bread for communion. His wife Amelia had to take charge of baking communion bread in the vicarage kitchen.[128]

In May 1836 two Chartists, Mr Kennedy and Joseph Burbage, gave notice of a motion to the vestry meeting that the salary of the chaplain to the workhouse be abolished. This led to a debate on whether there should be any kind of religious instruction for the poor in the workhouse and 'After some further discussion, in the source of which it was observed, that the vicar was so well paid for what he did for the rich, that he ought to provide for the poor, and that he should be requested to do so, the motion was carried.'[129] Mr Burbage was described as 'a humble mechanic' but he was an eloquent and effective public speaker who, one month later, roused a meeting at the Exchange Hall to thunderous applause for a speech on the Irish Municipal Bill in which he declared that the House of Lords had resolved 'that Ireland should never know anything but misery and woe'.[130]

In October 1836 another opportunity presented itself for assailing the Church of England's privileges, on this occasion through the agency of a public body. The Church had lost its public responsibility for the parish workhouse under the Poor Law Amendment Act of 1834. The Guardians of

[127] *An Autobiography*, Mary Howitt, 1898 quoted in The Anglican Church in the Industrialised Town, St Mary's Parish, Nottingham, 1779-1884, Mary W Bowen, 1997.
[128] Ibid.; *An Episode in the History of St Mary's Church, Nottingham*, A C Wood, in Transactions of the Thoroton Society, 1952.
[129] *Nottingham Review*, 6th May 1836.
[130] *Nottingham Review*, 10th June, 1836.

the new Nottingham Union Workhouse discussed the proposal to appoint a Church of England clergyman as Chaplain to the workhouse at a salary of £30 a year, the cost to be borne by the ratepayers. When the vote was taken 2 of the Guardians' votes were cast in favour and 9 against, with 2 abstentions. The chaplain was not appointed.

This was not a vote to establish a secular regime in the workhouse but to remove the privileges enjoyed by the Church and was successful because of the strength of non-conformist religions in the town among the middle class. Working class Chartists continued to promote their own interests and their own candidates in vestry elections, where they had the right to vote and could muster support. Joseph Burbage, and two other Chartists – the veteran framework knitting trade unionist Thomas Roper and Charles Withers, a smith from Radford – returned to the subject of the working of the Poor Law amendment Act at a vestry meeting at St Mary's in 1837, and Charles Withers continued to take on the Church over compulsory rates for several years, being one of the victors in one of the last reported 'adjournments' at Basford in 1841. He was still taking on the Christians, in the form of the Christian temperance movement, and defending working men against being stigmatised by them as 'drunken vagabonds', in 1854.[131]

In January 1837 a public meeting was arranged 'to consider the propriety of presenting Petitions to both Houses of Parliament, for the total and immediate Abolition of Church Rates'[132] The petition amassed 120 signatures and included many who were counted among the town's respectable middle class radicals of the time. Three members of the Nottingham Reform Association formed the previous year were included: Richard Sutton, editor of the *Nottingham Review;* William Cutts, who as a Town Councillor had seconded William Howitt, Quaker and author of the notorious *History of Priestcraft* to become an Alderman; and Francis Hart, librarian to the Artizans' Library. Thomas Kirk, printer and bookseller of St Peter's Gate was on the list and so too were Samuel Bean, in later years a supporter of the Complete Suffrage Union, and Thomas Wakefield, twice Mayor of Nottingham and President of the Artizans' Library. Jonathan Dunn, founder of the *Nottingham Mercury* in 1825 was also included, although his newspaper was not a mouthpiece of middle class radicalism but rather the voice of the Whigs.

[131] *Drink and Temperance in Nottingham 1830-1860,* J J Rowley, 1974.
[132] *Nottingham Review,* 27th January 1837.

The public meeting was held a week later and more than two hundred people attended. A rearguard action was mounted by a Mr Bradshaw who spoke against the calling of the meeting, cleverly combining his attack on the meeting with a condemnation of the Poor Law: 'The Poor Law Amendment Bill has robbed the poor of every hope and interest connected with this world, and now the same party wish, by taking away the Church rate to rob them of that religion which constituted their hopes of a hereafter. (Much disapprobation, with some cheers).'[133] The amendment from Mr Bradshaw was defeated by 158 votes to 56 on a show of hands. The same majority was then gained for the original resolution. 'The Church party here began to retire, and gave a parting three cheers for Church and King, which was met by three groans for the bishops.'

Despite their defeat by the Board of Guardians in October 1836 the Church of England did not give up on their attempt to have one of their party appointed Chaplain at the workhouse. In August 1838 a Vestry Meeting was called at St Mary's. One of the Chartist Woodhouse brothers contrasted the conduct of the Church ministers and the dissenting ministers in attending to the needs of the poor in the workhouse and another Chartist, Mr Kennedy, recalled that George Wilkins, Archdeacon at St Mary's, had attended the workhouse only once while a Guardian, a charge repeated in the columns of the *Nottingham Review* a year later: 'We never saw a clergyman there, except upon the one occasion when the Venerable Archdeacon Wilkins made an appearance at the Board of Guardians to support the motion for a salaried chaplain'.[134] There was discussion on refusing to pay the poor rate if a salaried chaplain was appointed. It was agreed to send a deputation 'to remonstrate with the Board of Guardians on the proposed measure'[135] and the deputation was admitted to the following meeting of the Guardians where, after a long discussion that lasted all morning, the Board voted by 8 votes to 6 to rescind the decision to appoint a paid chaplain.[136] Thereafter the services provided by a chaplain were paid for by voluntary contributions, the Anglicans performing two morning services on the Sabbath and an afternoon service performed by a dissenting minister.

[133] *Nottingham Review*, 3rd February 1837.
[134] *Nottingham Review*, 4th October 1839.
[135] *Nottingham Review*, 10th August 1838.
[136] *Nottingham Review*, 24th August 1838.

A vestry meeting, in Lenton in September, disposed of an attempt to raise a 9d Church rate, for the repair of the church wall. Facing defeat, the churchwarden moved a halfpenny rate instead, and this too was soundly rejected by the popular device of moving 'that the proposal be taken into consideration twelve months hence', which received 100 votes, with a mere 6 against. The victorious assembly then proceeded to enjoy themselves further by consuming 'a quantity of wine bought for administering the sacrament'.[137]

In October 1841 a vestry meeting was held in Basford to seek a Church rate to extend the burial ground, and although scheduled for a Thursday morning at 11.30am:

> 'three or four hundred were present, the affair seeming to attract great interest. The vicar of the parish, Rev Simpson, as is usual at all parochial meetings, took the chair ... a need for a new graveyard as the old one was full ... founded on the representations of the clerk, whose feelings were much hurt by the dreadful sights he was obliged to view ... coffins broken through ... a head was thrown out of a grave, with hair on it a foot long, and a comb in it.'[138]

The Duke of Newcastle had given some land adjacent to the church and it was proposed to stop up the footpath and erect a school for poor children into the bargain. A dissenter asked if dissenting ministers would be able to come in to the school and received a negative reply. The *Nottingham Review* continued:

> 'The great body of the persons present, who composed the lower classes of working men of the parish declared they had no obligation to pay for a burying ground for the church – they were quite rich enough to pay for it themselves, and condemned a rate altogether. Many called it cant and hypocrisy, to talk so much about the poor, when they did all they could to injure them ... The chairman then proceeded to put the motion [for a rate], whereupon a great uproar prevailed, the anti-rate party arguing that the amendment [for adjournment] should be put first ...' but they lost the argument. The motion was then put. For the rate about 29

---

[137] *Nottingham Review*, 28th September 1838.
[138] *Nottingham Review*, 29th October 1841.

hands were held up, for the amendment about 300 were shown. The anti-rate party immediately began to cheer, and the Vicar had no effect on stopping them, so great seemed their joy at being victorious.' [139]

By the close of the poll on the first day there were 71 for the rate and 139 against. The poll continued during the week and the rate was rejected.

Meanwhile the roof of St Mary's was becoming unsafe. In 1838 a bellman had been employed to rally parishioners to a vestry meeting to levy a rate for church repairs but only twelve parishioners voted for the rate and the meeting was adjourned. The church was subsequently refurbished, after £4,000 had been raised from private gifts, but the basic problems remained and four years later in 1842 it was discovered that the central tower was not built of solid masonry but consisted of an outer casing filled with builders' rubble and this was crumbling under the weight above it. To make matters worse it was found that the foundations of the tower had been weakened by the accommodation of a family tomb, and the vibration caused by the ringing of the church bells had further aggravated the situation. The Venerable Wilkins decided that the church was unsafe and closed it. The Church Patron, Earl Manvers, insisted that funds for restoration should come from the parish rate and an architect, Mr Lewis Cottingham, was engaged to report on the cost of repairs.

Wilkins had told the Bishop in 1839 that Church rate meetings had been abandoned as they could not be relied upon to obtain a compulsory rate, and he was reluctant to try that method of raising funds again. But he had no other choice. Circumstances conspired against him from the start. Churchwarden George Eddowes, a churchwarden originally selected by Wilkins, had not sought a Church rate for eight of the fourteen years in which he had held office and declared that he did not care whether a Church rate was granted or not.[140] The *Nottingham Review* reported the vestry meetings to obtain a Church rate for repairs in January 1843 and noted that George Eddowes had only put the proposition for a rate to the meeting because he was required to do so by the Ecclesiastical Court 'which he was bound to obey on pain of imprisonment.'[141] It has been suggested that James Sweet, the most prominent of the town's Chartists,

---

[139] Ibid.
[140] *Nineteenth Century Church and English Society*, Frances Knight, 1995.
[141] *Nottingham Review*, 20th January 1843.

intended to stand for election as a churchwarden with the sole intention of blocking any further attempts to raise a Church rate, although this appears not to have been proceeded with.[142]

Illustration 9: St. Mary's Church, Low Pavement.
Scene of body snatching, tumultuous meetings against Church rates,
'ribaldry and abuse'.

The most comprehensive and entertaining report of the vestry meeting appeared in the *Northern Star*. This was one of the few occasions on which the Chartist paper included news of Church rate protests in its pages but this one was taking place in one of the heartlands of Chartism and several well known local Chartists played a prominent role, one of whom was probably the correspondent to the *Northern Star*:

> 'Nottingham: the large parish of St Mary's was thrown into a state of great excitement when it was known that an attempt would be made to obtain a church rate on Thursday. The facts of the case are that St Mary's Church is cracked in its upper stories and the Reverend Dr Wilkins seemed to imagine that his parishioners were also cracked in their upper stories ... great numbers assembled ... due to church repairs the meeting was adjourned to the Town Hall ... £3,300 was wanted ... This information was greeted by loud cries of

---

[142]   *Nineteenth Century Church and English Society*, Frances Knight, 1995.

"Shame" "Shame" and produced a great deal of confusion ... increased when they learned that another £1,300 was wanted to pay off vestry debts ... Mr Beggs rose to move an amendment, but he was called to order by the chairman for calling church rates iniquitous; he objected to this rate both as to time and principle, for it was an outrage upon decency to attempt to attempt to obtain such a rate, whilst thousands around them were suffering the greatest privations and distress; and an insult to the people, for the Church received betwixt eight and ten millions per year to instruct the people, and yet told them they were too ignorant to exercise their rights – this Church had always been an enemy of the poor, and it was insulting them to ask for such a rate. He moved as an amendment "That this meeting regard all church rates as iniquitous and unjust, and therefore decide that the question be adjourned to that day twelve months." Mr Henry Newton seconded it, but the Reverend gentleman refused to put it to the meeting and the uproar increased – loud calls were made for him to leave the chair, which he refused to comply with, and he was greeted with cries of "they shall not steal", "more pigs and fewer parsons", "is this Christianity?", "he is certainly possessed of a devil", "the pastor feeding his flock", etc, etc. Mr Beggs rose again and told him that he had that day seen a fair specimen of priestcraft, and he moved that Dr Wilkins be respectfully requested to leave the chair, but he still refused to comply with it, and was proceeding to take the votes when Mr Beggs protested against it until a check was appointed. Mr R T Morrison was then appointed to check, and the poll continued until Saturday, at three o'clock, when there was For the Rate 145, For the amendment 921, majority for the Amendment 784. ... The announcement was received with loud cheers." [143]

The *Nottingham Mercury* also published a lengthy report of the proceedings from a reporter who had clearly enjoyed his evening's entertainment, adding an amusing account of the reaction to the news of the architect's report:

---

[143]   *Northern Star*, 21st January 1843.

'The Archdeacon [Rev Wilkins] offered to read the architect's report in full or in part ... "It was for the meeting to say whether they would hear the Report." (Cries of "No, no"). The Chairman: "Do not all speak at once". (Cries of "No, No, No report"). In consequence of these cries he would merely state that Mr Cottingham would undertake to complete the repairs for £3,300. (Cries of "Oh, oh" and loud laughter). "All he was stating was only a fact. The building might have fallen on the heads of those assembled for worship," and – A Voice – "No matter if it had". The Chairman – "Certainly you could not wish it to have fallen on the heads of your fellow-townsmen" (Cries of "no, no", and a voice "yes, if they had all been parsons")'.[144]

Illustration 10: George Wilkins, Vicar of St. Mary's 1817–1843, Archdeacon 1832-1865, a 'Pillar of "Old Mother Church"'.

The Editor added a final comment to reassure its respectable readers that the *Mercury* had not lost all sense of propriety, although even here the emphasis is upon the importance of preserving a historic building and not the right to levy a rate: 'The Poll will be re-opened this morning (Friday), when we trust that all who value church principles, and are desirous of sustaining the noble and beautiful fabric, which has for

---

[144] *Nottingham and Newark Mercury*, 13th January 1843

centuries been the glory of the town will record their votes in favour of the rate.'

The *Nottingham Review* commented in an editorial: 'We congratulate our townsmen on the defeat of the attempt to obtain a Church rate for the parish of St Mary. ... the result of the poll has rung the knell of church rates in Nottingham, and the effect will be felt, in the course of the year, not only in the adjacent parishes, but throughout the kingdom.'[145] The same edition also published a long letter from Mr R T Morrison denouncing the 'rabid' reporting by the Tory *Nottingham Journal* on the Church rate protests. The socialist *New Moral World* entered the fray, noting indignantly the 'base calumny' of the *Journal,* which 'in commenting on the violent and disgraceful proceedings at the polling for the church-rate, lately refused, thought proper to class the Socialists amongst other parties, as being actors in the outrageous scene which took place.'[146] Perchance fearful of exacerbating the tensions already noted amongst the members of the Nottingham branch, and losing some lucrative donors and 'influential individuals in the neighbourhood, who are friendly to our cause, and are prepared to assist us', the paper preferred to pay more positive attention to the 'state of excitement' in the town resulting from lectures 'on the new science of Mesmerism.'

George Wilkins was appalled by the vestry meeting. He had, he said, 'survived the most disgustful abuse and ribaldry that the worst passions of debased humanity could inflict'.[147]

In the same month of February 1843 Wilkins wrote to the Mayor to warn that recent gales had shaken the church and it was in imminent danger of collapse, but starved of cash for rebuilding, he partially re-opened the church for services.[148] Shortly afterwards in March he was preaching a sermon when the church resounded with a loud crack, which caused the parishioners to think the roof was collapsing above them and flee the building. The sound of cracking was found to have come from an umbrella falling onto the flagstones of the church floor, but the panic was genuine

---

[145] *Nottingham Review*, 20th January 1843.
[146] *New Moral World*, 11th February 1843
[147] *The Anglican Church in the Industrialised Town, St Mary's Parish, Nottingham, 1779-1884*, Mary W Bowen, 1997.
[148] *An Episode in the History of St Mary's Church, Nottingham*, A C Wood, in Transactions of the Thoroton Society, 1952.

enough and several were injured in the rush to leave the church.[149] Meanwhile 'crowds of Dissenters gathered on a neighbouring hill confident that it was about to collapse in ruin before their gaze.'[150]

The Archdeacon George Wilkins moved on from St Mary's in 1843 and was succeeded by Joshua Brooks, the scourge of Emma Martin. Wilkins had been Vicar there since 1817. He came from a family of architects with a strong personal interest in church buildings and his father was the estate architect to the Earl of Manvers, his patron as Archdeacon. His action in securing St Mary's restoration (though not from a compulsory Church rate), rather than its demolition, eventually secured the retention of one of the few medieval buildings remaining in the modern city, although the eventual cost after five years of restoration was £9,000, far in excess of the £3,300 sought from a Church rate in 1843.

Much of Wilkins' time at St Mary's was reputedly engaged with bothersome brides and grooms from other parishes wanting to be wed in his church, and he employed his sexton at 6d a time to check their places of residence before the banns were read. His vicar in Radford parish, the Reverend Samuel Cresswell, took a more laid-back position on marriages, which led to an irate Wilkins describing Radford as 'the Gretna Green of Nottinghamshire.' The Reverend George Wilkins himself, frustrated as a curate in earlier years by the failure of Earl Manvers to deliver on his promise of a 'lucrative parish' at St Mary's where he could have a decent wedding, was said to have eloped in protest with Amelia, to marry his affianced in the far distant parish of – Gretna Green.[151]

Notwithstanding the abject failure of the principal Anglican Church at St Mary's to secure the appointment of a chaplain at the Nottingham workhouse in 1836 and 1838, and the recent failure to levy a rate in January 1843, an attempt was made four months later in another Chartist

---

[149] *Nottingham St Mary*, Church of England, 2007.

[150] *The Anglican Church in the Industrialised Town, St Mary's Parish, Nottingham, 1779-1884*, Mary W Bowen, 1997.

[151] Ibid. and *Nineteenth Century Church and English Society*, Frances Knight, 1995. Michael Austin in *Minster People*, eds. S Chapman and D Walker, 2009, has challenged this widely disseminated tale, asserting that while Wilkins and Amelia may have eloped to Gretna Green, their marriage took place in Cambridge. He attributes the myth of their marriage in Gretna to the entry in the *Oxford Dictionary of National Biography* by a disgruntled relative of Wilkin's wife, the son of the vicar of Southwell who was made redundant when Wilkins abolished his post and created a new position of Rector at triple the salary – to which he then appointed his own son John Murray Wilkins.

stronghold, the village of Arnold in the same archdeanconry, to appoint an Anglican to the post of assistant overseer. Here the Chartists organised beforehand to attend the vestry meeting with a candidate of their own and sent a report of the event to the *Northern Star*:

> 'At the meeting on Tuesday Mr James Anthony, an uncompromising Chartist, was called to the chair ... and it was proposed that we should nominate Mr Daniel Mellar, an honest democrat and an unflinching Chartist as our candidate for the office ... At the vestry meeting on Thursday the Chartists were at their posts like men. The farmers and our would-be superiors mustered in their might. They were at the church before we got there. There was also a magistrate at their head. The vestry was crowded to suffocation, and many could no gain admittance. ... A person in the meeting proposed our Chartist candidate. ... our man was carried by above three to one.'[152]

Unwilling to accept the verdict of the vestry meeting, the Vicar put the proposition to a poll of parishioners. By the afternoon the backers of Thomas, 'supported by all the wealth and influence of the parish', was in the lead and had the church bells rung to proclaim their victory, but by the end of the poll it was found that the Chartist, Mellar, had been victorious by 228 votes to 203 for Thomas.[153]

The 'defeat of the church rate party' at Bulwell in 1844 was one of the last reports on Church rate protests in Nottingham and the *Nottingham Review*'s forecast that 'the result of the poll [at St Mary's] has rung the knell of Church rates in Nottingham, and the effect will be felt, in the course of the year' was proved correct.

There was one more report of a Church rate fiasco in the pages of the *Nottingham Review* before the churches gave up their attempts to secure compulsory rates, and that was in Radford in 1845. The vicar of St Peter's was experiencing a little local difficulty somewhat later than other parishes, which has been put down to the popularity of a garden scheme he had set up, open to dissenters as well as Anglicans.[154] The vicar, the Reverend Cresswell, called a vestry meeting and proposed a rate of one

---

[152] *Northern Star*, 20th May, 27th May 1843.
[153] Ibid.
[154] *Nineteenth Century Church and English Society*, Frances Knight, 1995.

penny farthing for the upkeep of the church and declared that it would be 'a sin in the face of the Almighty (loud laughter) to refuse it."[55] Among those present to move the amendment to adjourn the meeting were R T Morrison, the Chartist and opponent of capital punishment, and James Saunders, Chartist, present at the meeting in his capacity as a churchwarden elected by the parishioners, who declared that 'if the rate was obtained by such unfair means as refusing to put the amendment, he would not be a party to collect it (loud cheers).' At first the Reverend Cresswell refused to put the amendment to the vote on the grounds that it was 'contrary to his conscience' but eventually did so and admitted defeat as 'almost every hand [was] put up in its favour'.

Demands to abolish compulsory Church rates continued for another twenty years until eventually, in 1868, the Compulsory Church Rates Abolition Act was passed. This did not abolish the right of the Church of England to levy rates on householders in a parish, but it made the payment voluntary.

---

[55] *Nottingham Review*, 21st February 1845.

Chapter 6: For Freedom of Expression

On the evening of Saturday 17th February 1844, members of the National Charter Association arrived at Elmer Rollett's Temperance Hotel where Warser Gate met Queen Street to hear from Philip McGrath, elected to the NCA's Executive Committee the previous year. There was other important business on the agenda too, advertised in advance to readers of the *Nottingham Review,* which included the reading aloud of news from the *Northern Star* and other radical papers.

Public readings brought news cheaply to people of the town and to those who could neither read nor write, and helped to build an informed membership focussed on the challenges and priorities ahead of them. The socialists adopted similar arrangements for reading from the *New Moral World.* It was a practice which had endured for almost half a century, since the appearance of radical publications which were either too expensive for individual working men to buy on account of the government stamp duty applied to them, were politically or religiously unacceptable to the respectable middle class who sold newspapers for people like themselves, or were unstamped and sold surreptitiously by vendors who were at risk of being fined and sentenced to lengthy terms of imprisonment. They had also been places where publications deemed seditious or blasphemous could reach audiences that would have been unable to acquire individual copies. This was especially true outside of London.

Elmer Rollett was twenty six years old when he took over the coffee house in 1842, having previously been a framework knitter living in Woolpack Lane. He himself was a Chartist, the treasurer for his branch, and was nominated by the Nottingham members for a place on the National Charter Association's General Council that same year. He was continuing the work of another Rollett, Joshua, in providing a place for meetings of framework knitters and local radicals, and a venue from which support could be raised for brothers and sisters in the struggles of the day.

Joshua Rollett had been a local publican for many years and had similar connections with the radicals of the town. He had been the licensee of the Sir Isaac Newton in Howard Street since at least 1812, one of five public houses which had a news room and which had employed newspaper readers on Sunday mornings and certain weekday evenings. It had been the base from which Gravener Henson, a founder of the first framework knitters union, the United Committee of Framework Knitters, had from 1812 worked on campaigns to regulate the knitting trade and remove the threats from poor quality 'cut ups' through two decades of the new century.[156] And in 1820 it had been the meeting place of local 'Friends of Freedom and Toleration' who raised funds to support the radical publisher and printer Richard Carlile, imprisoned in Dorchester Gaol in 1819 for blasphemy for printing Thomas Paines' *Age of Reason,* and who subsequently collected subscriptions to a fund for Susannah Wright, a courageous woman from Nottingham whose contribution to freethought and a free press have been for too long overlooked.[157]

Richard Carlile, a tin plate worker from Devon, had arrived in London in 1813. He became a distributor of books and papers, including Thomas Wooler's *Black Dwarf,* which was launched in 1817 and soon proscribed by the Home Office. He re-printed Thomas Paine's *Age of Reason* and sold it in pamphlet form, and was present in Manchester in 1819 at the Peterloo massacre when a thousand cavalry, hundreds of infantrymen and yeomanry and four hundred special constables were ordered by the magistrates to be present at a public meeting in St Peter's Fields, where 50,000 people assembled to demand Parliamentary reform. The meeting had barely begun before an order was given to arrest the speakers, and the yeomanry and cavalry moved in, cutting people down with their sabres. Fifteen people were killed and about six hundred were wounded.[158]

The Home Secretary, Lord Sidmouth, sent a letter of congratulation to the magistrates for the actions they had ordered that day. He and Lord Castlereagh, an equally despised Leader of the House of Commons who promoted the repressive policies of the government, were forever excoriated in Shelley's poem *The Mask of Anarchy*:

> 'As I lay asleep in Italy,
> There came a voice from over the Sea,
> And with great power it forth led me,
> To walk in the visions of poesy.

---

[156] *Drink and the Public House,* J J Rowley, in Transactions of the Thoroton Society, 1975. The others were the Black Horse, Fox and Hounds, Rancliffe Arms and Rancliffe Tavern.

[157] *The She-Champion of Impiety: A Case Study of Female Radicalism,* Christina Parolin, in Unrespectable Radicals?, ed. Michael T Davies and Paul A Pickering, 2008. This is the most comprehensive account of the trials of Susannah Wright.

[158] Accounts of the number of deaths from the sabres, and being trampled underfoot, vary from eleven to sixteen.

I met Murder on the way -
He had a mask like Castlereagh -
Very smooth he looked, yet grim;
Seven blood-hounds followed him:

Clothed with the Bible, as with light,
And the shadows of the night,
Like Sidmouth, next, Hypocrisy
On a crocodile rode by."[159]

Richard Carlile was to have been one of the speakers that afternoon in St Peter's Fields but he succeeded in escaping arrest and took to London the first news of the massacre, and wrote an account of it that he published in Wooler's new publication *Sherwin's Political Register*. He was subsequently arrested and spent the first of many terms in prison. Sentenced for a total of two and a half years for publishing Paine's *Age of Reason* and Palmer's *Principles of Nature* he refused to pay the fines and securities imposed and was not released until six years had passed. So had begun a long running campaign to outwit and defeat those 'clothed with the bible and the shadows of the night' who sought to suppress the expression of views deemed seditious or blasphemous, and to persecute those who, like Richard Carlile and Susannah Wright, had the audacity and the courage to publish and sell them.

Susannah was a native of Nottingham, the daughter of Sarah and Robert Godber who lived in Kid Street, near the foot of Goosegate.[160] Her father was a framework knitter and, having served an apprenticeship, was a burgess of the town, entitled to vote in parliamentary elections under the system prevailing at that time. Her younger brother James was a cordwainer, a maker of fine leather shoes, and was enrolled as a burgess in 1824, a privilege he was entitled to as the oldest son of a burgess. She also had two sisters, Sarah and Elizabeth, and a third sister of whom there is no subsequent record. Susannah's date of birth is not known but she was described in reports of the time as a young woman, but 'well known here for many years."[161]

---

[159] *The Mask of Anarchy*, Percy Bysshe Shelley, 1819. Verses 1,2,6.
[160] Approximately where Nottingham City Council Housing Aid office stands in Lower Parliament Street, 2013.
[161] *Nottingham Journal*, 22nd February 1822. There is no record of Susannah's baptism and no further record of 'Sarah' Godber: I speculate that Susannah was the child baptised

Susannah later described herself as a lace mender and embroiderer during her time in Nottingham. Hers was clearly a family of intelligent working men and women where she was able to develop her political convictions and perhaps participate in political activity herself. Richard Carlile described her as 'a little mild and particularly civil woman, unless insulted.'[162] She credited her home town with providing the inspiration for her activism in 1823 in a letter of thanks to the group of supporters meeting in a room at the Sir Isaac Newton:

> 'Perhaps it is the distinguished spirit which the inhabitants of Nottingham have uniformly exhibited in the cause of Reform that I owed the formation of my present principles. It was from their example that my bosom caught the spirit to desire to extend the liberties of my country, and to burst the binds, while exploring the ignorance, which Kingcraft and Priestcraft entails upon mankind.'[163]

Susannah had married William Wright in Southwark in 1815 and at the time of her arrest in 1821 she was probably in her late twenties with two very young children, Henry William born in the summer of 1820 and Mary born in February 1821.[164] When Richard Carlile, and subsequently his wife Jane and his sister Mary Ann, were imprisoned for blasphemy, she offered to run the print shop at 55 Fleet Street and keep the publications flowing. She later explained how this had come about:

> 'Every day for more than a week I silently and privately followed the footsteps of Mrs Carlile into the Court of King's Bench to watch the conduct of the inhuman Judges, and her fate: and, fired with resentment at the result, I offered myself to Mr Carlile as a willing sacrifice to Corruption's shrine which stands emblazoned in Westminster Hall.'[165]

She did so with the support of her husband William until she too was charged with blasphemy for publishing two tracts written by Carlile from his prison cell in Dorchester. Her arrest in 1821 at Carlile's Fleet Street

---

'Sarah' in August 1792, that she or her parents subsequently adopted a different name, perhaps to avoid confusion with Sarah, her mother.

[162] *The Republican*, 4th Nov 1824.

[163] *The Republican*, 23rd August 1823 in a letter to Alfred Cox, Nottingham.

[164] The marriage between William Wright and Susannah Godber, took place on 25th December 1815 in Newington, Southwark.

[165] *The Republican*, 23rd August 1822.

premises followed the intervention of the Committee for the Suppression of Vice, amongst whose wealthy supporters were counted William Wilberforce, and she was indicted with being:

> 'an evil disposed and wicked person, and disregarding the Laws and Religion of this Realm, and wickedly and profanely devising, and intending to bring the Christian religion into disbelief and contempt among the people ... caused to be sold ... a certain scandalous, impious, blasphemous and profane libel'.[166]

Susannah conducted her own defence, in which she asserted the right to free expression, the separation of church and state, the iniquity of common law as 'whim, caprice and tyranny,' and the right of the people to make the laws of the country.[167] 'She felt,' she said, 'as the Christian martyrs – infatuated, but heroic victims of superstition – had felt when they had laid down their lives at the stake; and she submitted with joy to "this worse than Pagan persecution".'[168] Her defence lasted four hours with many interruptions from the Judge. The packed jury returned a verdict after conferring for just two minutes and she was sent to London's most notorious jail, at Newgate. Returning to Court for sentencing she declared:

> 'I come not with a plea of feigned humility and false penitence, but with a mind elated with pride, from the assurance that the cause which has brought me here has a common good, and not an evil to the community, nor an offence against known laws of the country.'[169]

Sentenced to eighteen months imprisonment, a fine of £100 and £200 sureties for good behaviour, she was sent to Cold Bath Fields prison, Clerkenwell. Her health and that of her third child who shared her cell were already impaired by the conditions she had endured while in Newgate Jail awaiting her last appearance in Court in 1823, and in April 1824 she wrote to her supporters in Nottingham, ending with a few words about her own health. 'I suffer much from fits and a variety of other complaints. ... If I take flight into another world, I shall leave nothing but

---

[166] *Report of the Trial of Mrs Susannah Wright*, R Carlile, 1822.
[167] Ibid.
[168] *Nottingham Journal*, 22nd February 1822.
[169] *Speech of Mrs Susannah Wright*, R Carlile, 1823.

my mantle behind'.[170] Her friends believed that her health was in serious decline. Carlile, writing from prison in Dorchester from where he continued to compose *The Republican* every week, reported her release in July 1824, one month before the end of her sentence: 'It has been a lingering struggle on the part of Eldon, Peel and Co to yield even this; and nothing but the fear of Mrs Wright's dying in prison has made them yield. She is a woman of very delicate health, and *truly all spirit and no matter.*'[171] The last thing that Eldon, the Lord Chancellor, and Peel, the Home Secretary, wanted was that she should die in prison and become a martyr to the causes she espoused.

Meanwhile others had been running Carlile's print shop and been sent to prison too. More than 150 people served prison sentences, calculated to have totalled 200 years in prison, until the Committee for the Suppression of Vice ran out of funds to pursue the growing number of perpetrators and gave up the battle against the publication of blasphemous libels. Prosecutions for selling unstamped papers continued.

Support for the prisoners came from groups around the country who had met regularly in news rooms to read *The Republican* and other journals, and collected subscriptions of 1d a week or more towards their subsistence. In March 1820 *The Republican*, in its second year of publication, and already being produced by volunteers, published a letter from Moses Colclough enclosing 'a small sub by a few friends at Mr Roltist's [sic], Sir Isaac Newton, Nottingham, for Mr Carlile towards supporting him in confinement.'[172] The sum raised was £7 13s 4d and further sums were sent during the following six years.

The succession of convictions against Carlile and his volunteers and the harassed and poorly paid workers were for blasphemy, but support for Carlile was understood to be important to secure freedom of expression, as another of the Nottingham 'Friends of Liberty', Joshua Doubleday, commented in February 1823: '[the] meeting is composed of many who differ in religious opinions with Richard Carlile, yet they all agree, that free discussion is the best, and ought to be the only, support of religion and liberty's.[173]

---

[170] *The Republican*, 9th April, 1824.
[171] *The Republican*, 16th July 1824 (original emphasis).
[172] *The Republican*, 3rd March, 1820.
[173] *The Republican*, 15th August 1823.

After her release Susannah remained in London with her family, including her third child born in September 1822 and named Thomas Paine Carlile Wright shortly after her conviction. Her husband William had been unwell and had been living at the home of B B Jones and his wife, who cared for him and the children while she was in Clerkenwell jail. William died in January 1826 at the age of 39 and it was after his death that she returned to Nottingham. Richard Carlile inserted a notice in *The Republican* in July 1826:

> 'Mrs Susannah Wright, now a widow, a native of Nottingham, will supply any persons in that town and neighbourhood with my publications, or with London publications generally, where an order is given and a deposit made as a security for being called for. Mrs Wright's present residence, until she can suit herself in a shop, is with her mother, Mrs Godber, at No. 10 Kid Street, Platt Street, Nottingham.'[174]

Illustration 11: Tradesmen's Mart, Parliament Street.
Where Susannah Wright had her first bookshop (photo 1898).

If Susannah or any of her Nottingham supporters had expected that her return to the town to open a bookshop would take place without comment from her adversaries, they were to be disappointed. Six months earlier

---

[174] *The Republican*, 28th July 1826.

when Richard Carlile was released from Dorchester Gaol, he received from William Harris of Nottingham – 'this hot-bed of religious enthusiasm' – a letter addressed to *The Republican*, fearful that 'those monsters of iniquity which have been your persecutors, are only meditating some more lasting, and if possible, more cruel punishment.'[175] More cruel punishment was indeed planned, but it was directed at Susannah rather than Carlile, and not in London but in Harris's own town of Nottingham.

Susannah opened for the business of selling books and papers in the last week in July at a stall in the Tradesmen's Mart on Parliament Street, moving on to more suitable premises in Goosegate a week later. Her enemies were waiting for her.

On the morning of Monday 31st July Susannah moved into her new shop in Goosegate. In the afternoon her new shop sign was delivered. By curious coincidence the landlord happened to be on the spot and objected to it being displayed, declaring that he would go to the Mayor if she insisted on putting it up. Susannah told him that he was 'a foolish man' to be looking for support in that quarter but away he went to see the Mayor, John Houseman Barber, returning later to say that the Mayor and magistrates had refused to intervene 'unless there was a riot.'

Susannah continued the story in *The Republican*:

> 'The crowd was very great round the window; but gratifying to say, remarkably quiet. After the shop had been shut about an hour and a quarter, my aunt and another person being with me, and two young men, that are kind enough to open the shop in the morning and close it at night, were just wishing me goodnight, when my door was burst open: one half of it is glass and a shutter over it – both *window and shutter came in,* my aunt ran to the door, and found my landlord Barber the broker ... He exclaimed, "I am glad of it, I wish they had broken every pane of glass in the window; for I have been to the magistrates, and they tell me that if we can breed a riot they can interfere, and we can get her out." '[176]

Challenging her landlord to admit his guilt in arranging the commotion he eventually agreed: 'at last, as if moved from his astonishment at my

---

[175] *The Republican*, 13th January 1826.
[176] *The Republican*, 11th August 1826 (original emphasis).

spirits, he replied: "indeed you are an ill-used woman, but I am beginning to get enlightened, I see that I have acted wrong". Do not these answers show that he was the instigation of those persons breaking open my house, or shop, at the time of ten minutes past eleven?'

A member of the Nottingham discussion and fundraising group, Lurus Smith[177], a young man of twenty four who had been born in Nottingham and spent most of his life there as a teacher of mathematics, wrote his comments on the state of siege in which Susannah had found herself in her first week in Goosegate:

> 'The town of Nottingham is in an uproar, the Saints are in a sweat, and all the bigots and blackguards are in a ferment – and for what? Because a woman is exposing Paine's *Age of Reason* and Palmer's *Principles of Nature* for public sale. The ire of the Christians is dreadful. The door has been broken open at midnight, and all the annoyance that a few illiterate knaves are capable of planning has been put into execution. Infidel publications have hitherto been sold in this town in a private way, and a public exhibition of these works has given an impetus to the mind of the multitude which will not speedily be forgotten."[178]

The *Nottingham Mercury* helpfully gave the shop some additional publicity, though not quite the kind that Susannah might have welcomed:

> 'We are extremely sorry to observe, that a shop has been opened, in this town, for the sale of those infidel publications which tend to disgrace and demoralise society; and we understand, that the person who keeps it is in the habit of disseminating (by way of controversy with curious enquirers) the most pernicious principles."[179]

Two weeks later the uproar had still not abated and Carlile, quoting from news sent by Susannah for *The Republican*, reported that:

> 'The Nottingham Christians destroy her property, as far as they can, in breaking the front of her shop, and threaten vengeance on her person, if they catch her alone. But she goes

---

[177] *The Republican*, 18th August 1826. The letter concludes 'Smith and Larus'. Lurus Smith census and BMD records exist, there are none for 'Larus'.
[178] *The Republican*, 18th August 1826.
[179] *Nottingham and Newark Mercury*, 16th August 1826.

bravely on, and will do a great deal of good in the town. The outcry is raised, and useful publications are selling there at a large rate. We want such a person in every town in the country.[180]

Carlile goes on to make the case for the benefits of an uncompromising approach: 'Knowledge can only be communicated by the shocking and removing of prejudices, and it is quite amusing to see the advantage, the power, which a mind set free from bad prejudice has over one that is not free.'

It is clear that the group of infidels and upholders of free expression that had existed for the past six years or more had now ventured out of the shadows of the Sir Isaac Newton. William Harris writes that 'were it not for the protection of friends, she would ere this have fallen a victim to the fury of fanaticism, and thus have added another crime to the black catalogue of Christian vices. ... no difficulties would induce us to renounce our project; we intend to achieve the victory and establish free discussion.'[181]

Having failed to foment a riot, or to intimidate Susannah into submission by threatened or actual violence, the organisers of the disturbances turned their minds to a prosecution for blasphemy. Lurus Smith had reported on the 10th August that a lawyer named Hopkinson had threatened her with prosecution 'but we fancy it mere vapour. This fellow is nicknamed *Brassy*, from his impudence and the hardness of his face.'[182] William Harris on the 19th August added 'we are well assured that a correspondence is carrying on with the most bigoted in this town and Pritchard of London. Our fate is yet unknown; but Old Brassy has given information of his intention to proceed as the law directs.'[183]

George Pritchard was a solicitor and secretary to the Committee for the Suppression of Vice, which had been engaged in hostilities with infidels since 1802 but had been virtually drained of funds in the long running battles with Richard Carlile, Susannah Wright, and more than a hundred and fifty others since 1819, and had by now practically abandoned the field. Knowing of Susannah's resolve and the frail state of health which

[180] *The Republican*, 1st September 1826.
[181] Ibid.
[182] *The Republican*, 18th August 1826 (original emphasis).
[183] *The Republican*, 1st September 1826.

had led to her premature release from Clerkenwell jail, the Committee would have been very wary of renewing proceedings against her. But Susannah and her friends could not have been sure of that, and Susannah told another solicitor who came to her shop that 'she had the promise of at least twenty ... to fill her place' should she be arrested.[184] The prospect of initiating costly and perhaps interminable proceedings against another twenty or more people, at least one of whom was an uncompromising woman, was a threat more powerful than any that could be used against Susannah herself and it marked a turning point in the relative fortunes of the oppressor and the oppressed.

The siege of the Goosegate bookshop lasted four weeks. On Tuesday 29th August Susannah wrote:

> 'My shop was broken open five or six times on Monday night, with several attempts to drag me out, which certainly would have been done but for my friends. The Christians got so furious, between nine and ten o'clock, that we found it necessary to call in the police. Two officers were soon on the spot, and fortunately caught a man in the act of bursting open the door. They soon lodged him in the *House of Correction*. Returning to my house one was dispatched to the *Mayor,* and one kept his post in the house. The Christians *thought he was gone*, and bursting open again, in came two of them. The officer closed the door, and kept them prisoners. The other returned with instructions to quell the riot if they could, if not, to call in more officers. This they were obliged to do, and succeeded in clearing the street by eleven o'clock.'[185]

The next day Susannah did not press charges against the men who had broken into the shop, but persuaded the magistrates to bind them over to keep the peace. 'The ringleader is not yet in custody; but there is a warrant out against him. This man I shall certainly prosecute, as he threatened my life again and again. The Magistrates said they should have him by Friday, and that we might attend at eleven o'clock on that day.' Meanwhile Susannah kept a pistol under the counter 'for they have attempted, even in the daytime, to drag me out ... Two youths came in and began to use the

---

[184] Ibid.
[185] Ibid. (original emphasis).

most dreadful language. I took up the pistol and very coolly asked them if they should like it fired at them ... They did not stay, but scampered off.' This was persecution worse than she had ever experienced before. There were, she said, at times 'more than two hundred throwing their curses and prayers alternately at me' but she knew that had she stayed inside her shop all day their courage and their ferocity would have grown greater still.[186] 'I never saw anything like it in London. The scenes here are not to be described'. The magistrates and police officers she commended for their willingness to do their duty to protect her, having acted 'with the greatest honour, for which I here publicly tender them my thanks."[187]

Two weeks later Susannah wrote to *The Republican* 'I have the pleasure to inform you, that *the victory is ours*, and that we have succeeded in establishing free discussion in the most fanatical and bigoted town in England. Yes, we are conquerors.' The tide had turned so swiftly that:

> 'the most bigoted would now be my friends, and invite me to their houses. *Even my old landlord, Mr Barber, has turned a customer.* ... The women are beginning to enquire, and we may soon expect to hear the greater part of them are Materialists. ... Our enemies blush at their own conduct towards me, and say, that they will now try to protect me from the more ignorant.'

If further proof were needed that the tide had indeed turned, she moved to larger premises further up Goosegate. 'I have no doubt that I shall yet do well."[188]

This is the last account of Susannah Wright and the bookshop in Goosegate. Whether she stayed in Nottingham or moved away, remained a widow or remarried, are at present mysteries unsolved, along with the year of her birth and the place and circumstances of her move to London. Richard Carlile makes no mention of her during his time in Nottingham in 1828 and would surely have lodged with her or visited her had she still been living in the town. Of her brother there is no record after 1825. Her mother Sarah died in 1829 at the age of 57. Of her two children little is known apart from their names and there is no trace of them in later UK census records.

---

[186] *The Republican*, 15th September 1826
[187] *The Republican*, 1st September 1826.
[188] *The Republican*, 15th September 1826 (original emphasis).

So who were the men and women who had been her opponents and her supporters? Some of them she named, others named themselves, many of her supporters remain hidden behind initials or pseudonyms to protect themselves and their families, if they identified themselves at all. The 'arrangements' which the Home Office had made in 1816 'for obtaining secret intelligence' were still in operation and remained so for many years to come, creating a real fear of arrest for sedition, blasphemy or being members of illegal combinations.[189]

Susannah named a few of her detractors in *The Republican*. One was "Old Brassy", the solicitor who threatened her with prosecution, so named 'from his impudence and the hardness of his face'[190] He was one Hopkinson, either George at Long Row, or William at Castle Gate, both solicitors, and both Church of England Tories. Another was a 'dastardly, methodistical pawnbroker, two or three doors from me, whose name is Hernick [sic], supposed to be one of the gang' which had organised the attacks on Susannah's shop on her first day of occupancy.[191] Samuel Herrick had been a pawnbroker in Goosegate for more than twenty years. His son William opened a grocery business there in the mid-1820s, was another Tory voter and supporter of the Tory candidate, John Smith Wright, in the Parliamentary election of June 1826, whose election agent was the lawyer, George Hopkinson. A third was her landlord, Barber, a furniture broker, whom she told was "a foolish man" for taking his complaints about her shop sign to the Mayor, and who had later agreed that she was indeed an "ill used woman".

Accompanying "Old Brassy" on his visit to her shop on opening day was 'a pillar of "Old Mother Church",' none other perhaps, than the George Wilkins, Vicar at St Mary's.[192] Wilkins had a passionate hatred of infidels and in December 1819, one month after the passage of the notorious Six Acts, he had written to the Home Secretary, Lord Sidmouth, about an unnamed man who had 'for some time disseminated tracts of the most abhorrent and blasphemous description', and 'for the wider distribution of them in the County, on Market day he keeps a stall in the Market Place for the same purpose.' Wilkins saw himself as a saviour of morality:

---

[189] *Home Office papers*, HO 41/42, 20th December 1816, National Archives.
[190] *The Republican*, 18th August 1826.
[191] *The Republican*, 11th August 1826.
[192] *The Republican*, 1st September 1826, in a letter from William Harris, Nottingham.

'The torrent is too important to be any longer tolerated. The Union Societies purchase largely for the sake both of distribution and exposition. The injury done against morality requires my best and most zealous endeavours to counteract and as the magistrates have <u>ostensibly</u> done nothing to stop the evil, it is my wish immediately to prosecute the vendor'.[193]

He would do, he said, all in his power 'to suppress and defeat the evil machinations of the seditious and profane both alike plotting the downfall of that government under which they might enjoy tranquillity and safety.'

Unfortunately George was a little strapped for cash and sought some pecuniary assistance. Wilkins' zeal, and the copy of the *Black Dwarf* he had enclosed, were gratefully acknowledged by Lord Sidmouth but his offer to prosecute was politely declined. Sidmouth did, however, direct that a list of articles 'which have been selected for Prosecution by the Attorney General' be sent to Wilkins and 'if you will cause any of these articles to be purchased at the shop, to which you allude, his Lordship will give directions for the Prosecution, and if any others are purchased which appear to you to be highly blasphemous and seditious the propriety of prosecuting them shall undergo consideration.'[194] The very next day Wilkins replied to Sidmouth, enclosing a copy of the *Medusa or Penny Politician* and the verbatim reports of Carlile's trial, which included extensive quotations from Paine's *Age of Reason*, which Carlile had had printed in the expectation that trial reports would not be treated as a blasphemy and enjoy unfettered circulation. Sidmouth responded that Carlile would be prosecuted on the basis of the editions Wilkins had forwarded.[195] On this occasion the vendor was not prosecuted, that would come later.

Susannah already had supporters in the town from her earliest days in Newgate jail. In August 1822, less than a month after her conviction for blasphemy, Alfred Cox, living at St Peter's Church Yard, formerly Assistant Writing Master at the Free Grammar School, sent £2, expressing 'the

---

[193] *Home Office papers*, HO 42/198, 1st December 1819, National Archives (original emphasis).
[194] *Home Office papers*, HO 41/5, 4th December 1819, National Archives.
[195] *Home Office papers*, HO 42/198, 5th December 1819, and HO 41/5, 11th December 1819, National Archives.

honest pride we feel in calling ourselves the townsmen of a woman so distinguished by her zeal and perseverance in advocating the cause of our country and of humankind'.[196] Susannah replied to the *Republican*: 'Be so good as to return my sincere thanks to the committee for the Management of the Nottingham Fund for the relief of persecuted reformers, for the sum of two pounds; and be assured that such a mark of approbation coming from my native town ... has been thrice pleasing and cheering to me.'[197]

The Nottingham 'Friends of Liberty' continued to send small sums to Susannah until she was released in July 1824, but some at least of the members of that group continued to meet and in November 1825 *The Republican* published a letter reporting a new discussion group, meeting on Sunday evenings at the Rancliffe's Head, Gedling Street, Nottingham. The letter bore the name of John Smith, of whom more was to be heard in the years to come.'[198]

The first name that came to light among the contributors to the relief fund after Carlile had been imprisoned was that of Moses Colclough, sending the proceeds of a collection of £7 13s 4d from the Sir Isaac Newton. In March 1822 he wrote again, enclosing £10 from 'The Friends of Freedom and Toleration, residing in this town and neighbourhood, feeling indignant at the merciless persecution inflicted on yourself and your family, for having fearlessly promulgated your sentiments on religious subjects'.[199] Moses Colclough lived in Dukes Place, Barker Gate, and was a burgess of the town, having qualified by serving seven years apprenticeship in his trade as a framework knitter. Donations from Nottingham to Richard Carlile's appeals in 1822 exceeded £26, which put the town fifth behind London, Manchester, Leeds and Edinburgh and ahead of fifty three other towns and villages.[200]

In August 1823 Moses Colclough sent £5 11 6d to Carlile and helpfully included the names of the contributors.[201] These included Joshua

[196] *A History of the Nottingham High School 1513-1953*, Adam W Thomas, 1957; *The Republican*, 23rd August 1822.
[197] Ibid.
[198] *The Republican*, 9th December 1825. The Rancliffe's Head was probably the Rancliffe Tavern in Gedling Street.
[199] *The Republican*, 29th March 1822.
[200] *The Republican*, 3rd Jan 1823.
[201] *The Republican*, 15th August 1823. Other names included are: Edward Sale, Sarah Sale,

Doubleday who was chairing the meetings of the Friends at the Sir Isaac Newton. He appears to have been a linen draper of Bottle Lane. Also listed was Benjamin Hind, a coal and iron merchant at Castle Lock Wharf; John Syniaed [Synyer], a framework knitter of Beck Lane; and John Crosby. In 1824 another name appeared, of John Walker who sent £5 from 'friends of tolerance and free discussion' meeting at the Duke of York. These were probably the nucleus of the group of men and women who collected funds for both Richard Carlile and Susannah Wright.

All of these men were burgesses, and they all appear in poll books for elections between 1820 and 1832. In the town Council elections in 1825 both Whig candidates had declared against enclosure of the common lands, but at the nomination meeting Thomas Wakefield expressed his doubts about their sincerity and nominated William Rowarth, who had avowed himself to be an implacable enemy of enclosure on the grounds that it was bad for health, unfair to burgesses, 'and the church, which looks after their own in this, would put in a claim to a large share' of the land, leaving the burgesses with 'nothing but the odds and ends and corners (applause)'.[202] Rowarth received only 25% of the votes cast but these included many of the radicals of the town, perhaps encouraged by the anti-clerical declamation by the candidate, or by his support for their rights as burgesses on the common land. Some of the radical burgesses gave one vote to Rowarth and another to one of the official Whig candidates: these included Benjamin Hind and Alfred Cox. Other burgesses cast only one vote, plumping for Rowarth: they included John Synyer, and James Godber of Kid Street, the brother of Susannah Wright.

Although Susannah's name disappears from records of events after 1826, the results of her work did not, as in 1828 the Reverend Joseph Gilbert conceded when he wrote to the *Nottingham Mercury*: 'Some time ago ... in consequence of very active efforts then employed, among the industrious classes especially, to subvert all confidence in revealed religion ... the evil had begun to infect the minds of many'.[203] Hearing that Carlile would be in Nottingham during a lecture tour of England, Gilbert challenged him to a debate.

Mary Sale, William Spray, Jesse Wright, R J Wright, Thomas Corer [Courah?], Zedekiah Moore, John Bradshaw.

[202] *Poll Book 1825*, Nottingham.
[203] *Nottingham and Newark Mercury*, 6th September 1828.

When Carlile arrived in the town 'a friendly silk-throwster, Mr Crosby, invited him home for tea.'[204] From Carlile's own account it is evident that he had known Mr Crosby prior to his arrival in Nottingham. 'I had several times seen the gentleman in London, had known him as a reader of my publications, and as a contributor to my Nottingham subscriptions.'[205] It is also clear that Mr Crosby was not a humble silk throwster but the proprietor of a silk warehouse, dye works, and twisting and spinning factory, probably the business which became Fellows & Crosby of High Pavement. Arriving at the Crosby house, Mrs Crosby refused to meet him in the library where she had prepared tea, and shouted at him from the safety of another room that he was a 'corrupter of the morals of youth'. Carlile later claimed that, apart from Mrs Crosby, no other respectable woman had insulted him during his time in the town. Called upon unexpectedly to defend his recently published *Every Woman's Book* with its advocacy of birth control, while spending a Sunday evening at the Royal Children public house he apparently did so. Although whether he outraged the decency of any respectable female company that might have been present by repeating in detail the method of tying a piece of sponge to a penny ribbon, or tying the sponge at both ends for extended gratification, and inserting it just before sexual intercourse – taking care to wash it before re-using – is open to conjecture.

At his first public meeting in the 'political reading room' at the Sir Isaac Newton, Carlile met the legendary Gravener Henson 'one of those men who has been connected with all the political mysteries of his neighbourhood' but who 'has been the constant discourager of my efforts, and would have excluded, if he had enough influence, my publications from the politics of Nottingham.'[206] Carlile appears to have been unnerved by Henson's presence and, well known for rudeness and tactlessness, described him as a power seeker, which 'disposition makes a man personally offensive to all who may be opposed to his narrow, paltry, and mischievous views.'[207] He also alluded cautiously to rumours that Henson was a police spy, suspicions that appear to be confirmed by later Borough records.[208]

---

[204] *'What Is Love? Richard Carlile's Philosophy of Sex*, M L Bush, 1998.
[205] *The Lion*, 15th August 1828.
[206] Ibid.
[207] *The Lion*, 27th August 1828.
[208] *Borough Records*, Volume 8, p 225.

Meanwhile the arrangements for the debate with the Reverend Gilbert descended into chaos and recrimination, with veiled attacks on Carlile's views on contraception arising from *Every Woman's Book*. Failing to come to an agreement with Gilbert over a venue, Carlile announced that he had 'obtained the consent of Messrs Kendall & Newell, to use their well enclosed yard on the Leenside, wherein to open his school for one day, on which he hopes to give as many of the respectable inhabitants of Nottingham and its Vicinity, *both* Ladies and Gentlemen, as may be pleased to attend, a very important Lecture and lesson.' The four hour lecture and lesson was to start at 3pm on the 8th September and admission would be by ticket at 1s each, on sale 'at Mr Synyer, New Sneinton.'[209] This was almost certainly Henry Synyer, a lacemaker and son of John Synyer who was listed among the donors to Carlile's appeal several years earlier in 1823, and with whom Carlile was now lodging.

Illustration 12: Richard Carlile.
Radical printer and publisher.

The lecture at the yard at Leenside took place as advertised. So long did it last that the August sun had set and darkness had fallen by the time it concluded. There were, by Carlile's later account, some thirty respectable women in the audience with whom he conducted a serious discussion. There were many more outside who were not to be counted among the respectable and who seem to have taken the lead in the attempts to disrupt the meeting. The *Nottingham Mercury* reported the occasion:

---

[209] *The Lion*, 15th August 1828 (original emphasis).

'At the hour of the meeting, a vast multitude, principally consisting of poor women, with a mixture of boys and youths, assembled about the gates of the yard, and on the canal bank, opposite to the wharf. The women were particularly vociferous; but as they were kept by the gates of the yard and the canal, at a considerable distance from the object of their abuse, but little interruption was given to Mr Carlile ...'[210]

Carlile's own description of events was very similar, but he added that the noisy women on the opposite side of the canal were led by the wife of his host. 'The amiable Mrs Crosby gave a holiday to the persons employed on her farm, with an encouragement, perhaps a direction, that they should come and insult me. Her head man was in the meadows on the other side of the canal, doing all that he could do ... he only got himself most heartily laughed at'.[211]

As darkness descended the crowd outside the yard increased. 'The drunken sexton of St Mary's Church, who on being found there drunk and noisy, was put out and reprobated for his conduct by the people who were on the outside of the yard.'[212] Goaded on by the women, a group of men tried to force the gates open. 'During the confusion about the gates, which drew the mob from the canal bank, a barge was swung across the road, and Mr Carlile, with a party of friends, made their escape.'[213]

Richard Carlile wrote his farewell to the people of Nottingham on the 8th September. He had been in the town for a month. He returned to Nottingham in later years on several occasions but his visits failed to generate the degree of controversy that had developed in the 1820s, not least because he was unable to book meeting rooms in which to speak. In 1829 in the course of one of his tours of the provinces, he wrote from the 'Infidel Mission Headquarters, Nottingham' that his letters to the Reverends Wilkins and Cresswell among others, and to dissenting ministers, had led only to the closing of doors against him. 'Up to this date we cannot get a suitable room for an oration in this town. We have engaged, paid for, and have been disappointed by subsequent refusal, in

---

[210] *Nottingham and Newark Mercury*, 25th October 1828.
[211] *The Lion*, 17th October 1828.
[212] Ibid.
[213] *Nottingham and Newark Mercury*, 25th October 1828.

no less than five places.'[214] None of the proprietors of large halls would accept his deposit, and even his landlady Miss Byrne, a milliner in Angel Row, was persuaded by his opponents to turn him out of his lodgings despite having been won over to his views. 'The aggregate state of mind in Nottingham is very low. There is no visible communication of useful knowledge to the working people. The public house mania and the chapel mania, both alike mischievous, are the chief features of the town.'[215]

It comes as a surprise then to find that in September 1831 a petition was delivered to the House of Commons with 1,200 signatures from Nottingham objecting to the 'injudicious prosecution of the Reverend Robert Taylor', colleague of Richard Carlile and known as the 'Devil's Chaplain', who had been sentenced in April to two years imprisonment for preaching blasphemous sermons at Carlile's radical meeting place, the Rotunda in London. Whilst there few who were willing to give support his views on religion – or contraception – there were clearly a substantial number in Nottingham who were prepared to speak out against the laws on blasphemy. The petition continued: 'That your petitioners also submit that prosecuting individuals for their religious opinion, is not only arbitrary, anti-Christian, and impolitic, but also unconstitutional.'[216] The petition went unnoticed by the three Nottingham newspapers.

In the years ahead the campaigns against compulsory Church rates absorbed much of the anti-clerical protest of earlier years while infidelism became associated with the socialists, of whom Carlile was not one. The socialist *New Moral World* was never prosecuted for blasphemy despite demands in the House of Lords by the Bishop of Exeter and, like Carlile's *Republican,* it was never an unstamped publication. After the unrest during the passage of the 1832 Reform Bill through Parliament, the government had less need for the repressive measures that had first been introduced after the Napoleonic Wars. Nevertheless, the threat of prosecution for sedition was raised a decade later against Feargus O'Connor's first attempt to gain legal protection for the Land Plan, and stamp duties on newspapers remained a powerful and practical exercise of state control over free thought and expression.

---

[214] *The Lion,* 12th June 1829.
[215] Ibid.
[216] *The Prompter,* 24th September 1831.

Chapter 7: The War of the Unstamped Press

The stamp duties, or 'taxes on knowledge', were part of a repressive government's attempts, in the aftermath of the Napoleonic Wars, to stifle discussion and debate, silence their critics, and literally 'stamp out' the radical press. They had been raised to 4d a copy on newspapers selling for less than 6d in 1815, and were extended in 1819 to include papers that published opinion as well as news. This extension was one of the provisions of the notorious Six Acts passed by Parliament in the wake of the Peterloo massacre and it remained on the statute book for almost forty years.

'There was one region', commented an early twentieth century historian of the struggle, 'in which the discontent of the working people does not seem to led to any struggle for the Freedom of the Press; that was the hosiery district, where unrest was chronic. Perhaps the workers there were as ill-educated as they were ill-paid'.[217] However, as the story of Susannah Wright has shown, the struggle did have its adherents in Nottingham from 1819 onwards and, though some were poor, they were not necessarily ill-educated, and the lack of publicity for their deeds was not of their own making.

In 1832 there was a scantily veiled reference in the *Nottingham Review* to the availability of unstamped papers in the town, at the celebrations arranged by the Town Council to mark the passing of the Reform Act. Opponents of the stamp duties and supporters of the unstamped press made a public appearance towards the end of the procession which made its way through the streets of Nottingham, displaying copies of unstamped papers attached to their banner. Emboldened perhaps by expectations of sweeping changes from a reformed Parliament ahead of them, and by the number of organisations that were coming out of the shadows to proclaim their existence and their purposes, the procession concluded with:

> 'the members of a small party, which meet weekly for the discussion of religious and moral subjects, accompanied with a few friends from Snenton – a large board with the inscription "Knowledge is Power" and immediately underneath were attached a variety of *cheap* weekly

---

[217] *The Struggle for the Freedom of the Press 1819-1832*, William Wickwar, 1928.

publications – those invaluable auxiliaries for accelerating the progress of the schoolmaster's influence through the wilderness of the mind including the *Review* and *Mercury* divested of the stamp – the badge of their thraldom; and underneath these was the injunction "Read, think, and judge for yourselves." ... on the reverse ... "The universal Diffusion of Knowledge" ... May its progress be soon unchecked by legal fetters, and become free as air'.[218]

It was to be several more years before their declarations of optimism were to be rewarded. Another event in the struggle also failed to find its way into any histories of the war of the unstamped until comparatively recently.

Illustration 13: Sir Isaac Newton Inn, Howard Street.
Meeting place of supporters of Richard Carlile and Susannah Wright and opponents of laws on blasphemy, sedition, and taxes on knowledge.

In April 1836 a party of about one hundred of 'the most intelligent men of the productive classes' ate 'an excellent dinner' and 'enjoyed themselves convivially to a late hour' at the Sir Isaac Newton to celebrate the release of the Dorchester labourers who had been transported to Australia in 1834.

---

[218] *Nottingham Review*, 10th August 1832 (original emphasis).

The toasts were numerous and no doubt each one was washed down with more of Joshua Rollett's ale. 'Gentlemen', said the Chairman rising from his seat:

> 'it is fashionable, we know, on occasions like the present, to give the King first, ... I will give you the majesty of the people, 2nd peace, liberty and moral improvement of the whole human race, 3rd unfettered literature – unlimited and absolute freedom of the press, 4th may the energies of Englishmen never be relaxed until Irishmen and Englishmen have attained the full measure of their rights.'

The toasts and the beer continued to flow until the eighth was reached, 'the speedy universality of British suffrage', followed by several more and finally 'Mr S's health being given'.[219]

The order of the toasts is instructive: after the first two general eulogies to the supremacy and advancement of the people, it is not the freedom of association in trade unions, for which the Dorchester labourers had been convicted, that takes third place but the freedom of the press, while the struggles for a free Ireland come fourth and universal suffrage is way down at eighth place. Then there is a final toast, to 'Mr S' So why this unusual statement of priorities? The answer may be that this was not a specifically socialist or Chartist celebration but a non-sectarian gathering of people who had supported the Dorchester labourers, which would have included socialists, Chartists and trade unionists, but many others too. At this time in 1836 the campaign for the release of the Dorchester labourers had been successful, now there were other campaigns to be waged. Ireland was topical: it was only two weeks since Daniel O'Connell had spoken in Nottingham on Catholic emancipation and Home Rule for Ireland. It was also an opportunity to raise support for another topical campaign which was of local importance to them all, the matter of a free press and the abolition on the stamp duties on newspapers.

Three months earlier the *Nottingham Review* had carried a report of the trial of John Smith, bookseller and newsagent of Parliament Street, who appeared before the Mayor, Thomas Wakefield, and Alderman John Heard, both radical Whigs and dissenters. John Smith had been charged with selling two unstamped newspapers, John Cleaves' *Weekly Police*

---

[219] *Nottingham Review*, 15th April 1836.

93

Gazette (its national weekly circulation currently 30-40,000 a week[220]) and Henry Hetherington's *Twopenny Dispatch and People's Police Register,* for which the maximum penalty was a fine of £20 for every offence or a prison sentence of six months. The only witness was a police informer who claimed to have bought the unstamped papers from him at the Tradesmen's Mart. Smith acknowledge that he had sold the papers, but declined to accept that it was the informer, Westbury, to whom he had sold them.

The sympathy in the Court towards John Smith is palpable. 'The defendant, who on account of ill-health was allowed to be seated' was asked by the Mayor whether he might stop selling unstamped papers until the law was changed. 'The Defendant considered that the ceasing to sell the publication would be an injury to the public and therefore he would make no promise.' The Town Clerk then suggested that the Court might impose the minimum fine of £5, and Smith could then make an appeal to the quarter sessions. Still Mr Smith refused to let the prosecution off the hook, saying that he had not the money to pay and would not appeal. The Mayor then ordered that he should pay £5 or be committed to prison one fortnight for each offence 'but as the defendant appeared to be in ill health, they would give him his choice of a place of confinement.' To which the defendant 'thanked them for their kindly feeling' and requested to be sent to the Town Jail 'which was complied with.'[221]

The proceedings were in more than one sense courtly. The reported exchanges convey a sense of ritual, of theatricality, in which the accused becomes the accuser, and arranges the place of confinement with which the Court complied. There is no sense that Mr Smith was a guilty man, simply an unfortunate man who had fallen foul of a police spy and of unjust and discriminatory laws passed by another class and party to maintain their interests and suppress the rights of others to a free press.[222]

A similar prosecution in Derby a month after John Smith's trial resulted in a very different outcome. At a Court hastily convened on a Saturday evening, the defendant, who refused to give his name, told the Court he

---

[220] *Dictionary of Nineteenth Century Journalism in Great Britain and Ireland,* Laurel Brake and Marysa Demoor, 2009.
[221] *Nottingham Review,* 29th January 1836.
[222] *Nottingham Review,* 15th April 1836. Three months later the magistrates refused to accept any more witness statements from Westbury as he had been found to be 'receiving money to compound his cases.'

was under no obligation to abide by a law he had no part in making, devised by Castlereagh 'of notorious memory' and now enforced by the Whigs. He had been imprisoned for selling unstamped papers in the past, he said, and was ready to go to prison again, and others would be waiting to take his place.[223] He refused to pay the fine and was sent to Derby Gaol for six months. The unnamed man was nineteen year old George Julian Harney who, having three years' experience in the war of the unstamped and two prison sentences for selling the *Poor Man's Guardian* in London behind him, was soon to be playing a leading role in Chartism.

Was 'Mr S', the man whose health had been toasted at the Sir Isaac Newton in April, the John Smith now languishing in the Town Jail for selling unstamped newspapers? It is very likely. It is also probable that this was the same John Smith who had written to Richard Carlile at *The Republican* in 1825 reporting a new discussion group at the Rancliffe's Head in Gedling Street commenting that the 'multitude are still in ignorance, they still yield implicit credence to a blood-sucking priesthood, a barbarous magistracy, and a corrupt government'.[224]

This may also have been 'J.S.' who had written to the *Mercury* in 1827 advocating 'the superior advantages of the Co-operative and Communal System of Society over the individual or competitive',[225] and the same John Smith who signed a letter to the *Review* in April 1832, along with Joshua Doubleday and John Crosby who had supported Richard Carlile and Susannah Wright ten years earlier, 'on behalf of the political clubs and associations which we virtually represent.'[226] It would seem likely that John Smith was also the man from whom the Reverend George Wilkins of St Mary's bought copies of the *Black Dwarf*, the *Medusa* and the reprints of Carlile's trial in 1819 when Wilkins was engaged in the business of being a Home office informer.[227]

The news of John Smith's arrest and conviction spread quickly. News arrived in London from a local middle class radical, John Clayton, the same John Clayton whom Richard Carlile had identified in 1828 as the publisher of an anonymous paper 'of the really religious and throat

---

[223] *Nottingham Review*, 5th February 1836; *Memoirs of a Social Atom*, W E Adams, 1903.
[224] *The Republican*, 22nd November 1825.
[225] *Nottingham and Newark Mercury*, 30th June 1827.
[226] *Nottingham and Newark Mercury*, 30th April 1831.
[227] *Home Office papers*, HO 42/198, 1st December 1819, National Archives.

cutting kind' when he was trying to find a place to debate with Reverend Gilbert.[228] On this occasion there were no problems in finding a meeting place. Clayton booked the Exchange Hall.[229] Chaired by the Mayor, the very same Thomas Wakefield who had presided over the Court which convicted John Smith, the platform consisted of many of the middle class radical, dissenting Whigs of the town, such as Alderman Howitt, Samuel Fox, William Cutts and George Gill. One of the speakers was Lurus Smith, a member of the support group for Richard Carlile and Susannah Wright and correspondent to Carlile's *Republican* ten years earlier, who seconded a proposition that the Town Council promote the motion for repeal of the newspaper stamp in Parliament. In a speech that drew comparisons with the oppression of the poor, uneducated, unrepresented black slaves of the United States by their white masters, he declared that in Britain 'political knowledge was most necessary of all for the working classes.'[230]

Lurus Smith clearly saw the repeal of the stamp duties as a political means to an end rather than an end in itself. Knowledge would convey power to those who were excluded from it, particularly the working class that had been betrayed by the Reform Act of 1832 which had given political dominance to the middle class. For Whigs, including radical ones such as Thomas Wakefield, there were always elements of hypocrisy and embarrassment about denouncing the stamp duties whilst enforcing the Stamp Acts. Feargus O'Connor summed up the situation in his inimitable style: 'The Whigs don't like the unstamped because, like the lady who refused to buy a looking glass, they make them look hideous.'[231]

Whig newspaper proprietors had other reasons for disliking them. 'The printer of the paper with the stamp, is much injured by the sale of the cheaper publications' sold unstamped, admitted the editor of the *Nottingham Review*, Richard Sutton.[232] Repeal of the stamp duties would benefit the stamped papers by enabling the proprietors to reduce their prices, and dispatch from the market place those cheap competitors with reputations for fearlessness that had kept the movement for repeal in the public eye. Market forces would succeed in doing what the Stamp Acts had failed to do, and indeed newspaper circulation did enjoy a period of

---

[228] *The Lion*, 12th September 1828.
[229] *The Pauper Press*, Patricia Hollis, 1970.
[230] *Nottingham Review*, 26th February 1836.
[231] *Nottingham Review*, 29th January, 1836.
[232] *Nottingham Review*, 22nd January 1836.

immediate and sustained growth after the reduction on the stamp duty to 1d in 1836, and the fortunes of the previously unstamped papers fell into decline.[233]

For working class radicals John Smith was not just a totem for repeal of the stamp duties. He was well known among working men and radicals of all persuasions in the town. He was a main source of stamped as well as unstamped radical papers, and his arrest was not only a personal misfortune but a political one too. His stall was one of only nine places outside of the capital that sold the socialist *New Moral World* which in March 1835 was advertising the availability of the paper, and 'A Splendid Portrait of Robert Owen', from 'Smith, Nottingham'.[234] In ill health he continued to sell papers on his release from jail, although by now most of the formerly unstamped papers were paying the 1d stamp. After his death sometime between 1836 and 1838 the newspaper stall continued to be run by his widow, Mary Ann, and became the main outlet for the *Northern Star* after its launch in 1838 which, it said, could be obtained from 'Mrs Smith, Tradesmen's Mart',[235] and which, two years later, reported that 'a box to receive contributions for our incarcerated brethren is fixed in Mrs Smith's shop, the news-agent for the *NS*, where they can deliver their mites'.[236]

The year 1836 marked the culmination of the campaign against stamp duties. Just as the numbers of willing victims of the laws of blasphemy had overwhelmed the resources of the Committee for the Suppression of Vice in the 1820's, so the numbers of willing victims of the stamp duties overwhelmed the resolve of Whig governments in the 1830s. It has been estimated that the circulation of the unstamped papers, selling at no more than 1d or 2d, had reached 200,000 copies a week by 1836.[237] Prosecutions were now counterproductive. 'So long as mere violence of language is employed without effect' said the Whig Prime Minister, Lord Melbourne, it was better not to add to the importance of 'these mob leaders' by prosecuting them.[238] Ultimately the campaign for abolition was successful in the lobbies of the House of Commons, but the real work was done in

---

[233] *The War of the Unstamped*, Joel Wiener, 1969.
[234] *New Moral World*, 7th March 1835.
[235] *Northern Star*, 10th November 1838.
[236] *Northern Star*, 5th December 1840.
[237] *Bread, Knowledge and Freedom*, David Vincent, 1981.
[238] *The Pauper Press*, Patricia Hollis, 1970.

the previous six years by those printers, publishers, vendors, many hundreds in number, who defied the law. John Smith's conviction in Nottingham was one of the last in a long running but successful campaign against the stamp duties on newspapers.

The campaign for complete abolition continued. In 1838 the Nottingham Working Men's Association drew up its Objects and third in the list of nine was 'To develop every possible means, and to use every exertion, to remove those cruel laws, that prevent the free circulation of thought, through the medium of a cheap and honest press'.[239] In 1849 a group of radical publishers in London formed the Newspaper Stamp Abolition Committee. The instigator of this committee was Henry Hetherington, in earlier years the publisher of the *Poor Man's Guardian* from 1831 to 1835, a 1d unstamped paper with a weekly circulation of more than 20,000, for which he had been imprisoned three times and in which upwards of five hundred persons had been imprisoned for selling it. Only after three and a half years did the Court of Exchequer declare the *Poor Man's Guardian* to be a legal publication and the persecution of Hetherington and his staff and supporters ceased, but Hetherington remained committed to the cause of complete repeal and, with George Jacob Holyoake, was among the founders of the Newspaper Stamp Abolition Committee in 1849. In December of that year the last session of the Chartist Conference adopted unanimously a resolution from George Julian Harney calling for the total repeal of the stamp duties. They were not finally abolished until 1855.

The government might have discarded the newspaper stamp as a means of controlling dissidence but the dissidents had by no means abandoned the radical press. Thoughts turned to publishing newspapers of their own.

The weekly *Northern Star,* launched by Feargus O'Connor in 1837, a year after the reduction in duty, was sold legally for 4½d, including the 1d stamp duty, still a considerable sum for a framework knitter earning less than 15/- per week. Within two years of its launch the *Northern Star* had developed a very substantial weekly circulation of 48,000, outselling *The Times* by a considerable margin, and for every individual subscriber there were many others who heard the news from the *Northern Star* at meetings such as that at Elmer Rollett's Coffee House and Temperance Hotel on a Saturday evening in February 1844.

---

[239] *Nottingham Review*, 10th August 1838.

The *Northern Star* gave good coverage of news of national and international events as well as news of Chartist activities, and it operated a policy of non-sectarian openness in the news, reports and correspondence that it carried, but there was a desire among organised framework knitters and Chartists in Nottingham for a regional paper under their own control which would give greater prominence to local news, and local news that did not include lengthy reports of bible tract societies, meetings of freemasons, and marriages among the gentry.

The middle class radical *Nottingham Review* did print extensive reports of local Chartist meetings and events, but its reports of the middle class Complete Suffrage Union were even more extensive, and reports on Anti-Corn Law League meetings more extensive still. Its treatment of local Chartist news was also on occasions questionable, and its attempts to identify 'physical force' Chartists and split the ranks of local Chartism were resented. And the editor had demonstrated the limits of his liberalism with the complete exclusion of news that his 'respectable' readers might find unpalatable, typical of which was the persecution imposed by local Christians upon Susannah Wright, and which he would repeat when Emma Martin came to town in August 1844 by imposing another news embargo, on two of the year's biggest public meetings in the Market Place. In creating an embargo on news about socialism and infidelism Richard Sutton was in the same company as his commercial rivals, the proprietors of the Whig *Nottingham Mercury* and the Tory *Journal*.

In April 1839 the *Nottingham Review* and the *Northern Star* had published a prospectus for *The Nottingham Chronicle & Midland Liberator*, intending to be a 'true Radical Newspaper' for the 150,000 working men in Nottinghamshire, Derbyshire and Leicestershire, with a broad platform of aims including abolition of Church rates, repeal of the Corn Laws, 'cheap and honest government' and a 'fair days wages for a fair day's work'.[240] Referring to the points of the Charter without mentioning it by name, it appealed for 'a restoration of the old English Constitution', and no taxation without representation. To be published as a profitable investment with a yield of 20%, the prospectus declared that 'all who purchase newspapers should be shareholders' and six thousand shares were to be sold at 6s each.

---

[240] *Nottingham Review*, 5th April 1839; *Northern Star*, 13th April, 1839.

Whether any working men took part in the drawing up of the prospectus – and the language of the prospectus suggests they were not – it was taken sufficiently seriously for Mr William Lilley, shoemaker and 'Chartist Drummer' who beat the drum at the front of what the *Mercury* disparagingly referred to as 'Chartist mobs', to be sent as a delegate from the Nottingham Democratic Association to a meeting in Derby to discuss the proposition. The Nottingham Democratic Association was one of ten such bodies in Britain, modelled on the London Democratic Association formed the previous year and representing the radical wing of London Chartism, with a reluctance to collaborate with middle class reformers. Shares in the paper were on sale from Mr Herbert Ingram, bookseller and letterpress printer of Chapel Bar, and Mr Lilley carried with him to Derby a letter from Mr Ingram asking to be appointed printer of the paper.[241]

The conclusion cannot be avoided that the proposition was a middle class intervention, for a paper that would have been beyond the reach of working men investors, with a radical remit that would not permit an honest declaration for the Charter and would extend no farther than the radicalism of the *Nottingham Review*. As no more news was published about the venture, it might be safely assumed that it advanced no further than the prospectus. Whether Mr Lilley was a supporter of such a venture is not known, but it would seem unlikely given the background of the Democratic Associations and his own later association with physical force Chartism, practising for which he suffered the ignominy of being accidentally shot in the chest by his wife.[242]

Although the plan for the *Liberator* came to nothing it established that there was thought to be a sufficient readership for a radical newspaper appealing to working class readers. The *Midland Counties Illuminator* was another, somewhat more successful, venture which did at least get off the drawing board in 1841 for sixteen editions. Published in Leicester and edited by Thomas Cooper, Chartist and teetotal campaigner, it had received the initial support of Feargus O'Connor. Nottingham Chartist James Sweet wrote a weekly column on subjects ranging from Chartism, the Poor Law, abolition of standing armies, the idle drones of the royal family to the politics of Chartists supporting a Tory candidate in the 1841

[241] *Nottingham Review*, 24th January 1840; *Nottingham and Newark Mercury*, 24th January 1840.
[242] Ibid.

elections. Three years later he contributed letters to another Leicester Chartist paper, *The Pilot*, edited by Jonathan Bairstow and Thomas Cooper, and by Cooper's wife Susannah while he was in prison on conviction of sedition. These were domains in which Sweet could express his thoughts without the restraint of his letters to the *Nottingham Review* and they give a hint of the different kind of newspaper that *The Nottingham Chronicle & Midland Liberator* might have become, had it succeeded in escaping the clutches of the middle class radicals and become a paper that was produced by and spoke to the working classes of the region.

A coincidental development was the remarriage of Mary Ann, the widow of John Smith. Still gaining a living from selling newspapers at the Tradesmen's Mart on Parliament Street where she had taken over her late husband's stall, she had opened a coffee house at the junction of Queen Street and Warser Gate with her son and three daughters, the Star Coffee Rooms. The wedding took place on the 21st January 1843 and her new husband was none other than the Chartist Elmer Rollett, with whom the previous chapter began.[243]

---

[243] *Northern Star*, 18th February, 1843.

Chapter 8: The Operatives' Libraries

On the evening of Wednesday 11th October 1844 'the members of the Operatives' Library No. 7, held at the sign of the White Swan, Alfreton Road, Radford, held a festival to commemorate the opening of the above institution', reported the *Nottingham Review*. This was the newest of the Operatives' Libraries, just five months old, one of seven then in existence and of which at least thirteen have been identified in or near to the town.[244] The first Operatives' Library at the Rancliffe Arms, founded in 1835, was now reporting the acquisition of 300 new books and a total stock of 1,600.

The libraries and news rooms at public houses and temperance coffee houses were associated with a development that is thought to have been almost unique to Nottingham: the establishment of a number of Operatives Libraries in the third decade of the nineteenth century, which represented another response by working men to the demand for unrestricted access to knowledge. If the laws on sedition and blasphemy, and the imposition of the stamp duties on newspapers and pamphlets, had been the instruments of control and coercion by the Church and the state, the Operatives' Libraries represented a new kind of response to a new and more subtle attempt to control the minds and thoughts of the operatives of the town.

Reading rooms had been in existence in the town at least since the previous century but they were established by and for the educated and professional elites of the town. A library had also existed in the town since 1744, and the town possessed (and still does) a prestigious Subscription Library at Bromley House, Angel Row, but a framework knitter, lacemaker or shoemaker would no more have entered the doors of the Subscription Library than enter the doors of the House of Commons.

The first known attempt to provide a library and reading room for working class readers was taken in 1824. This was a middle class initiative funded by the purchase of £5 shares, and resulted in the opening of the Artizans' Library in a large room at the top of the Exchange Hall, on the site of the present day Council House on the Market Square. Ordinary members paid a deposit of 2s 6d and a quarterly subscription of 1s 6d. It

---

[244] *The Operatives' Libraries of Nottingham: a Radical Community's Own Initiative*, Peter Hoare, 2002.

was open for two hours every evening. The library was planned at a time when the post-Napoleonic laws against sedition and blasphemy, and the extended provisions of the stamp duties, were being rigorously enforced and, more significantly, being systematically frustrated by volunteer printers, vendors and readers. The Combination Acts of 1799 which imposed penalties on nascent trade unionism were still in force and about to be abolished but, after the outbreak of strikes in 1824 including some well organised action among framework knitters in Derby and Derbyshire, were brought back into force again a year later in 1825. Rational middle class gentlemen living in a rapidly growing, industrial town were well aware that organised labour presented a formidable threat for the future and repressive measures alone would not be sufficient to quell unrest.

Adam Smith, author of *An Enquiry into the Nature and Causes of the Wealth of Nations* had drawn attention to what he described as 'gross ignorance and stupidity which, in a civilized society, seem so frequently to benumb the understandings of all the inferior ranks of people.' The solution to the problem lay in the instruction of those 'inferior ranks':

> 'The more they are instructed the less liable they are to the delusions of enthusiasm and superstition, which, among ignorant nations, frequently occasion the most dreadful disorders. ... They feel themselves, each individually, more respectable and more likely to obtain the respect of their lawful superiors, and they are therefore more disposed to respect those superiors.'[245]

The state was not yet ready to take on 'the instruction of the inferior ranks' but some of its leading citizens among the 'lawful superiors' in cities and towns such as Nottingham were ready to begin the process of educating and forming the opinions of its artisans by providing libraries and reading rooms.

In 1832 the Artizans' Library had a new librarian, Mr Valentine Kirk, who had also been librarian at the Bromley House Subscription Library.[246] In an ironical twist of fate his daytime occupation would find him in the role of Clerk at the Stamp Office, from which the 'taxes on knowledge' were regulated locally and from which the representative of the Stamp Commissioners in London stepped forth in 1836 to appear at the trial of

---

[245] *An Enquiry into the Nature and Causes of the Wealth of Nations*, Adam Smith, 1776.
[246] *Bromley House 1752-1991*, Rosalys T Coope and Jane Y Corbett, 1991.

John Smith for selling the unstamped. In 1833 the library had 2,658 books, the largest book stock in the town, and by 1837 it had 3,315. Until a fire in 1836 caused the library to move to alternative premises, it had shared some space with the Savings Bank, another middle class initiative intended to improve the habits of the working class, and equally unsuccessful in its mission, and the move to separate premises led to a temporary falling off in membership at the library.

The appeal of both institutions was greatest to clerks, shopmen, and young men in white collar working and lower middle class occupations. There were occasional connections between the Artizans' and the Operatives' Libraries in future years but the Artizans' appears in the guise of a first cousin, once removed. In 1845, along with the Mechanics' Institute and the Literary and Scientific Institution, the Artizans' Library was the object of – or the excuse for – one of the toasts at the annual dinner of Operatives' Library No. 2 at the King George on Horseback, a toast raised to a relation, somewhat *hoiti toiti*, absent, distant, over whom one could become sentimental only after imbibing numerous other drinks.

The evening opening hours of the Artizans' Library – closed on the Sabbath – and its scale of charges, were two frequent criticisms made about the library by many manual workers and artisans. In 1849 the Artizans' proposed raising its subscriptions from 6s a year to 10s, and changing the name from Artizans' to 'Tradesmen's', 'Commercial' or 'Tradesmen's and Commercial', moves that would finally exclude the few artisan and poorer workers from its ranks.[247] Indeed that appears to have been the intention, justified by the assertion that there were two other institutions for mechanics and none for the tradesmen.

A third point of contention was the library's restrictive practices on book selections. In 1825 the committee was exhorted not to order books 'which can in any way wound the feelings or excite the alarm of any Members'[248] In 1834 the library was asked by William Brooksbank, soon to become a founder of the first operatives' library, and later still the town's mace bearer and town crier, to buy William Howitt's *History of Priestcraft* and the committee refused. This was a dispute that would run and run at the

---

[247] *Nottingham Review*, 13th April 1849.
[248] *The Operatives' Libraries of Nottingham: a Radical Community's Own Initiative*, Peter Hoare, 2002.

Artizans' Library and there is evidence that some members were caucusing to change the acquisitions policy by changing the composition of the committee. In 1837 the rules on electing the committee were changed. Until then nominations were made prior to the Annual General Meeting by members submitting names of candidates in advance. 'It was contended that a great abuse of the old rule had taken place, and the Committee had been packed by parties who, prior to the Annual Meeting, had had pre-meetings at a public house, to arrange their voting lists, in order that such a Committee might be obtained, as would vote for a particular class of books.'[249] Despite the passing of the rule change in favour of oral nomination at the AGM, later in the meeting some of the opponents of the change were elected to the committee, including Francis Eames Jnr, a Unitarian, pawnbroker and silversmith of Goosegate, who had moved the amendment that the rule remain unchanged, but the most significant outcome of the dispute had already taken place when, in 1835, William Brooksbank and several other members had seceded from the library to set up Operatives' Library No. 1.

Attempts to exclude publications on politics and religion continued at other libraries set up for, but not by, working men. In early 1836 the Radford Artisans' Library 'founded for the benefit of the inhabitants of Radford and its vicinity' was opened for business and shortly afterwards there was a move to rent a neighbouring room 'in which the artizans of Radford might sit and read a few hours without interruption.'[250] Shares in the library cost £1, more than a week's wages for many of the parishioners, although mere subscribers could use the facilities for 1s a quarter, which was certainly cheaper than the town's Artizans' Library. The committee of twelve was elected in two equal parts by the shareholders and the subscribers. The Reverend Samuel Cresswell, his predecessor at St Peter's the Reverend Edward Cresswell, and the Reverend Thomas Keyworth were the Anglican presence on the committee, and the three Reverends were among the book donors. Samuel Cresswell was also the President. The moving spirit behind the founding of this library is unknown, but it likely to have been the Reverend Samuel Cresswell himself, the man responsible for turning Radford into 'the Gretna Green of

---

[249] *Nottingham Review*, 2nd June 1837.
[250] *The Library World of Nottinghamshire in the 18th and Early 19th Century*, Peter Hoare, in Transactions of the Thoroton Society, 2010; Nottingham Review, 12th February 1836.

Nottinghamshire.'[251] The ecclesiastic limits to freethought were made clear in Rule 8 and repeated in Rule 24:

'The funds for establishing this Library having been raised expressly on the condition that no book should be admitted, or remain in the Library, which was opposed to pure morals, or to the great doctrines of justification by faith alone, or to the divinity or atonement of Christ, this shall be considered a fundamental and unalterable rule of the institution.'[252]

It would seem that some mischievous inhabitants of Radford and its vicinity took exception to being told what they could and could not borrow from the library, as well as being deprived of the opportunity to change the 'unalterable' rule, and were not above infiltrating works of immorality and blasphemy onto its shelves. There was a rule to deal with that too, Rule 13: 'If at any time duplicates or objectionable works find their way into the Library by gift or otherwise, the committee shall at once remove them from the shelves, and dispose of them as they judge proper.'

The Mechanics' Institution was the most ambitious venture, opened in 1837, initially in a rented building at 17 St James Street. It had several classes of membership, including honorary and life, the latter costing 5 guineas. The library subscription was 1s a quarter, raised to 1s 6d, the same level as the Artizans' in 1840. With greater aspirations than the Artizans' Library it moved in 1845 to its own building in Milton Street, by which time its library stock had reached 40,000 volumes. A separate reading room was opened in 1848 with a separate subscription of 1s 6d per quarter.[253] It was also intended to provide educational classes, lectures, demonstrations of scientific experiments, dramatic, artistic and other events, but it was another institution established for, and not by, working men and its subscriptions, opening hours, and the exclusion of 'all matters tending to political or religious controversy',[254] made it an unattractive proposition for most mechanics and artisans, particularly those who were active in trade union or political activities. The education provided by Mechanics' Institutes was individualistic in its goals, having a

[251] See footnote 151.
[252] *Rules and Catalogue of the Artisans' Library, Radford, near Nottingham*, 1839, Nottingham Local Studies Collection.
[253] *History of the Nottingham Mechanics' Institution 1837-1887*, J Green, 1887.
[254] *The Mechanics' Institute: A Story in Pictures*, Volume 14, R Iliffe and W Baguley, 1975.

greater tendency to promote individual than general happiness, as Rowland Detrosier, a founder of the breakaway New Mechanics' Institution in Manchester, pointed out at the time. There was a world of difference between the individualism of the Mechanics' and the fellowship and self-organisation of the socialist Halls of Science and the Operatives' Libraries.[255]

The motivation for the Nottingham Mechanics' Institution had been clearly set out at its inception in the report of the Provisional Committee to a public meeting in the Guildhall at which a series of resolutions were passed, the second of which was an appeal to the enlightened self-interest of the middle classes:

> 'That it particularly behoves the wealthier, and more educated classes of the community, to lend their support to all institutions which have for their object the dissemination of knowledge, inasmuch as the rights of property are disregarded or respected, personal freedom circumscribed or extended, and the state of society discordant or harmonious, as the people are ignorant or enlightened.'[256]

Some of the less enlightened among the intended benefactors of the institution were suspicious or fearful of the enterprise, as the jubilee history of the Institution confirms, referring to 'the strongly pronounced feeling of hostility among the upper and middle classes to Mechanics' Institutions, as having inherent in their nature something of the revolutionary spirit', being 'hotbeds of sedition and irreligion.'[257] They need not have worried.

The permanent building in Milton Street opened in 1845 and was completed on a lavish scale, the front of the edifice dominated by 'a lofty portico, supported by fluted columns of the Corinthian style of architecture, imitated from the Temple of Sybil, at Tivoli'.[258] The interior presented 'an excellent specimen of the working of such institutions, and of the vast advantages which they convey to the class of persons for whose

---

[255] *Mechanics' Institutes of Lancashire and Yorkshire*, M Tylecote, 1957. However, in Mansfield, Mr Paulson and Thomas Rivers, consecutively secretaries of the socialist branch, were both active in the Mansfield Mechanics' Library: *Nottingham Review*, 31st May 1839.
[256] *The Mechanics' Institute: A Story in Pictures*, Volume 14, R Iliffe and W Baguley, 1975.
[257] *History of the Nottingham Mechanics' Institution 1837-1887*, J Green, 1887.
[258] *The Mechanics' Institute: A Story in Pictures*, Volume 14, R Iliffe and W Baguley, 1975.

moral and intellectual cultivation they have been established.' A passer-by might easily have mistaken the premises for a bank, and it is perhaps no coincidence that a Tory banker, John Smith Wright, was one of the prime movers in establishing the Institution. Most artisans found it intimidating and preferred the environment offered by the Rancliffe Arms or the Queen Adelaide at Sneinton to that of the Temple of Sybil at Tivoli.

Illustration 14: Mechanics' Institution, Milton Street (1844).

There was to be much wringing of hands over the years ahead by well meaning supporters of the Mechanics' who continued to be baffled by the absence of so many of the class of people for whom it had been intended. Seventeen years after it had first opened, Mr John Denison MP, at a joint meeting of forty delegates from the Mechanics' Institution and the Operatives Libraries, asked 'Why is the term Mechanics' Institution a misnomer?' Why had it been embraced by 'so small a portion of the class for whom institutions of this kind were originally intended?'[259] Messrs Burbage, Cope and Wall, three men with many years activity in the Operatives' Libraries, Chartism and the Chartist Land Company, replied that the 5/- entrance fee and the 1s 6d quarterly subscription had long been financial barriers to many working men and women, and 'that Sunday was the only day in which the operative could call his own, and on

---

[259] *Nottingham Review*, 25th January, 1850.

that day the Institution was closed, which compelled them to go to the public house library.'[260] The latter was probably intended as an appeal to the sentiments on religion and sobriety of the Member of Parliament rather than a criticism of the operatives' libraries at public houses, Mr Burbage being a past chairman of Operatives' Library No. 3, which met at the Pheasant public house in Charlotte Street.

An analysis of the Mechanics' Institution membership in 1850 showed that the largest category of members was that of clerks, shopmen and warehousemen (236) followed by shopkeepers and tradesmen (80). Lace and framework knitters (38) and other operatives artisans (75) were but a small part of the membership. Servants, labourers and gardeners were outnumbered by men from the manufacturing and professional classes. Women of all classes comprised less than 10% of the membership.[261] But for some, it would appear, the lack of operatives at the Institution was nothing to lose sleep over. Mr H Reid, the Principal of the Peoples College, said that it had always been a matter of regret with him that the operatives had not joined the Institution in the numbers expected but 'They must not conclude that because the operatives had not joined no good had been done by it. ...if they had never had a single working man among them, their Institution would have done much good...'[262]

The first Operatives' Library was established in August 1835 at the Rancliffe Arms, Turn-Calf Alley, Sussex Street in Leen Side. Its clientele would have been exclusively working class. This public house already had a radical history. Previously known as the Bull's Head, it had been bought in 1813 by a group of friends for John Blackner, framework knitter, author of the first substantial history of the town who completed it there in 1815, and one of the usual suspects in the search for the legendary Ned Ludd.[263] He remained landlord until he died there in 1816 when his wife became the publican.

---

[260] Ibid.
[261] *Education and Society in Nineteenth Century Nottingham*, David Wardle, 1971: Of 579 members in 1850, 64 were females, 56 youths, 10 were servants, labourers, gardeners, 20 in handicrafts, 35 smiths, engine or bobbin carriage makers, 10 joiners, plumbers, masons, painters, 38 lace and stocking makers, 236 clerks, warehousemen and shopmen, 80 shopkeepers and tradesmen, 16 professional and manufacturers.
[262] Ibid.
[263] *The Life of John Blackner*, J. C. Warren, in *Transactions of the Thoroton Society*, Volume 30, 1926; In *Old and New Nottingham*, 1853, William Wylie erroneously gives the address of the Rancliffe Arms as 'Ison Green'.

The founders of the library were William Brooksbank and nine other working men.[264] Their Rules set out their motivation and their intentions:

'Being deeply impressed with the importance of knowledge, we resolve to establish a book society, because as we progress in knowledge we must advance in freedom, knowledge being the only lever that can raise the working class into a fit condition to possess electoral privileges ... and ... as politics concern our welfare here, and religion affects our happiness hereafter, and as we believe that no political institution ought to stand which cannot bear examination, and no creed ought to be believed that cannot bear discussion, we therefore resolve to purchase books of every description, political and theological as well as those embracing history, science and literature.'[265]

This statement places the Operative Library in complete contradistinction to the Subscription Library, the Artizans' Library and the Artisans' of Radford, and to the future Mechanics' Institution. Knowledge was to be put to a collective purpose, and that purpose was to transform the political rights of the working class and the political life of the nation and, notwithstanding the reference to the 'hereafter', there were to be no religious or political barriers put in their way, 'books of every description' would be bought, and the first purchase would be the *History of Priestcraft* by William Howitt.

William Howitt proved to be less radical in politics than he was in religion, but 'he appeared in this book as the advocate of popular rights, and the liberal party at once seized upon Mr Howitt as a champion unexpectedly found'.[266] The *History of Priestcraft* appears in the oldest surviving catalogue from 1843, but there are also many other acquisitions which attest to the continuing commitment of the library members to a distinctive working class political culture. Besides many works of fiction and uncontroversial biographies, travelogues, poetry and scientific works, there were to be found the *Devil's Pulpit,* by the Reverend Robert Taylor, friend of Richard Carlile, which would have been regarded by the librarian

---

[264] William Wylie in *Old and New Nottingham* says five, David Wardle in *Education in Nineteenth Century Nottingham* says nine.
[265] *Education in Nineteenth Century Nottingham*, David Wardle, 1971.
[266] *Old and New Nottingham*, William Wylie, 1853.

at the Artizans' as even more scurrilous than Paine's work.[267] Thomas Paine's *Age of Reason* and *Political Works*; Sherwin's *Memoirs of the Life of Thomas Paine;* John Francis Bray's *Labour's Wrongs and Labour's Remedies;* William Godwin's *An Enquiry Concerning Political Justice;* John Minter Morgan's *Revolt of the Bees;* the *Cato Street Conspiracy;* Pestalozzi's *Letters;* various works by Robert Owen, William Cobbett, William Carpenter and Harriet Martineau; a report on the trials of the Chartists at Lancaster in 1843; these were all in the catalogue. There were also *Democratic Songs,* and *Corn Law Rhymes* by Ebenezer Elliott; the texts of Acts of Parliament such as the New Poor Law, and the Municipal Corporations Act; and periodicals, including the radical Whig *Tait's Edinburgh Magazine* which had been rejected by the Mechanics' Institute. Most of these publications remained in the 1857 catalogue; more recent purchases such as the *Democratic Review* by the Chartist and socialist George Julian Harney, and the *Miscellany,* by one of the later participants in Chartism, radical publisher George Reynolds, were now included.

Two of the periodicals stocked by the Operatives' Library No. 1 and the Artizans' were unstamped. One was the *Saturday Magazine.* This was published by the Society for the Propagation of Christian Knowledge. The other was the *Penny Magazine.* C D Collett, an active Chartist in 1848 and himself involved in the later stages of opposition to the stamp duties on newspapers, wrote many years later that as both publications frequently passed comment on Church and state, they should both have been stamped but they were never prosecuted 'presumably because the Lord Chancellor or the Chancellor of the Exchequer administered a judicious hint to the [Stamp] Commissioners'.[268] The *Penny Magazine* was reviled by the radical press 'and caricaturists sometimes represented Lord Brougham [Lord Chancellor] as thrusting it down the throats of its readers with a broomstick'.[269]

The fact that both libraries carried the *Penny Magazine* confirms that they did not expect it to be prosecuted, or they might also have found

---

[267] *Rules and Catalogue of the Artisans' Library, Radford, near Nottingham,* 1839. Nottingham Local Studies Collection. The catalogue lists 533 books and 5 periodicals of which 222 were history and voyages, and 143 were divinity or history. There were none indicative of infidelity or sedition, such as would have been found at Operatives' Library No. 1.

[268] *History of the Taxes on Knowledge,* C D Collett, 1899.

[269] Ibid.

themselves in Court for buying it. It was politically benign and Collett commented acidly that 'It is true that the news contained in the *Penny Magazine* was not the news of the day, but it was fresher than that of the *Spectator,* which was indebted for a good deal of its news to Socrates, Plato, Cicero and Marcus Aurelius.'[270] By stocking it the Operatives' Library proved the catholic nature of its acquisitions policy. Not even the Artizans' stocked the *Spectator.* Nevertheless, the cautious nature of the Operatives' Libraries when exposing themselves to public gaze is illustrated by the fact that they did not associate themselves with the local campaigns against the stamp duties until long after they had been made ineffectual. If there was a single legislative measure that might have benefited the libraries it would have been the abolition or reduction of the 'taxes on knowledge' that were imposed upon the newspapers and pamphlets which they purchased for their members to read. It was not until 1851 that the annual report of the Operatives' Library No, 1 reported that it would 'not be inconsistent with' their duty to 'call attention to the members to the taxes on knowledge, and the necessity of each member exerting themselves for their repeal'.[271]

The entrance fee at Operatives' Library No. 1 was 6d, half that of the Artizans' Library but the weekly subscription of 1d was the same, whilst the Mechanics' was charging 1½d. There were no grades of membership, no distinction between shareholders and subscribers, all members had a single vote in the election of the committee. It was a simple and democratic model that was familiar from working class culture, in benefit societies, trade unions, co-operative societies. They opened the library on Wednesday evenings from 8-9pm and on Sunday mornings from 12-1pm, fulfilling one of the frequent and unfulfilled demands of working men at the so-called artisans' libraries. Without the benefit of middle class philanthropy it started with a small stock of books but they were of their own choice, and not the choice of the committee on their behalf, but by a vote of the members of the society.[272]

Operatives' Library No. 1 remained at the Rancliffe Arms for the whole of its sixty year life. By 1853 it had 2,200 volumes and 4,000 in 1869. It was

---

[270] Ibid.
[271] *Nottinghamshire Guardian,* 13th February 1851.
[272] *Catalogue and Rules of the Operatives' Library No.1,* 1843, Nottingham Local Studies Collection.

always the operatives' library with the biggest stock, and it was also the catalyst for others.

The second operatives' library opened at the Seven Stars in Barker Gate in August 1837. It's origin has been said to derive at least partly from 'the indefatigable but unpaid exertions of a very poor artisan of Nottingham, William Fox, who was said to have played a role in founding some of the other Operatives' Libraries.'[273] Another founder was a man named Mellors, probably Samuel Mellors, who became the landlord of the King George on Horseback, one of the meeting places of the framework operatives, to which the library had moved by 1844. Its librarian in 1844 was a painter, Thomas Hart, probably the same Hart who had been one of the founders. The library catalogue in 1858 included several of the radical publications stocked by Library No. 1, including Sherwin's *Life of Thomas Paine* and the *Cato Street Conspiracy*, and a biography of Robert Emmett, the Irish patriot who was hung, drawn and quartered for his part in the rising by the United Irishmen against English rule in 1803.

Operatives' Library No. 3 was set up in March 1836 at the Queen Caroline, in Charlotte Street, later moving to the Pheasant in Charlotte Street. Its first purchase was not a freethought or political work but a literary journal, Chambers' *Journal of Popular Literature, Science and Arts*. Library No. 4 was established in 1840 at the Queen Adelaide in North Street, New Sneinton; No. 5 in 1844 at the White Swan, in Alfreton Road, New Radford, moving later to the Pelican Inn in Pelican Street, Radford; No. 6 in 1840 at the Cricket Players, in Hyson Green; No. 7 in 1844 at the White Swan in New Radford. Several moved from one public house to another in the same area, perhaps moving when the landlord moved. Landlords appear to have had a special relationship with the libraries, as they derived income from drink sales to library members and in most cases do not appear to have received rent for the library space. The treasurer of Library No. 2 was the pub landlord in 1858, according to the library catalogue of that year. The numbering of the libraries does not relate to their founding, and may indicate that some existed before joining a loose alliance and becoming numbered, whilst the New Lenton library was never numbered but was represented at functions with other libraries.

Besides the numbered libraries there were others at: the Castle Inn, Cross Street; the 'Philomathian Book Divan' at The Loggerheads, Narrow

---

[273] *History and Antiquities of Nottingham*, James Orange, 1840.

Marsh; the Sir John Borlase Warren, Canning Circus; the Lord Rancliffe (or Rancliffe's Head) in Gedling Street; and the New Lenton Operatives' Library founded in May 1844, at the house of Mr Rayner, the Smiths' Arms, New Lenton, which had recruited more than a hundred members in its first nine months of opening.[274] There was also the Temperance Operatives' Library in the town, founded in 1841 by William Smith at an address in Derby Road, moving with him to the coffee house he opened in Low Pavement, and later to larger premises a short distance away in Houndsgate.[275]

In addition to these libraries there were others, like the socialists' library set up in 1841. The existence of the socialist branch itself owed something to the freethinking, but not the political, views of William Howitt, as James Nixon reported to the *New Moral World*: 'The ground has in some instances been well prepared by the literary labours of William Howitt, whose *History of Priestcraft* – bold, fearless, and talented, has assisted in undermining the credit of that class.'[276] In August 1841 Nixon reported that they had accumulated 300 volumes, and charged an entrance fee of 3d and a weekly subscription of ½d. Reports of accessions of new books and new members continued to be sent until the branch suddenly ceased to exist in late 1843.[277]

Other libraries that are likely to have had a number of working class readers were those of the Oddfellows, although their allegiances probably fell more in the direction of the Artizans' than the Operatives' Libraries. In January 1845 the Operatives' Library No. 5 welcomed the news that the Manchester Society of Oddfellows intended to open a library for their members in the town, and it opened its doors in Barnsdall's Yard off Warser Gate four months later, and celebrated the opening with a ball at the Mechanics' Institute.[278]

All of the founders and committee members of the operative libraries were men, as far as records show. This would be partly a result of the libraries being held at public houses, although there is no mention of women at the Temperance Operatives' Library either.

---

[274] *Nottingham Review*, 17th January 1845.
[275] *The Library World of Nottinghamshire in the 18th and Early 19th Century*, Peter Hoare, in Transactions of the Thoroton Society, Volume 114, 2010.
[276] *New Moral World*, 10th July 1841.
[277] *New Moral World*, 9th January, 1842; 17th September 1842.
[278] *Nottingham Review*, 2nd May 1845.

A 'library for females' had opened in Houndsgate shortly after the Artizans' Library in 1824. Admission to membership required 'a reference from a respectable householder'. This, despite the low quarterly charge of 1s, would have deterred most literate working class women from using it. In 1834 a 'Young Woman's Library' was included in the *Directory* published by Pigott, with a stock of 'several hundred' volumes at 'Mrs German's, Spaniel Row.' Mrs German was probably the woman of the same name who was Matron at the House of Correction. The library was 'under the care of a committee of ladies' chosen annually by the subscribers, who paid 5/- a year.' Established in 1825, this might have been the same library set up in Houndsgate after the opening of the Artizans'.

The first mention of women being in any way involved in any of the libraries occurs in 1840 when 40 of the 130 members of Operatives' Library No. 3 attended the annual meeting at the Pheasant on Ash Wednesday. 'The female friends of the members partook of tea, after which the merry dance was kept up until a late hour'.[279] Social events combined with annual meetings were a familiar event at Operatives' Libraries. The following year the Sneinton Operatives' Library No. 4 members forsook the Queen Adelaide in North Street to hold their annual supper at the William the Fourth tavern in Manvers Street, where the size of the room would permit a social occasion to take place. Operatives' Library No. 1 held their sixth anniversary celebration in the library room at the Rancliffe Arms, where songs were sung 'and the ladies treated to a dance'.[280] The library room must have been of substantial size as dancing appears to have been a regular entertainment at their annual celebrations. In 1844 more than 80 members sat down to supper, followed by 'loyal and constitutional toasts' and dancing at 9pm. Whether the attendance figure included the wives and female friends of the members is not clear. Dancing also featured at the annual meetings of the Operatives' Library No. 2 at the King George on Horseback. In 1845, after the dinner and toasts 'about nine o'clock the room was prepared for the female friends of the institution to enjoy themselves with a dance' followed by the reappearance of some of the male members 'in theatrical costumes, giving the assemblage the appearance of a fancy dress ball.'[281]

---

[279] *Nottingham Review*, 13th March 1840.
[280] *Nottingham Review*, 13th August 1841.
[281] *Nottingham Review*, 12th September 1845.

Women do not appear in any of the reports in any other role than the guests of the male members at annual social occasions, although this is not to say that the libraries did not stock books that women would want to read or that husbands did not borrow books for wives and daughters.

It is not until 1850 that an annual report published in the *Nottingham Review* refers to the encouragement of women and children to become members, and then it is advocated more for the long-term benefit of the children than for the women members themselves: 'we should open the doors of our institution as wide as possible', reads the report from Operatives' Library No. 3, now resident at the Alderman Wood in Charlotte Street, 'the female and juvenile classes claim our special care: the latter will be the people of the future ... Many of the wise have said that the forming of the youthful mind depends on the female; if she be well informed, her children will be wise and virtuous.'[282] The following year's report suggests they have been successful as 'We have a large entry of members, both male and female.'[283]

Operatives' Library No. 1 had the *Boys' Own Book* in its catalogue in 1843 and Library No. 3 had also been among the first to draw attention to its 'juvenile members' in 1846, and to its arrangements for sick and unemployed members and members living in the workhouse, from which it would appear that the weekly subscription might have been waived.[284] The Operatives' Libraries were not just places for borrowing books, they embraced wider educational, social and welfare functions too.

When the Nottingham Working Men's Association brought into being a Central Radical Association in April 1839, it was to be 'composed of delegates appointed by the other associations and news rooms of the town and neighbourhood to direct the public mind in the attainment of the Charter'.[285] The libraries, and some of the news rooms, were held at the public houses at which Chartists, framework knitters, lace makers, shoemakers, met regularly, many of their landlords being Chartists themselves or sympathetic to the cause, including John Gibson at the Sir Isaac Newton's Head, Samuel Mellors at the King George on Horseback, William Thornton at the Seven Stars, and John Ellis at the King of the

---

[282] *Nottingham Review*, 1st February 1850.
[283] *Nottingham Review*, 24th January 1851.
[284] *Nottingham Review*, 16th January 1849.
[285] *Nottingham Review*, 26th April 1839.

French during the 1840s.[286] It would have been entirely natural to invite them to participate in the Association, although whether they did so is not clear.

How close the links were between the Operatives' Libraries and Chartism has been a source of some speculation.[287] When the Nottingham Working Men's Association had been formed in 1838 their eighth objective was 'To form a library of reference and useful information; and to maintain a place where they can associate for mental improvement.'[288] The language used in the libraries' annual reports, and the names of the committee members, suggest that there were few direct relationships between the two movements despite the common purposes of the libraries and the Chartists, their common venues and participants.

Annual reports of the libraries were on occasion somewhat overblown, lacking the simplicity and directness of Chartist pronouncements, tending towards the style adopted by the Mechanics' Institution, and appearing at times to be written for a middle class audience rather than the working class members who borrowed the books. This was evident at its most extreme in 1839 when Operatives' Library No. 1 placed a paid advertisement in the *Nottingham Review* to announce the presentation of Goldsmith's *She Stoops to Conquer* at The Theatre to raise additional funds for the library:

> 'Your Committee are aware that some may view with apprehension the establishment of Libraries like this, entirely under the management of Working Men, but we would ask them, are we become worse members of society, because we have cultivated a taste for reading?'[289]

Such a demeaning appeal could not have come from a Chartist such as James Sweet, probably the most frequent Chartist contributor to the *Review*'s letters page, who would write in the *Review* a few months later 'I acknowledge no man as my superior, unless he is more useful, more moral, or more virtuous'.[290] It was one thing to recognise that the majority

---

[286] *Some Organisational and Cultural Aspects of the Chartist Movement in Nottingham*, James Epstein, 1982.
[287] Ibid., and *The Operatives' Libraries of Nottingham: a Radical Community's Own Initiative*, Peter Hoare, 2002.
[288] *Nottingham Review*, 10th August 1838.
[289] *Nottingham Review*, 8th March 1839.
[290] *Nottingham Review*, 8th November 1839.

of the *Review's* readers were middle class, but quite another to plead with them.

Few of the operatives' library committee members named in annual reports appear as active Chartists or speakers at Chartist meetings: John Goodson, assistant librarian at Library No. 1 in 1839; Henry Cope, secretary of the Radford Operatives' Library No. 5; and Joseph Burbage at Library No. 3 in 1850 being three exceptions.[291] The complications of being involved with numerous organisations simultaneously would have been no less than they are in the 21st century, even greater given the long working hours of that time. Some specialisation of political and organisational commitments must have taken place as it does now, and the numbers of people available to do the regular work of cataloguing, repairing books, supervising the library room, and all the other jobs that needed to be done would have been limited, despite the membership continuing to grow. As the annual report of Operatives' Library No. 3, one of the most successful with 2,000 volumes and 300 members, recorded in 1852:

> 'When our first humble institution was formed it was thought that a *routine* of members would be found to undertake the care and management of the library; it has not been so; the labour has fallen upon a few who have devoted their time and attention to it almost from its commencement.'[292]

---

[291] From author's own database of participants in socialism, Chartism, libraries, infidelism, teetotalism etc.
[292] *Nottingham Review*, 30th January 1852.

Chapter 9: The Operatives' Hall

In December 1844 a meeting was held at the New Inn, Carrington to promote the opening of an Operatives' Hall that would serve the needs of all the working class organisations in the town and its neighbourhood. It was agreed that shares would be sold at 5/- with no shareholder having more than one vote, and the meeting then adjourned.[293]

The necessity for a meeting place owned by the working class was one that would have been admitted by few but the most radical members of the town's working population a decade or so earlier. Political and trade meetings were normally held in hired rooms at public houses and on most occasions these would have sufficed. It was the socialists who were the first non-religious organisations to build their own places for meetings, discussion, education, and social activities without selling alcoholic drinks on the premises. One of the earliest was the Social Institute in Great George Street, Salford and one of the largest was the Hall of Science opened by Robert Owen in 1840 in Manchester, which could accommodate 3,000 people, but halls of this size were dependent upon the philanthropy of the wealthy admirers of Owen and his ideas. The Manchester Hall had cost £7,000.

For a short time the Leicester socialists had their own Social Institute on a smaller scale, a room capable of holding two hundred people, above a grocer's shop in Hotel Street.[294] It was publicly opened in July 1839 by the Social Missionary George Fleming, who was followed a few weeks later by Robert Owen who gave four lectures in the Social Institute before moving on to Nottingham to lecture in The Theatre. James Rigby became the next Social Missionary to be stationed in Leicester where he attracted notoriety for his Deistic lectures and became a scourge of the itinerant Christian debater, James Brindley. Rigby was also lecturing in Nottingham, Mansfield and Arnold in the early months of 1840. Although the socialists themselves were a small group in Nottingham, and never succeeded in finding a suitable place to meet, they, and other radicals in the town, would certainly have been aware of the developments in Leicester, from Rigby and Owen and from the pages of the *New Moral World*, available at Mrs Smith at the Tradesmen's Mart in Parliament Street.

---

[293] *Nottingham Review*, 6th December 1844.
[294] *The History of the Leicester Secular Society*, F J Gould, 1900.

Despite the news embargoes in the middle class local newspapers, there would also have been a collective memory of the many occasions when meeting halls had been unavailable, deposits returned, booking fees rejected, speakers ejected from the halls. Richard Carlile had resorted to speaking in a yard on the bank of the canal in 1828, and in 1829 had been refused bookings at all the places with large rooms including the Thurland Hall; a chapel-like sporting hall called the Cockpit; the former Jewish synagogue; and the premises of the printer and publisher of the *Nottingham Mercury,* Samuel Bennet, leaving the town without being able to find a single large room available to him. In 1842 Henry Vincent's Chartist lectures were curtailed when The Theatre refused him permission to deliver any further lectures there, and the 'Conservative Hall' refused him too. His response was 'we are compelled to have our own chapel'.[295]

During the course of 1844 while the discussions on the proposed Operatives Hall were progressing, Emma Martin was ejected from the Assembly Rooms and spoke instead in the Market Place. But even the Market Place was not freely available. Permission for its use could be refused, and indeed was refused to the Chartists, with a threat to ban all speakers there on Sundays after Emma Martin's visit. In 1842 when 'a party of poor, starving, defenceless men, seated at their hard begged-for meal beneath a canopy of heaven and on the carpet provided by nature' were surrounded by police and dragoons, and four hundred arrested, handcuffed or roped together and marched into town 'when they are not committing the shadow of an illegal act,' the event entered folklore as the 'Battle of Mapperley Hills'.[296] Indoors or outdoors the right to assemble or speak publicly on political or religious issues that threatened the power structures of the time and place had not been won. Only when working men and women had their own meeting places, owned collectively by them and their organisations and under their own management, could they feel reasonably certain that subjects and speakers of their own choosing would find a place where they were welcome and safe.

As Chartism had spread through the town and villages of Nottinghamshire, Chartist groups had found public houses to meet, but they also sought to open their own meeting places, often referred to as 'chapels'. In Mansfield they opened 'the Chartist Chapel in the Bottoms'

---

[295] *Northern Star,* 10th April 1841.
[296] *Nottingham Review,* 2nd September 1842; *Nottingham Chartism,* Peter Wyncoll, 1966.

in December 1840.[297] In Arnold the Chartists had been meeting in a chapel but were evicted, and in December 1842 bookings at the Wesleyan and New Connexion chapels were withdrawn from Chartists planning a meeting in Hyson Green. In the town of Nottingham the situation changed for the better during the Chartists' occupation of the 'Democratic Chapel'.

When the Nottingham Working Men's Association was set up it met in the Chartist room 'at the end of Halifax Place' and it was there that NWMA meetings were held during 1838, and to which the Nottingham Female Political Union moved their meetings in January 1839 'in the room over the Engine house'.[298] It was here that the Central Radical Association met in April 1839 to discuss bringing together all the operatives' organisations and libraries in the campaign for the People's Charter. At some time during the next seven months the NMWA moved from Halifax Place to the 'Democratic Chapel' in Barker Gate. The first recorded use of that building was on the 11th November by the members of the Nottingham Female Political Union. But where exactly was the 'Democratic Chapel'?

The best guess is that it was previously known as the Salem Chapel. 'In November 1839 the Nottingham Chartists obtained the Democratic or Chartist Chapel which had formerly been a Methodist and then a Primitive Baptist Chapel' is the closest that any historian has come to identifying the building.[299]

The Salem Chapel was built in 1817 at a cost of £2,000 by a Mr Butcher, who retained ownership of the building and at first acted as the Minister in a voluntary capacity, to be succeeded by the Reverend James Orange. With a small and poverty stricken congregation it endured mounting debts until Mr Butcher died. By that time the debts had reached £900 and the creditors took possession and sold it to the Armenian Methodists in 1833 but after two years it was again in financial difficulties and was sold to a Mr Hine and a Mr Wallis who sold it on for £824 to a sect of Baptists, the New Testament Disciples, in 1839. William Wylie in 1853 wrote that 'this neat little place of worship is occupied by the New Testament Disciples'

---

[297] *Northern Star*, 5th December 184;
[298] *Nottingham Review*, 14th December 1843.
[299] *Some Organisational and Cultural Aspects of the Chartist Movement in Nottingham*, James Epstein, 1982.

and according to several sources Messrs Hine and Wallis were still acting as elders there in 1864.[300]

If the New Testament Disciples took possession of the chapel in 1839 and were still there years later, could it have been simultaneously in use as the Democratic Chapel? It is possible that only part of the chapel was rented to the Chartists, but it is unlikely that this 'neat little place' was of sufficient size for a part of it to have remained in use as a chapel while the remainder was sub-let to the Chartists. The Religious Census gives the seating capacity of the Salem Chapel as 650, and other sources suggest that the Democratic Chapel could accommodate 'around 800', which suggests that this was one and the same hall.[301] The most likely explanation is that the Chapel was rented to the Chartists soon after its purchase by the New Testament Disciples and that they took it back in late 1845 when the Chartists vacated it. The Primitive Baptists – if the New Testament Disciples were to be counted among them – had a reputation of being generally sympathetic to Chartism.[302]

During the period in which the Chartists occupied the Democratic Chapel it was only occasionally that the *Nottingham Review* referred to the 'Salem Chapel' and that was in 1841 when Mr Potchett, the librarian at the Mechanics' Institute, gave two lectures on astronomy and in December when the Mechanics' Institute chose it for their annual meeting, and again in October 1842 when the temperance lecturer Thomas Beggs spoke there. All three of these were events that were more likely to have been arranged by Chartists than by Baptists.[303] However, the Barker Gate Charity School continued to function throughout the period in which the Chartists occupied the Democratic Chapel, and the charity school was said to be located in 'the large Sunday school room attached to the Salem Chapel'.[304] The Reverend James Orange was a supporter of the charity school and he was certainly no Chartist. The mystery deepens with the

---

[300] *The Salem Chapel*, J H Walker, in Transactions of the Thoroton Society, 1927; *Religion in Victorian Nottinghamshire: the Religious Census of 1851*, M R Watts, 1998; *Old and New Nottingham*, W H Wylie, 1853; *Nottinghamshire History, Gazetteer & Directory*, Francis White, 1864.

[301] *Some Organisational and Cultural Aspects of the Chartist Movement in Nottingham*, James Epstein, 1982.

[302] *The Nottingham Baptists: The Political Scene*, F M W Harrison, in The Baptist Quarterly, 1978.

[303] *Nottingham Review*, 24th September 1841; 31st December 1841.

[304] *Dearden's Directory*, 1834.

listing in *White's Directory* of James Orange as the resident preacher for the New Testament Disciples at the Salem Chapel in 1844 – at a time when the Chartists were still in residence at the Democratic Chapel.[305] It is, perhaps, possible that the building was in shared use by Chartist and Baptists, although the absence of any reports of friction between the them would have to suggest an unusual degree of co-operation and compromise if this was the case.

Illustration 15: Site of the Democratic Chapel, Barker Gate. Pictured here in 2014.[306]

That the Chartists rented the Salem Chapel, in its entirety, in part, or as a shared space, for six years would still seem to be the most likely course of events, but there are some unexplained contrary indications such as the reference in *White's Directory*. It is regrettable that there is no mention of a Chartist interlude in any of the accounts of the history of the Salem Chapel, and regrettable too that there appear to be no accounts from the Chartists as to exactly how or when they acquired the building nor how, when or why they vacated it. For a building that saw some notable achievements, this is a disappointment. For those achievements we shall return after following the course of events to establish a permanent Operatives' Hall in the town.

---

[305] *White's Directory*, 1844. The description is taken from James Orange's *History and Antiquities of Nottingham*, 1840.

[306] The first publication of this book led to further scrutiny of maps and street directories. The site of the Democratic Chapel appears to have been where Gothic House (pictured) stands today, and not in the two storey building to the right.

In December 1844 when the promoters of an Operatives' Hall met at the New Inn at Carrington, Chartism had entered another period of decline. The biggest outdoor event of the year had been to mark the 'Battle of Mapperley Hills' at the end of August when a crowd said to be as large as 30,000 marched from the Market Place to the railway station to greet Feargus O'Connor and were led by brass bands from Sutton in Ashfield and Lambley to Mapperley Plains where James Sweet chaired the meeting addressed by O'Connor.[307] Other events included meetings and petitions seeking the release of Leicester Chartist Thomas Cooper from Stafford Gaol where he was imprisoned on charges of sedition. It was a time of looking back and taking stock. One outcome was probably a decline in the use of the Democratic Chapel and perhaps the beginning of financial pressures to meet the rent. The Nottingham economy had improved since the early years of the decade, and food prices had dropped, but the poverty of the town had been attested by the relatively small collection of £9 1s 6d collected for Chartism from the large crowd at the August meeting with Feargus O'Connor.[308] A permanent Operatives' Hall was an admirable ambition but it was perhaps not the best time to be setting out to bring it to fruition.

The Hall proposition had been made in the previous year when Chartist activity was still in full swing, at a meeting in May 1843 at the Shoulder of Mutton to discuss setting up a central Working Men's Hall and Library.[309] According to the promoters of the meeting, the Operatives' Libraries in the town had between them about 700 members and 3,300 books. The promoters included Messrs R T Morrison and John Skeritt, both Chartists; Mr J Wright who may have been the Chartist John Wright but is more likely to have been the former temperance missionary J B Wright; and Mr Wesson whose name does not appear in any other connection. The outline of a plan from R T Morrison was approved and handbills were agreed to be circulated, which led to the meeting at the New Inn.[310] When the meeting in 1844 at the New Inn was adjourned, it did so as the Operatives' Hall Society with a new Secretary pro-tem, the redoubtable Chartist James Sweet.

---

[307] *Nottingham Chartism*, Peter Wyncoll, 1966.
[308] *Northern Star*, 31st August 1844.
[309] *Northern Star*, 13th May 1843.
[310] *Nottingham Review*, 12th May 1843.

In January 1845 James Sweet wrote to the *Nottingham Review*: 'A large room is very much wanted at the present time, there not being one in the town available to the wants of the labouring portion of the population'. The Town Hall was not suitable for meetings of working men and too expensive to hire. 'The chapels and other large buildings are closed against them, even when they are willing to pay the extortionate price usually demanded for their use'.[311]

Combining the libraries in one place would increase the total stock available to any member, enable the members to use the library without feeling obliged to buy alcoholic drinks, and make it welcoming to women and children, 'a place where children can be taught a knowledge of their rights', in the words of another promoter, Henry Dorman.[312] Already the proposal had grown from a hall to a hall and library, and the vision was soon to expand even further.

Henry Dorman was a 'former drunkard hailing from East Anglia' who had become a Primitive Methodist and a devout adherent of temperance, settling in Nottingham in 1839.[313] He begins to appear in reports of Chartist meetings in 1841 chairing lectures at The Theatre. If he was not among the promoters of the first Operatives Hall meeting, he arrived on the scene at a fortuitous moment, for he had been involved in similar activity during his time in Leicester ten years earlier when Thomas Ryley Perry, the socialist and Leicester agent for the unstamped newspapers in the town, called a public meeting 'for the purpose of establishing a Reading Room for the working classes, without resorting to a public house' where 'the Christian ... and the infidel, or man of no religion at all, would be equally welcome.'[314] It was at Mr Dorman's Temperance House in Clare Street that the Nottingham committee held its next meeting in April 1845 where they agreed that the Hall should include an elementary day school, library and reading room, and a meeting room for lectures on science, history and politics, a place where working men could air their grievances, whether social or political.[315]

With the objectives agreed, it was time to call a public meeting, which

---

[311] *Nottingham Review*, 17th January 1845.
[312] Ibid.
[313] *Drink and Temperance in Nottingham 1830-1860*, J J Rowley, 1974.
[314] *The Gauntlet*, 10th November 1833.
[315] *Nottingham Review*, 4th April 1845.

took place on the evening of Monday 27th April at the Town Hall which had been provided free of charge for the occasion, attended by an impressive list of names, including many Chartists, some middle class Chartist supporters, and some names that have not occurred in other connections.[316] It was a coming together of different parts of the working class movement with radical liberals from the middle class and such a meeting, while appearing to share a common objective, would have encompassed any number of competing objectives, rivalries and hostilities. For some clues to the eventual outcome and its success or failure it is worth looking in detail at who was there and what they represented.

Mr Wright was called to the chair. He was, according to the *Northern Star*, a cotton merchant, and a former temperance missionary in the town.[317] Acting as secretary was Mr Gregory, probably Daniel Gregory, from the Carrington Chartist locality. The meeting opened with an address by Mr Dorman. 'Nottingham has 60,000 inhabitants' he said 'and yet contained no place which the working classes could call their own to meet'. The Mechanics' Institution was expensive and there were 'obstacles in their way which would effectually prevent the working classes from using them.' Daniel Gregory gave the report of the committee's work to date. Similar ventures in Staffordshire and Lancashire had been contacted, 400 shares of 5/- had been sold, Operatives' Libraries, Oddfellows' lodges, sick clubs and co-operative stores had been told that they could also become shareholders.

The meeting then proceeded to elect officers and committee. James Sweet was elected general secretary and George Parkin treasurer. Other Chartists elected to the committee were: Joseph (or James) Saunders, Job Atterbury, William Treece, Christopher Bell, Daniel Gregory, John Moss, Mr Barton and John Wall. In addition to these 10 Chartists there were: John Lee from Operatives' Library No. 1; Mr Farrow, Library No. 2; Henry Ford, Library No. 3; Henry Norris, Library No. 4; Francis Eames from the Artizans' Library; Mr Wright; and seven men whose allegiances are unknown.[318] There were also three middle class men who gave conditional

---

[316] *Nottingham Review*, 2nd May 1845.
[317] *Northern Star*, 3rd May 1845; *Drink and the Public House*, J J Rowley, in Transactions of the Thoroton Society, 1975.
[318] Messrs Randall, Cape, Carnelly, Potter, Killingly, Anthony, Simons.

support to the Charter but were principally supporters of the Complete Suffrage Union: Samuel Bean, lace manufacturer; Thomas Beggs and George Gill, all of whom had worked with Chartists on Chartism, and in campaigns against capital punishment, slavery, Church rates, and in support of temperance. A committee of twenty six.

Defining class or political allegiances is a hazardous activity, but George Parkin, a middle class baker in Hockley, a 'gentleman' who had provided £50 bail for James Woodhouse after his arrest following Chartist activity in 1839, has on account of this been included here as a Chartist. Two of the seven men whose allegiances have not been assumed could also have been Chartists: Mr Anthony may have been James Anthony 'an uncompromising Chartist'[319] from Arnold, and Simons may have been Joseph Simons, both Chartists with occasional mentions in press reports. With one or more of the delegates from the libraries, or from among those whose names are unfamiliar, this might have given the more radical members a bare majority had votes been taken on any issue.

Other Chartists who spoke at the meeting but did not join the committee, whether because they did not stand or because they were unsuccessful in a contested election is not known, included Henry Dorman, well known as a Chartist and as the proprietor of a temperance hotel; Jonathan Barber, one of the best known of local Chartists, accused by the *Review* of being in favour of 'physical force' to get the Charter; and Abraham Widdowson, a lacemaker from Carrington, active in the Chartist Land Company.

James Sweet's letter to the *Review* in January had stressed the need for a meeting hall 'for the labouring portion of the population' and ended with an appeal to working men: 'It therefore becomes the duty of the operatives generally to look to themselves – to do their own work – to depend upon no other class doing it for them'.[320] James Sweet was a man who would work with anyone of any class who shared the same objectives and he was respected for doing so, but he was not inclined to compromise with middle class supporters on the basic principles of the project. The basis upon which he, and the NCA as the successors to the Nottingham Working Men's Association, functioned was in line with the Objects of the NMWA, number 9 being a statement that they would 'co-operate with

---

[319]   *Nottingham Review*, 20th May 1843.
[320]   *Nottingham Review*, 17th January 1845.

all those who seek to promote the happiness of the multitude' but they would 'elect their members as far as possible, from the working classes.'[321] Dedicated, dependable, methodical, honest, and generally – though not always – restrained in his expressions, he was clear in his belief that it was by the actions of the working class that an Operatives' Hall should be achieved. His comments were an appeal but they were also a warning.

The report of the committee published in the *Nottingham Review* in April prior to the large public meeting also contained an unambiguous warning:

> 'It is confidently expected that those who make liberal professions will give the managing committee as little unnecessary trouble as possible, but come forward with their advice, influence, and money and thereby prove their sincerity, and promote the accomplishment of an object they have so long seemed to desire and approve.'[322]

The reporter is not named, but it is certainly not James Sweet, even if he approved of the sentiments. They were sentiments which had been aired since the first appearance of Mechanics' Institutes: *The Co-operative Magazine and Monthly Herald* had warned in 1826 that 'The employers of the operative classes, as well as others of the benevolent rich, have in many places come forward with their money books, and instruments to aid in the establishment of your institutions. But let not this class of persons expect *power* in return for their gifts.'[323]

The size and the composition of the new committee can be seen as a tribute to diversity, or as a taking up of battle positions. It was probably both. James Sweet had been elected unanimously as committee secretary but still he felt it necessary to voice his awareness of 'the prejudices against him' in the meeting.[324] Thomas Beggs had been applauded after objecting to working men being 'driven to public houses' to attend meetings, but he went on to say that 'if there was the least of party or sect connected with the building he would not have anything to do with it.' There is a strong sense that there are tensions simmering just below the surface.

---

[321] *Nottingham Review*, 10th August 1838.
[322] *Nottingham Review*, 4th April 1845.
[323] *The Co-operative Magazine and Monthly Record*, January 1826 (original emphasis).
[324] *Nottingham Review*, 2nd May 1845.

The committee met in July at Mr Rayners', the Smith's Arms, a beer house in Willoughby Street, New Lenton, and home of the New Lenton Operatives' Library, and again in September at the Democratic Chapel. At the latter meeting Mr Roper chaired, probably Thomas Roper, a veteran of working class struggles for more than forty years since the days of Luddism. Other meetings were scheduled to take place at The Greyhound in Castle Gate, at the Marquis of Anglesey in St James' Street, and in the Sneinton Operatives' Library rooms at the Queen Adelaide and the Pheasant in Charlotte Street. In October it was announced that the number of shares issued had reached 1,000, but another 3,000 would need to be sold before the project could be completed.

Perhaps it was at this point that some of the members realised that at least another four years work would be required to raise sufficient funds, even with an estimate of the building costs as low as £1,000. In November 1845 the committee reported that 'We are happy to state that some of the middle classes, seeing the necessity of such a building as the one contemplated, have come forward to assist the working classes, by taking shares.'[325] Three further meetings of the committee, at the Skinner's Arms in Mortimer Street and the Rancliffe Arms in Turn-Calf Alley were announced in 1845 and at Mr Flack's Drury Hill coffee house in January 1846. After that no more is heard of the Operatives' Hall or its committee.

The successor to the Operatives' Hall project was the People's Hall in Beck Street.[326] In October 1853 the *Nottingham* Review announced that the former School of Design had been bought by Mr George Gill, whose object was to convert it to 'a hall for working men' and a year later it opened as 'The People's Hall'. Although it dispensed with the restrictions on politics and religion which had been bones of contention at the Mechanics' Institute and the Artizans' Library, it was once again an institution created largely by middle class philanthropy for deserving working class users.

The People's Hall also represented the culmination of the efforts of Thomas Beggs for a Temperance Hall in the town where working men and their sick clubs and other organisations could meet without the temptation and the expense of drinking alcohol. Between 1850 and 1852 the simmering antagonisms between religious and non-religious

---

[325] *Nottingham Review,* 7th November 1845.
[326] That part of Beck Street south of Parliament Street is now known as Heathcote Street.

temperance advocates had been resolved when the religious members of the old Temperance Society rid themselves of their members 'professing Infidel principles' by the forming the Nottingham Christian Temperance Society, to which only members of the evangelical churches were welcome, and by the parallel establishment of the Nottingham Secular Society.[327] This paved the way for the religiously motivated temperance activists to associate themselves with a working men's hall committed to temperance without being tainted by what they would have regarded as the long-standing blight of working class infidelism.

Illustration 16: People's Hall, Heathcote Street.
Pictured here in 2013, now a grade 2 listed building.

Early in April 1853 Mr J B Wright, the temperance missionary who had been active in the Operatives' Hall Society, had revived the call for a Temperance Hall at the anniversary dinner of the Christian Temperance Society, and in May the Hall was said to be on the horizon. The Temperance Hall, for which architects' drawings had been prepared, was never built, but in October 1854 the People's Hall opened – and its first manager was Mr J B Wright.

The People's Hall was never the success its promoters had hoped for. The Operatives' Libraries did not transfer their stocks to the People's Hall's library and remained independent. Henry Cope, secretary of the

---

[327] *Drink and Temperance in Nottingham 1830-1860,* J J Rowley, 1974.

Radford Operatives' Library had written in the fourth annual report in 1847 that they had survived a year of 'unparalleled sufferings and privations' yet their income had exceeded their outgoings and their future was secure. 'This proves that when the working classes take their affairs into their own hands they and they alone know best how to manage them.'[328] Even the Nottingham Artizans' Library remained independent of the People's Hall, although its librarian Francis Eames did make a gift of books. The intention of making it the home of local co-operative societies was never realised and the only organisation admitted under that heading was the Temperance Society.

The membership of the People's Hall reached a plateau of 400 in 1856, followed by a decline to 300 by 1869.[329]The Christian temperance movement's aims may have been met, but for Chartists, socialists and working men and women, temperance was never an end in itself, only a means to an end. Robert Owen had described temperance as 'in reality part of socialism, as only the sober can practice it'.[330] Mr Gill and the *Nottingham Review* thought otherwise. 'One of the main features of the new institution, however, will be, entire freedom from Socialistic principles' he declared.[331] The boundaries had been set down at the outset. The best that can be said of the People's Hall as the outcome of an attempt to create a permanent institution under working class ownership and control was that it represented a truce between the enduring struggles of working class and middle class cultures and aspirations.

---

[328] *Nottingham Review*, 15th October 1847.
[329] *Drink and the Public House*, J J Rowley, in Transactions of the Thoroton Society, 1975.
[330] *New Moral World*, 20th November 1841.
[331] *Nottingham Review*, 14th October 1853.

Chapter 10: The Democratic Chapel

The last recorded meeting at the Democratic Chapel was that of the Operatives' Hall Society in September 1845 at which the sale of 1,000 shares had been announced. Although it was not recognised at the time, the Democratic Chapel represented the summit of achievement in the creation of a working class political and social centre in Nottingham.

Temperance was not itself a campaigning issue for most Chartists but it did play a part in the success of the Democratic Chapel during the six years in which the Chartists were in residence. Temperance coffee houses and hotels were enjoying popularity in Nottingham as the middle of the nineteenth century approached and were frequently run and used by Chartist and other working class organisations. *Orange's Directory of Nottingham* in 1840 had listed just two 'teetotal meeting places', William Holt's Teetotal Coffee Room in Rigley's Yard, Long Row, and William Baker in Middle Pavement who sold 'Wine (Teetotal)' or 'unfermented juice of the grape'. Four years later Mr Baker the grape juice salesman was at Greyhound Yard, and had been joined by eight other temperance hotels and eating places in White's *Directory*, including Henry Dorman's hotel at 16, Clare Street, William M'Garr's boarding house at Castle Gate, William Swann's coffee house at Drury Hill and William Smith's eating house at Low Pavement. Not mentioned was the new coffee house at Warser Gate run by Elmer and Mary Ann Rollett.

Temperance coffee houses did not always weigh very highly on the health and efficiency scales at this time. Dr F R Lees, temperance campaigner, was critical of temperance hotels 'where we blush to take friends, or to be seen ourselves'.[332] George Jacob Holyoake was scathing about them. He thought there were only 'half a dozen Temperance Hotels in the country in which a traveller would desire to appear twice, with no beverage except water that anybody could drink.'[333] And this at a time when even drinking water was often unsafe to drink. The absence of alcohol was a mixed blessing:

> 'In the majority of provincial Temperance Hotels you find yourself in a cloud of narcotic smoke, reminding you of Pandemonium, where pallid men are puffing most

---

[332] *The Book of True Temperance*, Dr F R Lees, 1871.
[333] *The Social Means of Promoting Temperance*, G J Holyoake, 1859.

malodorous fumes, and drinking coffee of the most equivocal mocha. Certainly there are victims of temperance as well as intemperance'.[334]

If the situation was dire in the provinces, in London it was even more intolerable. There, he claimed, tongue held firmly in cheek, the coffee was made from 'diseased cows reared by gaslight.'

The Democratic Chapel did not sell intoxicating liquors but did not promote itself as a temperance meeting place. The working men epitomised by James Sweet would not have subscribed to a middle class evangelist belief that drunkenness was a sign of personal inadequacy and the cause of poverty. On the contrary, drinking was often seen to be the result, not the cause, of poverty. Sobriety was preferable because it enabled men to act rationally and change social conditions, it was a handmaiden to collective self help. Some commentators would later claim that temperance flourished because the working class were becoming individualistic, seeking respectability, setting out to attract middle class sympathy and support, and even that temperance was responsible for saving the country from revolution.[335] An alternative view from a west country vicar was that temperance enthusiasts consisted of 'Jews, Turks, heathens, Infidels, Socialists, Chartists, Arians, Socinians or Antinomians, of liars, slanderers, Sabbath breakers, adulterers, robbers and manslayers.'[336] Most of the men and women who frequented the Democratic Chapel would have been very pleased to be known by at least one of these terms.

The *Poor Man's Guardian* had mused upon the connection between public houses and the supposed attitudes of women to politics several years before:

> 'Women dislike politics in general because they are apt to distract husbands from the scene of domestic duties, and to make them neglect their wives for the club-room and public house. Women very naturally like their husbands to stay at home in the evenings, and not to spend their money or get drunk at the public house. ... Let us therefore, my friends, when we meet to discuss politics, avoid the public house and

---

[334] Ibid.
[335] *Drink and the Victorians*, Brian Harrison, 1970.
[336] *The Water Drinkers: a History of Temperance*, Norman Longmate, 1968.

make our sittings as short as possible ... take them with you ... show them the results of your time spent ... like children, they are dazzled by success'.[337]

This was a man's view addressed to other men and they would have not forgiven him had he suggested that some women might have preferred their husbands to stay sober and stay out. Being free from alcohol the Democratic Chapel was able to provide a more welcoming place for women and children, a place where husbands and fathers need not desert their families of an evening, and an environment that promoted economy, morality and health, among adults and children. It would have appealed to the writer for the *Poor Man's Guardian*.

A description of how the Democratic Chapel had been acquired and how it was used when at its zenith was given by 'a Chartist shopkeeper' in the *Midland Counties Illuminator* in February 1841. The writer explains:

'like our brethren in most other towns, the Chartists of Nottingham had great difficulty in obtaining a room to hold their meetings in; all the large ones being in the hands of persons whose minds were prejudiced against us on account of our being called "Chartists", and our having been misrepresented as a reckless body of men, and as wishing to plunder and destroy property'.[338]

But, he continues 'thanks to the determined patriotism and perseverance of 2 or 3 individuals who manfully combated the arguments brought forward by the enemies of the people, we succeeded in obtaining a chapel, the rent of which is £19 per year.'

Using religious terminology that was in common use and using it here to describe secular activity, he reports that:

'This chapel is open for religious services on Sunday, and the whole truth is preached therein. On Monday evenings the "Charter Association" transact their business; on Tuesday evenings the "Chartist Total Abstinence Society" meets in the same place; on Wednesday evenings the singing class meets to practice; and on Saturday evenings our friends meet for mutual instruction, and to read the newspapers etc. A "Tract

---

[337] *Poor Man's Guardian*, 14th September 1833.
[338] *Midland Counties Illuminator*, 27th February 1841.

Society" for the spread of political information amongst the poor is forming; and also a library of useful and instructive works, which will materially assist us in our onward progress to establish practical religion and liberty. In the daytime, the chapel is occupied by one of our brethren as a school room; and the school, I am proud to say, is progressing as well as can be expected from the extreme poverty of the great body of the working classes ... An adult school is also forming. The adults meet two or three evenings in the week to receive instruction in reading, writing, and the principles of the Charter'.[339]

The description of activities is not so different to those taking place among the Nottingham socialists in 1842, or in Manchester or London at the socialist Halls of Science, except that the socialists were perhaps better at introducing entertainments such as 'social aquatic steam excursions' (boat trips) and demonstrations of laughing gas to attract the curious, but on the other hand the Democratic Chapel spared them the burden of being instructed in 'rules of propriety' and 'rational politeness'. There is no mention of 'a want of cleanliness in the dress' of the people using the Democratic Chapel and no complaints that men and women 'keep on their hats, to the great inconvenience of those who sit behind them', to which Robert Owen drew attention in a message to the Social Missionaries in 1839.[340] The Mechanics' Institute, the Artizans' Library, the Savings Bank and other middle class institutions for the artisan had made the 'man in a fustian jacket' feel uncomfortable and aware of his poverty. Women would have been unwelcome, hat or no hat. At the Democratic Chapel they were all welcome.

Apart from Susannah Wright, Mary Ann Smith and a few others, the names of local working class women have been conspicuous by their absence from the records of political campaigns prior to Chartism but, for the first time in October 1838, not only do women become visible but a women's Chartist organisation appears, the Nottingham Female Political Union. This was only nine months after the Nottingham Working Men's Association first appeared, and less than two weeks before the first public demonstration in Nottingham on 5th November in support of what had become the People's Charter.

---

[339] Ibid.
[340] *New Moral World*, 13th July 1839.

Women had been prominent in one of the very first large political reform meetings, at Cronkeyshaw Common near Rochdale in 1808, when 5,000 women led the procession of reformers.[341] Societies of women for political reform began to appear again in 1818 in Yorkshire and 'an entirely novel and portentous circumstance was the formation of a Female Reform Society at Blackburn, near Manchester' in 1819.[342] At Peterloo in August of 1819 'two clubs of female reformers advanced, one of them numbering more than 150 members and bearing a white silk banner'.[343]

The repression which followed Peterloo put an end to overt political reform societies but women were on occasions mentioned as taking part in political activities. In 1820 an 'Address of the female inhabitants of Nottingham' to Queen Caroline, assuring her of their loyalty on her return to England, was signed by 7,800 women of Nottingham and its vicinity which, if correct, would equate to nearly 10% of the female population of the county.[344] In 1834 at a meeting on the Forest 'a band of female unionists joined the multitude' in support of a petition to King and Parliament to revoke the sentences of transportation on the Dorchester labourers.[345] Female associations reappeared in number after the publication of the People's Charter in May 1838, and the Female Political Union in Nottingham was formed at the end of October.

The *Nottingham Review* reported that a Mrs Butler was called to the chair at the first meeting on 22nd October, and the event was 'electrified by the able and energetic address of Mrs Oakland.' Two men from the Nottingham Working Men's Association, William Lilley and Mr Smith then addressed the meeting.[346] It was agreed that the Nottingham FPU would co-operate with the Birmingham FPU. The meeting would then have moved on to prepare for their participation in the November demonstration at which a National Petition would be considered and a delegate elected to the first National Convention.

The NFPU was in the forefront of the procession as it moved on from the Sir Isaac Newton in Howard Street. After the Nottingham Reformers Band came the NFPU with a banner proclaiming 'The Nottingham Female

---

[341] *Weavers of Dreams*, David J Thompson, 2012.
[342] *The Annual Register, or, A View of the History, Politics and Literature for the Year 1819.*
[343] *A History of the Chartist Movement*, Julius West, 1920.
[344] *The Republican*, 7th July 1820.
[345] *Nottingham and Newark Mercury*, 5th April 1834.
[346] *Nottingham Review*, 16th October 1838.

Association for obtaining the People's Charter' that led the parade as it passed through the town, making its way to the Forest.

The demonstration was immediately followed that same evening by a public meeting for women in the large room of the Hope and Anchor at Parliament Street 'which was so densely crowded that many were unable to gain admission. Mr Salt from Birmingham addressed the meeting.'[347] Mr Thomas Clutton Salt had been a founder of the first Birmingham Political Union in 1832 and rejoined when the Association was revived in 1837. His presence in the new movement was short lived but in April 1838 he was responsible for calling a meeting at the Birmingham Town Hall attended by many thousands of women. His speech at the Hope and Anchor can be imagined from a letter he wrote to the Sheffield radical Ebenezer Elliott about the Birmingham meeting:

> 'I alone of Birmingham reformers, dared convene or attend it. The experiment was triumphant. Not only was the vast Hall full, but even its spacious lobbies were crowded. There could not have been less than 12,000 women there. A more beautiful and moving sight was never seen; a meeting more enthusiastic and orderly never was assembled. It was evident that the iron had entered into their souls; that they felt deeply, and resolved religiously, that their children's children should not be trampled upon as they had been ... I believe, (I might say I know,) that hitherto, the women have thought so little upon politics, and being so utterly ignorant of the connexion of our system with their poverty and degradation, that they have either not interfered, or persuaded their husbands from meddling with politics, as a thing of no profit. We cannot afford their neutrality or hostility; they must be our enthusiastic friends.'[348]

Mr Salt's contribution to the meeting at the Hope and Anchor was doubtless an inspirational address and at the end of the meeting the Nottingham FPU enrolled fifty new members.

A week later they held their second meeting. Some resolutions were passed and accounts were presented, the *Northern Star* and the *Nottingham Review* were read, and Mr William Lilley spoke on the current

---

[347] *Nottingham Review*, 9th November 1838.
[348] *Ebenezer Elliott*, The Ebenezer Foundry of Research.

agitation for the Charter. They arranged to hold a public meeting the following Tuesday, the 20th November at the Hope and Anchor, open to both men and women where they intended to 'adopt measures to alleviate the worse than negro slavery now endured by a poor woman, 72 years of age, who may be see daily breaking stones on the highway leading from Nottingham to Eastwood ... a practice disgraceful in the country which enfranchised the slave.'[349]

This was an astute campaign to have taken on, combining the plight of an elderly woman, the cruelty of the Poor Law, sympathy for slaves, and exclusion from the franchise of both women and men. It also drew a line between the humanity of the Chartists and those paladins of Christian reforming zeal such as William Wilberforce, fêted for leading the movement for the abolition of slavery in the colonies and protecting the rights of animals at home whilst persecuting the radical press by his support for the Committee for the Suppression of Vice and opposing the extension of the franchise to working men and women. The final sentence of the report, just to make the point even clearer, was printed in capitals: 'BUT, UNHAPPILY, THE VISION OF MANY OF OUR SLAVE ABOLITIONISTS, IS TOO EXTENSIVE TO SEE THE MISERY, DISTRESS, AND HORRIBLE PRIVATIONS OF THE WORKING CLASSES AT HOME.'[350]

The outcome of the public meeting was the appointment of a deputation to enquire into the circumstances endured by Susan Robinson, which visited her home in Nuthall. It was subsequently agreed that a report of the deputation be given to the next meeting of the NFPU on the 17th December, which resolved that warm clothing be procured, the parish authorities be censured, and a subscription be raised for her. Should the parish fail to find 'more congenial employment or enable her to spend the remainder of her days in a more comfortable and Christian-like manner or if they should attempt to drag her from her friends and home, to linger the remainder of her days in a Poor Law Bastille' the committee would arrange another public meeting to take the matter further.[351]

At this point the story of Susan Robinson ends, the lack of further activity implying that the story ended happily. It was after the publication

---

[349] *Nottingham Review*, 16th November 1838.
[350] Ibid. (original emphasis).
[351] *Nottingham Review*, 14th and 21st December 1838.

by Robert Lowery of his *Address* some time in the summer or autumn of 1839 that the Nottingham Female Radical Association [NFRA], as it was now known, found a cause which linked the bread and butter issues of a working woman's life to the cause of Chartism: exclusive dealing and co-operative trading.[352] Meanwhile, areas beyond the town of Nottingham were experiencing the involvement of women in Chartism.

In February 1840 Sutton in Ashfield Chartists held a public meeting in the General Baptist Chapel and filled all 500 seats. It was a smart move on the part of the men to put the women upstairs, 'the large gallery being appropriated for females', or there would have been insufficient room for all the men downstairs.[353] In April 1841 Mrs Vincent was presented with 'a cap, some gloves, and other articles of the manufactures of this place' by the women of Arnold attending the opening by her husband Henry, the Chartist lecturer, of the Chartist chapel in Arnold. In July Chartists walked from the village of Calverton to Arnold, a distance of four miles, to welcome two speakers from Belper. 'There were several hundreds in the procession, a great portion of whom were respectably attired, healthy, spirited Chartist ladies.'[354] In October in Hucknall Torkard 'a female lecturer, named Huish, of Hucknall, was astonishing her audience with her harangues on Chartism'.[355]

The year 1842 began with 'a most excellent supper' provided by Mr and Mrs Jacques, 'both sterling Chartists', at which 'a party of male and female Chartists' participated, but little more is heard of the female Chartists that year. Whether this resulted from a decline in their activities or a lack of reporting is not clear, but in 1843 the number of reports of women's activity increases. In May 1843 there is a reference to a meeting in their room in St Anne's Street where a lecture was given (whether by a man or woman is not stated) on the political rights of women, and every member was invited to bring a woman friend with them. It is evident that the group was seeking to expand membership by recruiting from the friends of existing women members and not solely from the families of male Chartists.

---

[352] *Address ... on the System of Exclusive Dealing*, Robert Lowery, 1839, in Robert Lowery: Radical and Chartist, Brian Harrison and Patricia Hollis, 1979.
[353] *Northern Star*, 21st February 1840.
[354] *Northern Star*, 17th April 1841; 24th July 1841.
[355] *Nottingham Review*, 29th October 1841. There was one adult female named Huish in Hucknall in the 1841 census, Hannah, 35, wife of a framesmith, of Belle Isle Close.

This was also the first occasion on which the political rights of women are specifically referred to. This may represent a development in their thinking, beyond the supporting role they had adopted in 1838 when they were said to be determined to support 'their husbands, brothers, etc, in their present arduous struggle to establish the People's Charter.'[356] However, evidence that there were advocates of universal suffrage from the beginning of the NFPU might be conjectured from the decisions of their very first meeting in 1838 when they declared that 'As all consumers and producers in this city are taxpayers, so ought all to be represented'.[357]

The meeting in St Anne's Street in May 1843 was described as crowded, and at the close a collection was taken to buy books for the 'Female's Adult and Children's School' at the Democratic Chapel.[358] A further meeting was held later in May which suggests that they were still holding regular fortnightly Monday meetings.

In November 1843 one of the members, Miss Eliza Blatherwick, gave a talk at the Democratic Chapel, on the distressed state of the country. The Democratic Chapel could hold more than 600 people, and on Monday evenings it was reserved for meetings of the Nottingham branch of the National Charter Association [NNCA], which suggests that it was a meeting consisting of men and women that Eliza Blatherwick addressed. For any woman to be addressing a mixed meeting would have been unusual, for a working class woman to be doing so would have been highly unusual at that time. The audience was described as crowded and her address as 'able and soul searching'. The meeting again closed with a collection for the school fund.[359]

Miss Blatherwick remained in the Chartist movement much longer than many other participants, and in 1847 was present at the annual meeting of republicans and Chartists, contributing songs and recitations to an evening of at least sixteen toasts, and speeches so numerous that the pub must surely have run out of beer before the business was concluded. Although the event sounds very much like a drunken gathering of maudlin men, one of the last toasts – a vote of thanks 'to the ladies for their attendance upon the occasion' – confirms the presence of women,

---

[356] *Nottingham Review*, 26th October 1838.
[357] Ibid.
[358] *Northern Star*, 6th May 1843.
[359] *Northern Star*, 20th May 1843; 3rd June 1843.

but whether they were present in their own right, as the wives or guests of men, or were present to serve the food and beer is not entirely clear.[360]

In July 1843 the names of seven members of the NFRA are given in the nominations to the NCA General Council for Nottinghamshire.[361] In August the women again met at the Democratic Chapel and agreed to dine together the following Monday at 2pm at Mapperley, to commemorate the first anniversary of the Battle of Mapperley Hills.[362] Meetings of the NFRA continued in 1844 at the Democratic Chapel on Tuesdays, and Eliza Blatherwick gave further talks at the Democratic Chapel in October and December, but reports of their activities cease to appear in the *Nottingham Review* or *Northern Star*, and it would seem that their fortunes followed those of the Chartist movement generally into a period of despondency and decline.

Of twenty one names of Nottingham women Chartists which appear in the press between 1839 and 1843 most appear to be married women, but six do not share surnames with active male Chartists who appeared in press reports of Chartist meetings, as speakers, or delegates to other bodies.[363] Another four were unmarried, including Eliza Blatherwick, whose sister Caroline and father John were active Chartists, and the two Abbott sisters who do not appear to have had fathers or brothers prominently involved in Chartism. As a sample of all women Chartists in Nottingham the numbers are too small to draw any firm conclusions, but they do not seem to conform to the generally accepted view that most women participating in female Chartist associations did so as wives or sisters of male Chartists.

The Abbott sisters, Mary Ann and Jane, have probably attracted more notice than most of the women involved in Nottingham Chartism for their roles in running the children's Sunday school. Education, both formal and informal, played an important role in the life of the Democratic Chapel. Besides the Sunday sermons and hymns, discussion evenings, the library,

---

[360] *Some Organisational and Cultural Aspects of the Chartist Movement in Nottingham*, James Epstein, 1982.
[361] *Northern Star*, 8th July 1843: Martha Sweet; Hannah Barnett; Maria Ellis; Susannah Wainwright; Eliza Watkins; Mary Ann Ellis, sub-treasurer; Mary Ann Abbott, sub-Secretary.
[362] *Northern Star*, 19th August 1843.
[363] Mrs Oakland, Mrs Daniels, Mrs Tracy, Mrs Colton, Mrs Blunston, Mrs Keeland. From the author's database of names.

readings of newspapers, and the newspaper reading room supported by voluntary contributions, there were formal classes for children and for adult men and women. The daytime school was run by William Russell but the Sunday school was run by Mary Ann Abbott, the school for which the Nottingham Female Radical Association had been collecting subscriptions. In May 1844 at a gathering of children, parents and teachers, the scholars were 'examined' by James Sweet and Henry Dorman who proposed 'That the best thanks of this meeting are due, and is hereby given, to Miss Abbott, for the uniform kindness and attention which she has evinced on behalf of the school connected with the Democratic Chapel.'[364]

It would be unwise to regard either of the Abbott sisters as the leading figures among women Chartists in Nottingham as some commentators have done on the basis of very limited historical data. That they played an important role in the Sunday school for children is certainly true but the reputations of Mary Ann and Jane Abbott – and Eliza Blatherwick – have been enhanced by the attention given them in the *Northern Star* at the expense of many other women for whom only their names have survived, and of those who were active but remained nameless. This is especially the case with women Chartists as they do not appear in reports of other organisations such as the trades unions, co-operative and temperance societies, and are less likely to write letters to newspapers or sign petitions than men. When they do become visible they become so in one dimension only. Those who were married to Chartists also suffer the disadvantage of being in the shadows of their husbands, and this was the fate of Martha Sweet, wife of James, who was also an active Chartist in her own right.

Some historians have seen the social and educational activities of Chartism as part of a clever plan to inveigle wary artisans into a political movement, as a covert means to a political end. But the Charter was always a political means to a social end, universal (male) suffrage and the other five points of the Charter being the instruments by which the working class or 'the people' would gain political power to improve their lives and change the relations between the classes. Sometimes the immediate priorities of a Chartist would seem to confirm the views of the sceptic, as in the justification for educational classes in the Democratic Chapel provided by the 'Chartist shopkeeper' in the *Midland Counties*

---

[364] *Northern Star*, 1st June 1844.

Illuminator. However, even in this piece of writing it is the duties to society, and the relative values of people and things that are stressed first, politics being introduced 'in due time':

> 'There the children are taught their duty to one another, and to society in general; and will be taught to put a proper value upon men and things. In due time they will hear *when and how* their forefathers were plundered of their liberty and property; – of the struggles which have taken place from time to time to regain their rights; – of the rise and progress of the Chartist movement; – and the principles which are embodied in the document entitled "The People's Charter", will be fully shewn them. ... by the time they leave the school, they will be enabled to meet a Whig or Tory in fair argument, and beat them into the bargain.'[365]

It had been the fourth objective of the forerunner of organised Chartism in Nottingham, the Nottingham Working Men's Association, 'To promote, by all available means, the education of the rising generation; and to eradicate those systems which tend to fetter and enslave mankind.'[366] The dual aims contained here attest to a desire for a different kind of education and a different regime of schooling.

When the Democratic Chapel opened in 1839 there were very few opportunities for young children to receive any kind of education and only three infant schools in the town worthy of mention when James Orange wrote *History and Antiquities of Nottingham* in 1840.[367] One of these was in St Anne's Street, under the teaching authority of Mr J R Brown, who came, by invitation, to Nottingham from Samuel Wilderspin's infant school in Spitalfields, London, expressly for the purpose of opening the school in St Anne's Street.[368] Mr C H Clarke, secretary to the St Anne's school, explained at the opening ceremony in April 1827 that the educational system was one which traced its roots from the school established at New Lanark by Robert Owen:

---

[365] *Midland Counties Illuminator*, 27th February 1841 (original emphasis).
[366] *Nottingham Review*, 10th August 1838.
[367] *History and Antiquities of Nottingham*, James Orange 1840.
[368] *Nottingham and Newark Mercury*, 14th April 1827. Three more infant schools on the Wilderspin pattern were opened subsequently, in Rutland Street, Independent Street and Canaan Street. The school at St Anne's Street appears in the 1835 *Pigott's Directory* but is not listed in *Orange's Directory* of 1840 or in later Directories.

'By the system pursued, the ideas of children were called into play without bewildering their minds, and the restraint, so injurious to health as well as to the mental powers, usually enforced in schools upon the old system, was in this superseded by allowing rational freedom, and rendering instruction a species of amusement rather than a laborious task; it was also calculated to inculcate obedience and tractability'.[369]

Illustration 17: School at New Lanark (c.1820).
A dancing class at the school.

With the exception of the final few words, this could equally have been a report from the co-operative school at Salford in 1831 onwards or the system practised later at the socialist community at Queenwood. The language employed by Mr Clarke, his references to 'the old system' and 'rational freedom' do suggest that Clarke himself had a background in Owenite socialism. This is quite possible, as there had been a close connection between Robert Owen and the School at Spitalfields. Owen had part financed an infant school in Westminster in 1820 in conjunction with the philosopher James Mill and radical politician Lord Brougham, and he appointed James Buchanan, the teacher he had employed at New Lanark, to run the school. It was the result of Wilderspin's introduction to

---

[369] Ibid. Mr C H Clarke was still in Nottingham in 1839 when he chaired a teetotal festival at the Exchange Hall: *Nottingham Review*, 5th April 1839.

James Buchanan and the Westminster school that Wilderspin's own school in Spitalfields was planned and opened.[370]

The principles which lay behind the socialist schooling are neatly set out in the constitution for the school established in 1834 within the Labour Exchange in Charlotte Street, London. This was the only one of the labour exchanges for which Robert Owen later accepted any personal responsibility. It was a place where the labour theory of value was practised, where goods were brought in and exchanged or bought using 'labour notes'. Half of the fees payable for the education of the children in the school were paid by labour notes. The six principles of the school's constitution are worth stating, as every single one of them is a challenge to the prevailing practices in the schools of the time:

> Every pupil shall be encouraged to express his or her opinion.
> No creed or dogma shall be imposed upon any child.
> Admitted fact alone shall be placed before the pupils; from which they shall be allowed to draw their own deductions.
> No distinction whatever shall exist.
> Neither praise nor blame, merit or demerit, reward or punishment, shall be awarded to any: kindness and love to be the only ruling powers.
> Both sexes shall have equal opportunities of acquiring useful knowledge.[371]

An educational regime of a very different kind was advised by William Thompson in the *Chartist Circular*:

> 'The first thing to be done when you employ your own teachers, is to get a Chartist catechism prepared and published for the use of families and schools. By question and answer, it may simply, correctly, and minutely elucidate all the principles of the Charter. ... Children should commit a portion of it to memory every day at school, until they have mastered it; and parents ought to catechise their families in it, at least once a week'.[372]

---

[370] *Robert Owen*, Peter Gordon, 1994.

[371] *Crisis*, 4th January 1834, quoted in *The Educational Innovators 1750-1880*, W A C Stewart and W P McCann, 1967. See also articles in *The Co-operative Magazine*, November 1827 on the Westminster Infant School and Pestallozian infant schools.

[372] *Chartist Circular*, 14th March 1840.

Most of the socialist and Chartist schools probably occupied a space somewhere between these two poles of purpose and teaching method. In his commendation of Mary Ann Abbott in May 1844 it was the quality of kindness which Henry Dorman chose to remark upon in his address at the Democratic Chapel. He was referring to the conduct of the Sunday school and there is no record of the day classes, but unsmiling discipline and learning by rote are unlikely to have been evident among the teaching methods there.

Chapter 11: The New Poor Law

The year 1844 was memorable in local Chartist history for two separate campaigns against the New Poor Law, in Nottingham and Basford. In March 1844 the *Nottingham Review* reminded its readers that elections for the Poor Law Guardians would be taking place soon and 'we would remind the ratepayers that these elections are the nearest approach to complete suffrage, inasmuch as every householder, male or female, possess the right to voting, if the poor rates have been paid up to the last six months'.[373]

The kindness of Mary Ann Abbott at the Sunday school in the Democratic Chapel, remarked upon by Henry Dorman, was not a political ideal that was much spoken of, but it was inherent in the values which motivated most of the opponents of the New Poor Law. The word used most frequently to describe the 1834 Poor Law Amendment Act was at the opposite end of the scale. It was 'cruel'.

The ban on providing relief to unemployed workers unless they were admitted to the workhouse; the degrading conditions of workhouse life; and the separation of husbands, wives and children, were the most feared and hated aspects of the New Poor Law. Within three months of the New Poor Law being introduced to Nottinghamshire, one of the first relieving officers to be appointed in the Basford Union resigned his post after one day:

> 'We understand that Mr William Smith, who was last week appointed relieving officer of the first district of the Basford Union, has resigned his situation, being satisfied, after one day's attempt to fulfil the duties of the office, that no man, possessed of feelings like his, and unaccustomed to the scenes of distress and misery such officer is doomed to witness, can efficiently perform the duties required.'[374]

In many parts of the country it was the Poor Law which brought into being the first organised protests and campaigns since the days of the Reform Bill in 1832 and frequently brought together those campaigners

---

[373] *Nottingham Review*, 15th March 1844.
[374] *Nottingham Review*, 10th June 1836. Was this the same William Smith who was socialist branch secretary, and the same William Smith who kept the coffee house on Low Pavement? It is one of many unanswered questions.

who went on to form the working men's associations and branches of the National Charter Association. In Nottingham the campaigns against the Poor Law began later than in some areas and came to a peak after the founding of the Nottingham Working Men's Association in 1838, which might explain why the repeal of the Poor Law Amendment Act and local opposition to it are not included among the Objects of the NMWA.

Workhouses had been introduced in parts of England long before the Poor Law Amendment Act of 1834, and the workings of the systems introduced in Bingham by the Reverend Robert Lowe in 1818 and by Thomas Becher in Southwell, had provided welcome evidence of the correctness of Malthusian doctrines for the Poor Law Commission set up in 1832 to look for ways of overhauling the Speenhamland System of outdoor relief. George Nicholls, honorary overseer of the Southwell workhouse from 1821 to 1824, whose own writings appear to have been the source of Becher's *The Anti-Pauper System* which received much attention after its publication in 1828, had stated unashamedly: 'I wish to see the Poor House looked to with dread by our labouring class, and the reproach for being an inmate of it extend downward from father to son ... for without this, where is the stimulus to industry?'[375] This was not just an attack on the 'undeserving poor' but a calculated assault on an entire class of working people and for all time to come. He was rewarded by being appointed one of the first Poor Law Commissioners, a post in which he remained for the full thirteen years from the inception of the New Poor Law in 1834 to the abolition of the Commission in 1847.

The New Poor Law had been motivated by the belief that poverty was a consequence of idleness and personal inadequacy and that cash payments to unemployed and destitute people encouraged laziness and dependency by removing the incentive to find work, and placed an unnecessary burden upon the ratepayers. The principle of 'less eligibility' in poor relief would ensure that the condition of the pauper would always be less favourable than that of even the poorest workers outside, lest the latter should find the workhouse an attractive proposition. By providing relief only by admission to the workhouse the paupers would have their families separated from them, they would wear workhouse clothes, be allowed no

---

[375] *In the Shadow of the Workhouse: Implementation of the New Poor Law Throughout Nottinghamshire, 1836-1846*, Maurice Caplan, 1984; *John Thomas Becher*, Michael Austin, in Minster People, eds. S Chapman and D Walker, 2009.

visitors, have alcohol and tobacco taken from them, subjected to a nightly curfew, and forced to do hard, degrading or unproductive work in the daytime lest they should begin to enjoy their idleness. Their situation would in turn create fear among those outside the workhouse that they too might one day find themselves inside it, and the fear would breed a respect for hard work, independence and self reliance. Those who were admitted on account of age or infirmity would have to understand that their poverty in the workhouse was necessary to teach those outside it to make personal provision for their old age and infirmities.

The New Poor Law had come to Nottingham in 1836 with the appointment of Edward Gulson as Assistant Commissioner for Nottinghamshire, charged with the responsibility of creating Poor Law Unions from groups of parishes and creating new or enlarged workhouses for each of them. At first everything went to plan. Gulson reported to the Poor Law Commissioners in London that the Guardians were carrying out their duties under the Act with greater co-operation than he had experienced anywhere. Credit for this has been laid at the door of Absalom Barnett, who was workhouse manager for St Mary's and had written a pamphlet on the Poor Law in 1833, which the Whig *Nottingham Mercury* had reviewed favourably. Barnett was in favour of the workhouse test; of measures to enforce 'moral discipline in workhouses'; to secure instruction to the children; and encourage industry and economy.[376]

Within months of Gulson's arrival the workhouses of St Peter's and St Nicholas' parishes had been closed and St Mary's workhouse had been taken over by the new Nottingham Union. Aware of the past political history of Nottingham and the burning of the Castle in 1831, Gulson proceeded with stealth and the first elections for the new Guardians passed off quietly. By 1837 the downturn in trade with the United States had led to a growth in unemployment in Nottingham. St Mary's workhouse could accommodate 520 men and women and it was soon full. With the sick, the children and the elderly moved to the workhouses recently closed and now re-opened, there was room for 700, but these places were soon filled.

Gulson was completely opposed to paying relief to anyone outside the workhouse and pressed ahead with plans for a new workhouse capable of accommodating 1,000 adults and children. There was public opposition to

---

[376] *Nottingham and Newark Mercury*, 27th April 1833.

this, and the Poor Law Commission in London authorised a reluctant Gulson to suspend the rule on payments to able-bodied unemployed men outside the workhouse, although under no circumstances would payments be made to make up wages to those whose income was so low as to make them effectively destitute. By August 1837 there were 900 people in the workhouses of the Nottingham Union and other able-bodied men were receiving outdoor relief.[377]

In 1840 Gulson revealed the plans for the new workhouse with places for 1,000 men, women and children at York Street. William Rowarth, the Mayor of Nottingham, called a public meeting at the Exchange Hall at which almost every speaker condemned the plans. James Withers, who 'lived by the labour of his own hands', and who had signed an appeal the previous year against physical force Chartism and supported collaboration between the working and middle classes to 'abolish the Corn Laws and gain universal suffrage', spoke up to support the new workhouse because he was opposed to the overcrowding in the old workhouse and wanted better conditions for the aged and infirm. He was in a small minority and was continually interrupted with calls to 'put him out', and a motion that the new workhouse was 'wholly unnecessary and a waste of public money' was adopted overwhelmingly.[378] The construction of the new workhouse went ahead regardless of the strength of opposition, and by the time of the election of Guardians in 1841 it was almost complete and ready for occupation.

The meeting at the Exchange Hall had also adopted a motion to set up a ratepayers' association to arrange slates of candidates opposed to the new workhouse for the three parish wards of the Nottingham Poor Law Union and a committee was elected to put this into effect. Among the members was James Sweet. In his regular column in the *Midland Counties Illuminator* he reported that:

'In consequence of a majority of the Board of Guardians in this Union being "Liberal Whigs", and withal very pious men, they have determined to build at a very great expense, a splendid new Bastille ... The great majority of the ratepayers

---

[377] *In the Shadow of the Workhouse: Implementation of the New Poor Law Throughout Nottinghamshire, 1836-1846*, Maurice Caplan, 1984; *Unemployment in Nottingham (1837-38)*, Parliamentary papers, XXXI, 1837.
[378] *Observations on the Administration of the Poor Law in Nottingham*, W Rowarth, 1840.

having some old fashioned notions of right reasoning ... said that such a receptacle was unnecessary ... Bastille was built ... in which they intend to immure honest poverty, and also to shew them their "Christian love" to their poor brethren, by exercising a little "moral restraint" over them'.[379]

Sweet argued that a Board of Guardians should be elected which would 'dissolve the Union' and abandon the workhouse, 'The building would then do for the Queen to put her ponies in, and for her husband's dogs'. He continues: 'yet the wicked shall not go unpunished, and the same measure which they mete out to us, shall be measured to them again.'[380] This is James Sweet at his most unrestrained, speaking to his own audience, and giving a glimpse of the language and the emotions that were usually withheld from public scrutiny.

In April 1841 James Sweet appeared among the nominees for five of the Poor Law Union candidates for St Mary's parish, including George Gill, and Richard Sutton, editor of the *Nottingham Review*. George Eddowes, churchwarden of St Mary's, nominated by John Hicklin, editor of the *Nottingham Journal,* received the highest number of votes for the those in favour of the new workhouse, but Eddowes and all the other pro-workhouse candidates were soundly defeated in all three of the town's parishes. James Sweet wrote triumphantly in the *Midland Counties Illuminator* that 'The "no Bastille party" have been declared duly elected by an overwhelming majority; the highest Bastiller being in the minority of upwards of 850.'[381]

The Guardians maintained their opposition to the new workhouse until a child died in the old overcrowded workhouse and the pressure upon them to close it mounted. An enquiry by Poor Law Commissioner Henry Hancock reported favourably on the new premises and also reduced the permitted capacity of the old workhouse to 240. At that point the Guardians gave up the battle and took over the new workhouse.

The campaign against the new workhouse had failed, but the success of the electoral campaign was not forgotten. James Sweet appended his

---

[379] *Midland Counties Illuminator*, 20th March 1841.
[380] Ibid.
[381] *Midland Counties Illuminator*, 24th April 1841. Highest vote for the ratepayer slate was 1,934 for Brewster and lowest was 1,263 for Yates; highest for pro-workhouse candidates was 651 for Eddowes.

report to the *Midland Counties Illuminator* with a postscript: *'Circumstances now require* that the Radicals of Nottingham should do their duty, and paralyse the base Whig faction, who have so long tyrannized over the People.'[382] It was a message taken up by editor Thomas Cooper who declared that the 'resolution of the Nottingham Chartists is as sagacious as it is patriotic.'

Illustration 18: Nottingham Workhouse, York Street (1898).
The 'new' workhouse, which opened in 1841.

The electoral tactic of swinging working class support for an anti-Whig candidate – in this case by supporting a Tory – was used again by Nottingham Chartists in the April parliamentary bye-election when Chartist support for radical Tory candidate John Walter, editor of *The Times*, caused the defeat of the Whig candidate George Larpent. An editorial in the *Midland Counties Illuminator* described this as a:

> 'combined act of the working classes – of the 300 who went up in banded array before them in the morning – was an open and avowed one ... Every Chartist elector proclaimed his unchangeable hatred of Toryism, while resolving to vote for the Tory candidate ... in a resolve to deal a death blow at Whiggery ... .'[383]

---

[382] Ibid.
[383] *Midland Counties Illuminator*, 1st May 1841.

It goes on to quote a man who said to Walter, 'I tell you without hesitation, that our chief purpose, as a party, is to make use of you to cut the throat of the Whigs, – and when that is done, we intend to make use of *them* to cut your throat, politically speaking, and the general throat of your party!' Explaining the logic of this was not an easy matter, as explaining and justifying a political *volte-face* seldom is. James Sweet sought to enlarge upon the treachery of the Whigs by combining their support for the New Poor Law with their imprisonment of Chartists following the uprisings of 1840: 'Now for the causes which have induced the Chartists to assist Walter in preference to a Liberty-professing, but Freedom-hating Whig; in the first place you Liberal Whigs have imprisoned nearly 500 Chartists for attempting to carry out the principles on which you took office'.[384]

In Basford there was a similar growth in unemployment after 1837 and the Reverend Padley in Bulwell urged Gulson to allow outdoor relief for the able-bodied, but was refused. The Basford Union workhouse with 400 places was full during the winters of 1837 and 1838 and the Basford Guardians provided outdoor relief in the form of bread despite being threatened with personal surcharges for doing so. Eventually the Commissioners had to acquiesce to outdoor relief, but insisted that the recipients be engaged on some kind of public work which had at least the semblance of being useful.

It was this ruling which was responsible for 72 year old Susan Robinson being made to break stones on the highway in return for parish relief, and which became the first campaign of the Nottingham Female Political Union. When the workhouse became overcrowded again in 1844 the Commissioners formally refused another request for permission to provide outdoor relief and the chairman of the Board of Guardians resigned.[385]

The year 1844 was also memorable in the history of Chartism for the 'Basford Union Workhouse Affair', in which Chartists were at the forefront. In January the *Nottingham Review* reported that the editor had received correspondence from some present and former inmates of the Basford workhouse alleging that they had suffered from ill treatment and wretched conditions there. These included allegations that they had to

---

[384] *Midland Counties Illuminator*, 15th May 1841 (original emphasis).
[385] *The Poor Law in Nottinghamshire, 1836-1871*, Maurice Caplan, 1970.

wash plates and cutlery in buckets used to dispose of urine, had been refused clean clothes and sheets, had to wear the same stockings for up to ten months without them being washed, feared they would be refused food if they appeared in the dining room stockingless and in bare feet, and were afraid to complain lest they be punished by Colonel Rolleston, chairman of the Board, in his capacity as a magistrate. The *Review* also noted tellingly that the Guardians had refused to allow newspaper reporters to attend their meetings.[386]

When the Guardians met, all twenty four of them present, George Harrison, a Guardian elected by the ratepayers in Calverton, took the lead in the discussion. Harrison was a Primitive Methodist preacher and a Chartist who had represented Nottingham at the 1842 Chartist Convention. He brought to Nottingham Chartism the vengeful wrath of a Christ aggrieved by the sins of the money-grubbing Whigs and the inhumanity of their Poor Law. He preached regularly at the Democratic Chapel on Sundays and at open air Chartist meetings. When he delivered a funeral oration for 27 year old Samuel Holberry, the Sheffield Chartist who had been born in Gamston in Nottinghamshire, and who died of tuberculosis in York prison after conviction for incitement to riot and sedition, 10,000 people assembled on the Forest to hear him speak.[387]

The documents referred to the Board of Guardians by Harrison were in some cases written by others on behalf of illiterate paupers who had signed them with a cross. The names of James Saunders, druggist, of Denman Street and William Norman, dyer, of Bottoms Buildings, both members of the Radford Chartist locality, were attached to some of them. The workhouse rule was quoted: 'That every pauper in the workhouse shall have clean linen and stockings once a week, and that all beds be kept in a clean and wholesome state.'[388] William Eaton, a pauper who appeared before them as a witness said 'We have had one pair of sheets for ten weeks together' and 'Now, sir, I ask you, what those people are to do who are liable to sweaty feet? I wore my stockings from the middle of August to the middle of November.'[389] A complaint was also heard against the Medical Officer. The discussion continued for some time before the

---

[386] *Nottingham Review*, 26th January 1844.
[387] *Some Organisational and Cultural Aspects of the Chartist Movement in Nottingham*, James Epstein, 1982.
[388] *Nottingham Review*, 16th February 1844.
[389] Ibid.

Guardians agreed to ask the Commissioners to conduct an enquiry and if the allegations were found to be incorrect 'to punish the author thereof'.[390]

An enquiry was rapidly arranged and conducted over a period of three days by Assistant Poor Law Commissioner Robert Weale, and a 131 page report presented to the March meeting of the Board of Guardians.[391] The report concluded that 'the charges made in the papers are not substantiated'.[392] One of the complainants was committed for trial on a charge of perjury and other witness statements were declared to be invalid. However, the practice of washing eating utensils in the urine buckets was discontinued, the medical officer was reprimanded, and some other minor changes were made to workhouse practices.[393] George Harrison, who was not present at the meeting, bore the brunt of the other Guardians' ire for having wasted time and money on what they regarded as frivolous complaints, but they were not in a position to 'punish' him.

In the eyes of many, however, Harrison was considered a hero for championing the rights of the workhouse inmates, and at a public meeting at the Fox and Hounds in Basford, both he and the editor of the *Nottingham Review* were congratulated for bringing the complaints to public notice. Harrison was pressed upon to stand again in the elections for the Board of Guardians. He did so and was returned at the top of the poll.[394] At the first meeting of the new Board he was appointed an overseer, responsible for collecting the poor rate.

Harrison's campaign centred upon the indignities perpetrated against the workhouse inmates, the deprivation of their control over their own circumstances, and the unhealthy conditions they were made to endure. The lack of respect for human beings, their souls and their bodies had been at the forefront of the earliest hostilities against the Poor Law reformers even before the Act was on the statute book. Those objections were connected with the widespread contempt for doctors, surgeons and medicine in general, with the treachery of the Reform Act, and the Anatomy Bill which found its way through Parliament in 1832.

---

[390] *Nottingham Review*, 2nd February 1844.
[391] *Ministry of Health, Basford Board of Guardians*, MH/12/9234/41, National Archives.
[392] *Nottingham Review*, 8th March 1844.
[393] *Chartism and Opposition to the New, Poor Law in Nottinghamshire: the Basford Union Workhouse Affair of 1844*, Colin Griffin, 1974.
[394] *Nottingham Review*, 29th March 1844. Harrison 433 votes, Farrands 382, Cheetham 375, Richards 114. All elected.

Local concern over the increasing regularity of body snatching had arisen in the late 1820s. Robberies of recently interred corpses had increased during the latter part of the eighteenth and the early nineteenth centuries. They were most prevalent in towns with anatomy schools in the vicinity, which did not include Nottingham. Nonetheless, in January 1827 'the town was greatly horrified by the discovery of an organised system of despoiling the sanctuaries of the dead, by a gang of "resurrection men", who were in the habit of selling the bodies, for the purpose of dissection.'[395] When some body snatchers were apprehended after the remains of an old woman and a young boy were intercepted in a package destined for London, people started digging up the graves of their relatives in St Mary's churchyard to check they were still there. Quite a few were missing. The Reverend Wilkins responded by preaching a special sermon on the Violation of the Dead and had it published for good measure. The following month a vestry meeting was treated to a demonstration of a coffin from Bedford. 'Its principal features were a new screw to secure the lid of the coffin, and a method of preventing the removal of the coffin from the earth.' [396] By 1832 an examination of the churchyard revealed that thirty four recently buried bodies had been surreptitiously removed from the burial grounds of St Mary's.[397]

The public dissection of the corpse of a criminal as a punishment after hanging had existed for centuries, but from 1752 hanged murderers could be supplied to the surgeons for the purpose of anatomical dissection. The first case in Nottinghamshire was recorded in 1827 when the body of an Ollerton man, hanged for the murder of another, was passed on to surgeons for dissection.[398] Dissection roused various responses. Some feared that the dissected bodies would be unable to rise on the day of judgement. Others feared that the remains would be melted down to make candles and soap, a fear originating in Lambeth not far from Price's candle factory. For most it was probably a simple wish that the bodies of the dead should be allowed to rest in peace.

The use of the bodies of paupers for dissection was first proposed in 1819 by John Abernethy, the founder of the medical school at St Bartholomews

---

[395] *Nottingham Date Book*, 1852.
[396] *Nottingham and Newark Mercury*, 31st January; 5th May 1827.
[397] *The Anglican Church in the Industrialised Town, St Mary's Parish, Nottingham, 1779-1884*, Mary Wendy Bowen, 1997.
[398] *Nottingham and Newark Mercury*, 31st March 1827.

hospital in London. Jeremy Bentham took up the idea and produced a draft Bill for Parliament which would have provided free treatment for the poor in a charity hospital in return for their corpse for dissection, unless a relative claimed the body within 24 hours of death. The first Bill foundered in 1829 but was reintroduced in 1832 with 'anatomical examination' replacing the term 'dissection' to obscure the association between the dissection of hanged murderers and those of dead paupers. The passage of the Anatomy Act did not escape public notice despite preoccupation with the Reform Bill and led to riots in some towns, although Nottingham was not one of them.

It was after the Poor Law Amendment Act of 1834 that connections with the Anatomy Act became evident. Accusations were made that the Poor Law was a device of the medical fraternity to make poverty a criminal offence and so reward themselves with an abundant supply of cadavers for dissection. The right of relatives to claim the body within seven days of death in a workhouse was for many a spurious one as there was no effective way of making known the death to all close relatives, and the cost of retrieving the body, paying for a coffin and a burial was beyond the means of many whose families were also poor or who were themselves the inmates of a workhouse. Unclaimed bodies, which were the majority, were then sold by the workhouses for medical dissection, and it has been estimated that less than half of one per cent of all bodies dissected after the 1834 Act came from anywhere but poor law institutions.[399] The dire reputation of the medical profession had not been improved by the catastrophe which had struck Nottingham just a few years earlier.

When cholera arrived in Nottingham in the summer of 1832 it found a town ideally hospitable to its requirements. A large population in densely occupied back to back houses in narrow streets and courtyards, with poor sanitation and polluted water supplies, streets filled with accumulated rubbish of all descriptions, damp houses in Narrow Marsh and Broadmarsh, inadequate hospitals and overcrowded burial grounds, were all ideal conditions for cholera. Life expectancy in Broadmarsh and Narrow Marsh were already said to be lower than in Calcutta or anywhere else in the British Empire.[400] At first the newspapers tried to minimise

---

[399] *Death, Dissection and the Destitute*, Ruth Richardson, 1988.
[400] *The Press and the Nottingham Cholera Outbreak of 1832*, Peter Foster, in Nottinghamshire Historian, Autumn/Winter 1989.

occurrences of the disease, being wary of the public response, although the response proved to be fear rather than anger. 'Nothing in the memory of man produced so much alarm and consternation as this dreadful plague' wrote a contemporary observer.[401]

The causes of cholera were not then known and attempts to stem the outbreak, by burning pitch for example, were often motivated by a mistaken belief that the disease was spread by the air, while remedies recommended in reports and advertisements in the local newspapers were liable to contain mixtures of laudanum and nitrous acid as well as benign additions of peppermint and sal volatile. The unstamped *Poor Man's Advocate* published a poem entitled *The Cholera Morbus:*

> The doctors combined had found a way,
> To diddle their patients out of their pay,
> For if in your bowels you ever feel queer,
> They tell you the Cholera Morbus is here.
> With the doctors' consent, I will give them advice,
> and though it is simple, yet may suffice,
> For the very best way this infection to cure,
> *Is to feed all the hungry, and clothe all the poor.*[402]

This was not mere rhetoric. Hunger was not the cause of the disease but it did contribute to the deaths from it. In the analysis of deaths in the town it was noted that they were most numerous towards the end of the week, before pay day when the sufferers had the least to eat, and least numerous towards the west of the town where the inhabitants were wealthier and lived in conditions that were less crowded and insanitary.[403]

The ignorance of the medical establishment, and the appearance of specious medications, did not encourage faith in the medical and public authorities, and in Mansfield a rumour got under way that doctors were being paid a guinea for every fatality they registered and that the doctors were killing for profit.[404] In Nottingham it was alleged that live bodies were being disposed of in a trench dug in Carter Gate to accommodate

---

[401] *History and Antiquities of Nottingham*, James Orange, 1840.
[402] *Poor Man's Advocate*, John Doherty, 31st March 1832 (original emphasis).
[403] *The Press and the Nottingham Cholera Outbreak of 1832*, Peter Foster, in Nottinghamshire Historian, Autumn/Winter 1989.
[404] Ibid.

cholera victims.[405] The dead – and allegedly the living – were being disposed of with the same lack of concern for human dignity and respect for the dead that would soon be evident in the workhouse and in the disposal of the bodies of the workhouse paupers.

The cholera epidemic in Nottingham claimed 930 people of whom 330 died. A disproportionate number died in St Mary's workhouse where the death toll was 40.[406] The worst affected areas were in St Mary's parish, where overcrowding and unsanitary living conditions were at their worst.

The prime role of the doctors in the cholera epidemic was not to cure the sick but to record the deaths and dispose of the bodies. The failure of the medical profession to understand or curtail the cholera epidemic contributed to a continuing, and healthy, scepticism of their value to society. Hospitals were valued, but their roots were in the community, whilst those of the physicians were in the service of the aristocracy. The medical profession was often included in a trilogy of demons that preyed on the people. John Doherty, at that time running a radical bookshop and printing press in Manchester, and under attack from the clergy and the government for his publications, wrote an article in 1832 entitled 'The Parsons, The Lawyers, and the Doctors, Against the *Poor Man's Advocate*',[407] and in 1835 the *New Moral World* castigated the:

'Lawyers and magistrates – whose business, in this Old Immoral World, is, to confound all notions of right and wrong ... Priests, who fill the minds of all with folly and madness ... Physicians, who produce no wealth, and little knowledge ... occupied in curing, or attempting to cure, diseases, which ought to be prevented or cured by the knowledge which should be given to each individual.'[408]

James Sweet, as late as 1850, would have had them all transported to Australia:

'all the parsons, because they are not only useless, but very mischievous. All the lawyers, because their trade is to mystify that which ought to be clear and indisputable. Three fourths

---

[405]   *The Nottingham Cholera Epidemic of 1832*, Martyn A Walker, in Transactions of the Thoroton Society, 1991.
[406]   Ibid.
[407]   *Poor Man's Advocate*, 14th April 1832.
[408]   *New Moral World*, 14th November 1835.

of doctors might accompany them, as very few only would be required when the people were taught to live in accordance with natural laws.'[409]

The right to health and the right and the ability to be one's own physician was becoming increasingly asserted. For some that meant self medication by use of any of the varied pills and potions being advertised on the front pages of the local newspapers, for others it was to be found in enclosure of the common lands and better housing, in allotment gardens or a return to living on the land as a smallholder or a member of a community, in improved education, in the abstention from alcoholic liquors, in a vegetarian diet, in unadulterated food, in the opening of coffee houses, parks and libraries on the Sabbath, in a reduction in working hours and a better and healthier standard of living, in membership of sick and burial societies. Even mental illness was not beyond simple cure: when asked 'where are the lunatics' in your system, Robert Owen replied to his questioner in Leicester 'We shall have no lunatics – all will be trained to become rational and intelligent beings.'[410] It was a holistic view of health which required a degree of control over one's own environment and the spirit of self help.[411]

---

[409]   *Northern Star*, 5th January 1850.
[410]   *Leicester Chronicle*, 18th August 1838.
[411]   *Disease, Medicine and Society in England 1550-1860*, Roy Porter, 1987.

Chapter 12: Friendly and Co-operative Societies

On the 15th April 1844 the members of the Carrington Co-operative Society held their quarterly general meeting and received the report of their auditors, two members of the society, William Anderson and Benjamin Douse, the latter a prominent member of the Chartist locality which met at the New Inn.[412] The society had completed its fourth year in business, its trade with members reaching £2,380, an average of £45 a week. The profit for the year was £133, of which all but £11 was distributed as a dividend to approximately 100 members at the rate of 6s 1d on shares.

The level of weekly sales and a rate of return equivalent to 5.5% on sales or 30% on members' capital indicates that this was a commercially successful joint stock co-operative society, one of many of which little trace has been left in the histories of Co-operation nationally or locally.[413]

The Carrington society did not practice open membership, having a limit on membership of 124 members, and returned surpluses to members in proportion to their shares, not in proportion to their spending. Nevertheless, the Carrington society seems to have lasted much longer than most of this type of joint-stock venture. It appears in directories of Nottingham with the names of its manager John Scott in 1855, secretary Richard Rudd and storekeeper Henry Skelton in 1866 and 1868. Most similar societies did not survive the Chartist period and failed to develop into a movement. The founding of a movement was to be the legacy of the Rochdale Society of Equitable Pioneers, and it was their success which placed the birth of Co-operation in Rochdale in December 1844 and overshadowed the co-operatives with different roots extending back some seventy years.

Some of the earliest co-operative endeavours had their roots in the friendly societies, and friendly societies were often a screen behind which working people combined to protect their livelihoods and maintain their wages or the price of their manufactures in an early form of trade union.

---

[412] *Nottingham Review*, 19th April 1844.
[413] There are records surviving of two societies in Carrington. It is not clear whether the society referred to in the text is either of these: the *Nottingham, Carrington and Sherwood No 1 Trading Association*, FS8/571/236; the *Carrington Co-operative Industrial Society*, FS8/33/1634, National Archives. It is possible that the 'Carrington Co-operative Society' founded in 1840 was registered as the former under the Friendly Societies Act and as the latter under the 1851 Industrial and Provident Societies Act.

These practices were evident in the Ayrshire village of Fenwick from 1761 and in the following years the weavers of that village expanded their activities to include buying and selling food, establishing a library, and organising an emigration society, and it is the Fenwick Weavers Society that is now widely accepted as the earliest recorded co-operative.

Fenwick weavers began meeting by the village pump around 1759. The pump was an innocuous place for a conversation but as their numbers were unusually large and their discussions longer than the time it took to fill a pail, they posted lookouts on the adjoining roads. Two years later they had drawn up a charter and on a Tuesday evening on 14th of March 1761 sixteen weavers and apprentices met together in the safe haven of the parish Church to sign a foundation charter in which 'all with one consent Erect and unite ourselves together into a Society to be called from henceforth The Society of Weavers in Finnick', in which they pledged loyalty to each other and to 'make good & sufficient work and exact neither higher nor lower prices than are accustomed', setting purchase prices for yarns and selling prices for their cloths to which they would all adhere.[414]

From their mutual fund, supported by an admission fee of 2s 6d for weavers and 1s for apprentices, the two Headsmen elected annually by the members would 'give out and apply the same as the Trade or a Majority of the shall think fitt', as well as making quarterly donations to the poor of the village. On Thursday 9th November 1769 they agreed that funds from the 'box' would be used to buy provisions which they would sell to their members and to non-members, putting the profit back into the box. It was this decision to engage in mutual trading that has been taken to mark the start of their activities as a co-operative society.

Six years after the founding of the Fenwick Weavers' Society in Scotland the Blue Ball Club was established at the New Inn at the village of Blidworth in Nottinghamshire, on Saturday 3rd January 1767. Two years after the Fenwick Weavers bought their first sack of oatmeal in 1769, the members of the Blue Ball Club at Blidworth in the autumn of 1771 bought their first cheese for £28 7s 11d from the Goose Fair in Nottingham for resale to their members. They also bought a bag of thurds for £2 6s 0d,

---

[414] *A History of the Fenwick Weavers*, John McFadzean and John Smith, 2008. A transcript of the Charter, now held at the National Library of Scotland, can be found online. See Bibliography.

although there is naught to say on what they were or why they wanted them.

Neither society began as a co-operative retail trading society and neither ever became one. Their primary functions lay elsewhere. But if Fenwick was the birthplace of Co-operation in Scotland in 1769, Blidworth has an arguable claim to be the birthplace of Co-operation in Nottinghamshire, if not in England, in 1771.[415]

The Blue Ball Club was a friendly society for the support of members in times of sickness.[416] Meeting monthly in the club room of the New Inn, the men paid their subscriptions, plus 2d for beer.[417] The members elected a Master and two Headmen or stewards annually, and they were the keyholders for the 'box', in which the members' funds were kept. There was an admission fee in addition to the weekly subscription, and a charge of 3d for the rule book, which from the outset contained twenty six rules including several which detailed the fines to be imposed for drunkenness, swearing, betting, speaking on politics, and other misdemeanours. There was also an annual feast on Tuesday in Whitsun Week which all members were required to attend on pain of exclusion from the society, and for which the charge was 1s 7d, at which the Master and Stewards would appear wearing sashes, with ribbons in their hats, carrying staves in their gloved hands behind a banner and brass band. From a membership of 36 in 1770 the numbers rose to a height of 121, attracting members from the surrounding villages and as far away as Mansfield.

Friendly societies had existed in England since at least the sixteenth century, and the scope of the Blue Ball Club's rules suggests a prior knowledge of other societies which preceded theirs. With no provision for legal protection or registration with local magistrates until an Act of Parliament in 1793, many of the early societies disappeared without trace. The Fenwick Weavers' Society and the Blue Ball Club are both known to us because they registered under the 1793 Act, and their rule books, accounts and documents have been preserved. By registering under the

---

[415] Flour and bread societies in England have been dated back to 1759. See *Eighteenth and Nineteenth Century Consumer-Owned Community Flour and Bread Societies: Collective Response to Market Failure*, Joshua Bamfield, 1996.

[416] *Blidworth: the History of a Forest Town*, J C Whitworth, 1973; *Blidworth at Work and Play*, Will Richards, 1993; *Friendly Societies in Nottingham*, Julie O'Neill, in Nottinghamshire Historian, Autumn/Winter 1988.

[417] The Blue Ball was renamed the Crispin Arms and later still the New Inn.

Act they could benefit from some limited privileges, such as having the right to sue as a legally recognised body, but they were not obliged to register and many did not. Some would have had difficulty dealing with the registration process and others would have been reluctant to reveal their business to the magistrates.

The rules of the Blue Ball Club were typical of friendly societies of the time. Differences between societies' practices included rotation in office by all members instead of by election, the misdemeanours for which members might be fined, the inclusion or exclusion of references to religion and attendance at church services, and the admission or exclusion of women members. The Claypole Friendly Society, for example, allowed 2d per person to be taken from the box for beer 'when all business shall be gone through, and not before', provided no benefit for a member suffering with a venereal disease, and required of members that they attend 'divine service' on the day of the feast, and besides the President and two Stewards they elected nine directors to manage their affairs.[418] The Swarm Friendly Society in Arnold had a narrow age band for new members of 18 to 30, required that 'every member shall serve the office of Steward in his turn', paid a salary to their clerk, ruled that 'no money shall be expended on feasting, hat band, flags etc' and provided that a hefty fine of 2s be imposed on any member daring to suggest any such a violation of this rule.[419]

Most of the societies at this time met at public houses, and it was there that the box would normally be kept in the care of the landlord, who would benefit from the mandatory attendance of members spending their tuppences on beer. Almost all societies met at public houses. Most were societies of men but there were some mixed societies, and by the beginning of the nineteenth century there were 23 female friendly societies in existence in Nottinghamshire, including the first female society, founded at the Green Dragon in Hucknall in 1792, and another in Blidworth, which also met at the home of the Blue Ball Club, the New Inn.[420] Successful moves were made to set up a friendly society committed to temperance, and the Rock of Horeb branch of the Independent Order of Rechabites friendly society, which held tea meetings at William Holt's

---

[418] *Claypole Friendly Society, Rules*, C/QDC/1/1, Nottinghamshire County Archives.
[419] *Swarm Friendly Society, Rules*, DD/959/1-3, Nottinghamshire County Archives.
[420] *In the Club: Female Friendly Societies in Nottinghamshire 1792-1913*, Julie O'Neill, 2001.

temperance hotel in Greyhound Yard, Long Row East, was the result in 1840, but this remained an exception to normal practice. A 'tent' of the United Order of Female Rechabites, known as the 'United Sisters' was set up in 1842 but disappeared within four years.[421]

According to one of the few historians of the friendly societies it was 'extremely probable that had they trusted solely to the sense of duty – the duty of insuring against sickness – and merely required members to pay their weekly contributions to a collector, very few societies of the kind would have remained in existence'[422] but Absalom Barnett, the Overseer for the Nottingham Poor Law Union, said of friendly societies that 'In most instances the funds are inadequate to the promised payments. Partly because a considerable portion is drunk in ale ... The Club is an allurement to the ale-house; love of company combined with love of liquor is an occasion for a periodical debauch'.[423] The accounts of the Swarm Friendly Society show that 15/6 was spent on 'club ale' at each monthly meeting in 1826, a considerable sum for a small society. The 1827 Royal Commission on Friendly Societies was particularly concerned about the presence of women in public houses drinking alcoholic beverages, for drunkenness and debauchery were not restricted to men's societies. In 1851 a particularly memorable event occurred when crowds gathered to watch as the police arrived to deal with a crowd of drunken women outside the Queen Adelaide in Sneinton, following the annual supper of the Sneinton Female Burial Society.[424]

Despite middle class concerns about the consumption of alcohol at friendly society meetings and feasts, and continuing suspicions that they were fronts for illegal combinations, there was another school of thought which rose to ascendancy, and that was that friendly societies encouraged respectability, taught thrift, and kept the poor out of the poor house, to the great benefit of the ratepayers. The Poor Law Report of 1817 had spoken of the virtues of friendly societies and, in seeking leave to introduce his Friendly Society and Parochial Benefit Bill in 1819 the mover, Thomas Courtenay MP, said 'Many persons thought this mode of providing for the wants of the poor so desirable that its operation ought

---

[421] *Drink and Temperance in Nottingham 1830-1860*, J J Rowley, 1974.
[422] *Self Help: Voluntary Associations in 19th Century Britain*, P H J Gosden, 1973.
[423] *The Spirit of Independence: Friendly Societies in Nottinghamshire 1724-1913*, Julie O'Neill, 2001.
[424] *Drink and Temperance in Nottingham 1830-1860*, J J Rowley, 1974.

not to be left to the voluntary acts of individuals, but that the poor should be compelled to resort to it.'[425] This was his second attempt to introduce coercion into the membership of friendly societies. 'It had been proposed', he recalled, 'to establish this compulsion by inviting persons to enter into such societies, and then by refusing parochial relief to those who had not done so.' The outcomes of such a measure would be, in modern parlance, a 'win-win' situation for the ratepayers. Those who joined a friendly society would not need poor relief and those who were unable or refused to join would be denied it.

Although the Bill passed into law, measures to enforce membership of friendly societies upon the poor were not enforced, but friendly societies as a means of forcing the poor to bear the costs of relieving their own poverty remained popular among poor law reformers. Evidence presented to the House of Lords Select Committee on the Poor Laws in 1831 noted the connection between a high incidence of friendly society membership and the lower claims made upon poor relief: Lincolnshire, where an above average level of 16% of households were in membership of a friendly society, was contrasted with the low level of 7% of households receiving poor relief.

There is no local evidence that the fear of the workhouse after the passage of the 1834 Poor Law Amendment Act led to any significant growth in the number of new societies being formed, nor to any growth in the membership of existing societies.[426] For many people whose income was low or irregular the friendly society was not an option. The dinners, feasts and ceremonies, and the use of rituals and regalia, has often been noted as being a demonstration of fellowship, but it was also a declaration of independence, of a sense of difference from those who were not able to benefit from the advantages of membership.[427]

Often favoured with the patronage of the landed gentry and the church, the friendly societies tended to exhibit an outward deference to the established order, requiring regular attendance at church and levying fines for taking the name of God in vain. They would generally stand aside from other manifestations of working class self-organised activity,

[425] *House of Commons Debates*, 25 March 1819, Volume 39, CC1159-61.
[426] *The Spirit of Independence: Friendly Societies in Nottinghamshire 1724-1913*, Julie O'Neill 2001.
[427] *Self Help: Voluntary Associations in 19th Century Britain*, P H J Gosden, 1973.

especially in rural areas, but friendly societies were, nonetheless, on occasions to be seen among the political demonstrations of the working classes of the town of Nottingham.

After the passage of the Reform Act, some thirty friendly societies and branches of affiliated orders such as the Oddfellows, Foresters and the Ancient order of Druids, took part with their banners in the celebratory procession through the town in August 1832. The members of the Beehive Friendly Society were there, 'wearing medals and with a banner, suspended by a crimson riband, with a purple flag, yellow border, 'Earl Grey and the people'. On the reverse a beehive, with the inscription, 'working bees and no drones'.[428] Other friendly societies present included the Bulls Head Friendly Society, and the Black Horse Amicable Society with four banners, on which were displayed Earl Grey, the union jack and a tricolour. The 'Society at the Half Moon, Carter Gate' appeared with a banner displaying the Rose, Shamrock and Thistle United. The Hyson Green Friendly Society was present with its banner proclaiming 'United and Free'. In 1838 the Hyson Green Friendly Society paraded again with its banner at the first of the public processions to the Forest to demand the six points of the Charter.

The early co-operative societies for the mutual purchase of foodstuffs for members borrowed much from the friendly societies, in terms of their organisation, rules, and practices. The earliest to appear in Nottinghamshire appears to have been set up in Hucknall in 1828 or 1829. A historian of Hucknall recorded the date as 1828 when a shop was opened in Ball's Yard, West Street by founder members Jarvis Cartledge and James Buck and managed at the outset by John Hall. By 1835 William Calladine was the manager, moving with the store to South Street in 1840, and then to premises at the junction of the Market Place and High Street.[429]

William Calladine had been born in 1803 in Melbourne and moved to Nottingham some years later. As a young man he was present in Hucknall at the time of a Baptist revival, and was one of sixteen members enrolled into the Hucknall Baptist Society in 1827, another being Reuben Cale. Both men maintained a long association with the Baptist Chapel in Hucknall and both were associated with the co-operative society. William

[428]   *Nottingham Review*, 10th August 1832.
[429]   *History of Hucknall Torkard*, J H Beardsmore, 1909; *White's Directory*, 1832; *White's Directory*, 1844; *Kelly's PO Directory*, 1855.

Calladine continued to manage the co-operative store for more than twenty five years. In 1864 it appears to have been run under the agency of Reuben Cale, who was by now a successful Shetland shawl manufacturer.[430] The last manager of the society is said to have been Roby Rowe, who found that the strength of the society had been sapped by extended credit to members, and supervised the winding up of the society in 1865, although he was still listed as manager of the co-operative store in Hucknall in 1869, four years after its supposed demise, and five years after the founding of the Rochdale-model co-operative society in Hucknall which maintained an independent existence until 1968.[431] Despite its eventual dissolution, the first Hucknall co-operative society had outlasted most others founded during the period of co-operative enthusiasm in the late 1820s. Few of those independent societies, isolated from each other, unsupported by a central agency, and sharing no common values or goals, could boast a life approaching forty years.

Despite the discrepancies of recorded dates and places, that society might have been the First Hucknall Torkard Friendly Co-operative Trading Association. That society is known to us because it registered under the Friendly Societies Acts in 1842 and recorded in its rule book the date of foundation as the 21st July 1829, in the schoolroom at Half Moon Yard.[432] In 1842 it was putting half of its profits back into the society and paying a dividend on purchases of 8d in the pound, provided a minimum spending of £4 for married or £2 for single members had been reached. Unlike many of the co-operative societies formed in the period before the Rochdale model had become established, this was not a joint stock company distributing profits to shares but distributed surpluses on purchases, although that might not have been the case when it was originally founded in 1829.

The earliest co-operative society in the town of Nottingham may have been formed in 1827 when a group of admirers of Robert Owen's plans for communities met to set up their own community society. 'In Nottingham', reported the *Nottingham Mercury*, 'a Society has been formed, the members of which meet to discuss the merits of the System, and they have

---

[430] *Wright's Directory*, 1864.
[431] *Morris and Co., Directory*, 1869.
[432] First Hucknall Torkard Friendly Co-operative Trading Association, *Rules*, 1842, FS1/571/245, National Archives.

for some time past regularly appropriated some portion of their weekly earnings for the purpose of forming a fund to enable them to join a Co-operative Community.'[433]

Co-operatives for joint purchasing were frequently an adjunct to plans to establish communities. The *Mercury* had published an account from a correspondent on the Devon and Exeter Community which was intending to raise 2s in the pound from the profits of co-operative retail trading among their members to fund the purchase of land for their community, and the *Mercury*'s editor was troubled by the prospect of this being part of the Nottingham plan. 'The plan the correspondent mentions may appear objectionable, as it tends in a great measure to destroy the profits of retail dealers' the editor declared.[434] Although there is no explicit reference in the *Mercury* report of a co-operative trading society being formed to raise funds for the Nottingham project, many years later G J Holyoake did include a society in Nottingham in 1827 in his chapter on 'eccentric and singular societies'.[435] He also cited societies formed in Derby in 1827, Mansfield and Leicester in 1829, and Newark in 1831.

The business of friendly societies posed no threat to the middle class, who stood to gain from a reduction in the poor rate when the poor made provision for their own sickness and unemployment, but co-operative provision societies posed a clear threat to existing shopkeepers, many of whom were £10 copyholders who had been given the vote from the 1832 Reform Act. These were the 'Ten Pound Aristocracy' whom James Sweet described as 'the *greatest enemy* the Working Classes have to deal with.'[436] Magistrates of this class for many years to come were not averse to refusing poor relief to men and women who were known to be members of co-operative societies until they had spent any money in their share accounts.

In January 1839 the *Nottingham Review* reported that 'On Monday the 21st instant, the Hyson Green Co-operative Trading Association held its ninth anniversary dinner at Mr Mayfield's, the Sign of the Lumley Castle' on Radford Road. 'They partook of an excellent supper, and were afterwards greatly gratified by the information communicated to them

---

[433] *Nottingham and Newark Mercury*, 19th May 1827.
[434] Ibid.
[435] *The History of Co-operation*, G J Holyoake, 1908.
[436] *Midland Counties Illuminator*, 3rd April 1841 (original emphasis).

respecting the cause of that unexampled success which has constantly attended this society from its commencement' in 1830.'[437]

Another society in existence at this time was a provision society 'of about 64 members, with a small trading fund, and a store of provisions etc, in Milton Street, from which they purchase what they consume in their families, and divide the profits quarterly'.[438] The society's agent was Thomas Haddon. It is the only evidence of the existence of this society, although the fact of being almost invisible might suggest that there were many others of which no evidence at all survives.

Mansfield had two co-operative societies, both established in 1830 'each having about 30 members, a retail store, and a sick fund.'[439] One was situated at Westgate and the other at Ratcliffgate, their agents being William Taylor and William Bust respectively. William Taylor was still managing a grocery store at Westgate in 1842, although not, it would appear, on behalf of the co-operative society.[440]

Few of the societies, estimated to be at least 600, formed in Britain in the period from 1828 to 1834 survived the first period of co-operative activity which ended with the collapse of the Grand National Consolidated Trade Union. The *New Moral World*, which began publication in November 1834 had little to say on co-operative societies, apart from the news that the 'First Female Co-operative Association, formed ... for the purpose of facilitating social arrangements by enabling the members to live in contiguous dwellings' was making progress and had 'lately determined to employ the capital already acquired, in trading in Tea, Coffee etc'.[441] and, in an appeal touched with desperation in 1835, that a 'Handsome Suit for Four Pounds, or in exchange for anything that is useful' could be had from the Operative Tailors at The Strand.[442]

---

[437] *Nottingham Review*, 25th January 1839. The society's address is given as 1 Union Row and its agent as William Bronson in *White's Directory*, 1832 and *Dearden's Directory* 1834. Union Row was off Cornhill Street. The Mayfield Arms was at the corner of Cornhill Street and Radford Road. The buildings were demolished in the 1960s for the construction of the Hyson Green flats, which were in turn demolished in the 1990s to make way for Asda.

[438] *White's Directory*, 1832.

[439] *White's Directory*, 1832.

[440] *Pigott's Directory*, 1842.

[441] *New Moral World*, 20th December 1834.

[442] *New Moral World*, 21st March 1835.

The socialist movement which had encouraged their formation formally abandoned co-operative societies as an immediate instrument of reform in 1837, describing the past history of the societies as:

'little more than a detail of experiments unsuccessful in the realization of their anticipated object ... The breaking up of the various Co-operative Societies, the unfortunate progress and termination of the Labour Exchange, and the dismemberment of the great Trade Union, all within a few years, have in the opinion of the Directors, caused such distrust among the working classes, that some time must elapse before sufficient confidence will be restored as to induce them once more to turn to *co-operation* as the only means of rescuing them from their numerous grievances.'[443]

The Hyson Green co-operative society had proved an exception to the rule, affected neither by disillusionment nor by distrust according to the report published by the *Nottingham Review*. Although there is no evidence that it was connected to the socialist movement, the inspiration for its existence may well have come from the enthusiasm for co-operative experimentation that swept across England at that time. It was not registered as a friendly society and no records of its existence survive.

The next period of co-operative activity began towards the end of the decade, when the Chartist movement took up the call for 'exclusive dealing'. Feargus O'Connor had raised the subject in April 1838 at a meeting of the London Working Men's Association, and it became a subject of debate in some Chartist circles in the months that followed.[444] In November the newly formed 'Nottingham Female Political Association'[445] issued an 'Address to the Patriotic Women of England' in which exclusive dealing was advocated as an important role for the women involved in Chartism. Identifying the middle classes with the shopkeepers, the shopocrats 'priding themselves on their importance behind their counters, with as little claim to your respect as possible', and identifying the women as those best fitted to take them on, the Address declared:

---

[443] *New Moral World*, 6th May 1837 (original emphasis).
[444] *Exclusive Dealing in the Chartist Movement*, Peter Gurney, in Labour History Review, April 2009.
[445] The regular title was Nottingham Female Political Union.

'Let every shop and shopkeeper be noted in a book kept for the purpose, stating name, residence, trade, and whether Whig or Tory; also, another book containing the names of those friendly to the cause of the people ... encourage each other by mutual dealings in the way of trading, and not to spend your hard earnings with men opposed to the bettering of our common country.'[446]

It was the women of Mansfield who seemed to be first to act on this advice. The *Northern Star* quoted Feargus O'Connor during his tour of Nottinghamshire in 1839 as saying that 'at no part of the country was exclusive dealing carried to such perfection as it was at Mansfield.'[447]

It was not until the following year that the Chartist Convention in 1839, at which James Woodhouse was present as the Nottingham delegate, adopted exclusive dealing as one of a number of 'ulterior measures' to be used if the Chartist national petition was rejected by Parliament.

By this time Bronterre O'Brien, a former editor of the *Poor Man's Guardian,* who had given a half-hearted nod in the direction of exclusive dealing the previous summer, describing it as 'a potent lever in its way', now seemed to turn against it.[448] Speaking in Nottingham in July 1839 in support of a 'national holiday' or general strike, he recommended that workers instead 'borrow' food to survive the event.[449] Whether the women of the Nottingham Female Political Union had already adopted exclusive dealing since their declaration of the previous November is not clear, but probably not, as there were no complaining letters from shopkeepers in the local newspapers to suggest that they had, and in August 1839, disregarding Bronterre's recent comments, they resolved unanimously 'that exclusive dealing be immediately commenced.'[450]

In November 1839 in another address they spoke directly 'to the middle classes and shopkeepers' and reminded Chartists of their duty to 'keep your money out of the enemy's tills for this will effectually find their brains'.[451] The *Nottingham Review,* paper for the radical middle class,

---

[446] *Northern Star*, 8th December 1838.
[447] *Northern Star*, 6th July 1839.
[448] *Northern Star*, 14th July 1838.
[449] *Exclusive Dealing in the Chartist Movement*, Peter Gurney, in Labour History Review, April 2009.
[450] *Nottingham Review*, 23rd August 1839.
[451] *Northern Star*, 23rd November 1839.

which normally carried news of NFPU meetings, did not publish this report.

Chartists were now moving on from exclusive dealing towards creating their own joint stock co-operatives and opening stores, the first of which is believed to have been initiated in Hull in April 1839 when the *Northern Star* reported that 'a large number of the working classes in this town have formed a Society for the sale of Provisions, in shares of £1 each; and they are making great progress in arranging their plan of operation. The working classes will do well to join this society, as it will bring the shopocrats to their senses.'[452] Their store was eventually opened eight months later on the first Saturday in December 'with a good selection of beef, mutton, pork, potatoes, soap, candles, and other necessaries, which was all sold early in the evening, leaving a good profit for the benefit of the company.'[453]

By this time others societies were forming in Tyne and Wear and some had already started trading. In June it was reported that the private shopkeepers of Winlaton, a few miles west of Gateshead, at a public meeting addressed by George Julian Harney and others, 'gave various sins of compunction for their evil doings. Probably they have been awakened to a sense of their folly by a joint-stock shop, which has existed for many weeks in the village, and which affords every man who puts in 10s, no less than 12s worth of "household stuff" at the shopkeepers' prices.'[454] Societies in Sunderland were reported to be forming in September and said to be doing good business. The Sunderland Chartists had visions of opening meeting halls and bringing enlightenment through their co-operatives, and saw co-operative societies as an attractive alternative to 'the attempt being made to decoy working men into the National Loan Fund humbug' of Feargus O'Connor.[455]

In August 1839 the Chartist Northern Political Union [NPU] based in Newcastle placed lengthy advertisements in its weekly paper setting out its proposals for a Joint Stock Provision Stores. This was an ambitious project requiring the sale of 2,000 shares at 10s each, the society to begin trading when 1,000 had been sold. Within two months 'spacious premises'

---

[452] *Northern Star*, 6th April 1839.
[453] *Northern Star*, 14th December 1839.
[454] *The Charter*, 23rd June 1839.
[455] *The Charter*, 6th October 1839.

had been acquired and a festival for shareholders was held there, the two warehouses decked out for the occasion with banners and bunting. William Thomason, one of the NPU Committee who had been arrested in August and charged with unlawful and seditious assembly, told the shareholders that this was no 'speculation of pounds, shillings and pence; it had in view a nobler object – the regeneration and happiness of the human race.'[456] Their store opened in November and in the first four weeks of trading the 'receipts had considerably exceeded £4,000.'[457]

In April 1840 the 'North of England Joint Stock Co-operative Society' as it was restyled, registered under the Friendly Societies Act. This was still a joint stock company, in which the shareholders benefited from the distributed profits, but it's trading success demonstrated that it was also attractive to non-shareholders. It also had grander aims than mere profit making. Object number one was:

> 'to make arrangements for the production and distribution of wealth, by establishing workshops for the employment of the members; by purchasing land and other property, and by establishing bazaars and shops for the sale of various productions of nature and art; and supporting all such measures as have for their object the promotion of the happiness of the members.'[458]

Another society, formed in October 1839, was the Durham County Social Institute. It's unique and distinctive title suggests Owenite influence, and it received fulsome praise from the *New Moral World*, which welcomed what it saw as a change of direction 'among that section of the population lately engaged in agitating for political changes'.[459] Chartist festivals, reading rooms, schools, meeting halls, public lectures, and co-operative stores were seen as a move by the Chartists towards a wider social reform, and this Institute in particular was praised for its plans to do all these things and more and, in their final objective, to 'ultimately establish a community, in which Production and Distribution will be combined and regulated on the most equitable principles.'[460]

---

[456] *Northern Liberator*, 26th October 1839.
[457] Ibid., 14th December 1839.
[458] Ibid., 4th April 1840.
[459] *New Moral World*, 23rd November 1839.
[460] *Northern Liberator*, 5th October 1839.

If the references to regeneration, to a future in community, and the promotion of the happiness of the members evoked the spirit of socialism, there were also strong Chartist reasons for supporting co-operative provision stores. William Thomason declared to much laughter and applause from his audience in September that 'they had already established Universal Suffrage, those who had one share had one vote, and no man had more. Vote by Ballot they should go upon in electing Directors; and as for property Qualification they would never trouble them about it.'[461] A week later Thomas Devyr borrowed his words, calling on every man in Tyne and Wear to take up 1s a week in shares 'under the management of men elected by Universal Suffrage, Vote by ballot, and No Property Qualification, and it would at once sweep social misery and political tyranny from the face of the land' he declared to cheers and laughter.[462]

In late October or early November 1839 Robert Lowery, former tailor, bookseller and vendor of unstamped newspapers, and an active Chartist in Newcastle, who had also been one of the 53 delegates to the first Convention and spent several months before the Convention travelling around Britain collecting signatures for the first Chartist petition, wrote a pamphlet with a very long title which was advertised in the *Northern Star* by a very small advert: ' "Rich and be Wise, Rich and Free". Just published, price 1d. AN ADDRESS ON EXCLUSIVE DEALING, with Plans for the formation of Joint Stock Companies. By Robert Lowery. Sold at his shop, 16 Nun's Street, Newcastle.'[463]

It's full title was an 'Address to the Fathers and Mothers, Sons and Daughters, of the Working Classes, on the System of Exclusive Dealing, and the Formation of Joint Stock Provision Companies, Shewing How the People May Free Themselves from Oppression.'[464] The length of its title has frequently caused it to be abbreviated, by others as well as by Lowery, to an Address on Exclusive Dealing, and it is exclusive dealing has attracted most comment from historians. However, less than a quarter of the pamphlet is devoted to that subject compared with more than half to the formation of joint stock provision societies. Of the eleven items listed

---

[461] *Northern Liberator*, 14th September 1839.
[462] *Northern Liberator*, 21st September 1839.
[463] *Northern Star*, 9th November 1839 (original emphasis).
[464] *Address to the Fathers and Mothers ...*, Robert Lowery, in Northern Liberator, 1839.

under 'THE PLANS' only the first – 'Wherever there are Radical shopkeepers, deal with them immediately in preference to those that are opposed to us' – refers to exclusive dealing and that as a preparatory step to the next ten which set out the principles on which co-operative stores should be founded. Lowery's plans appear to owe much to the writings of Dr William King in *The Co-operator* between 1828 and 1830.[465] Lowery's version was, perhaps, the last time that such precepts were proclaimed before the 'Rochdale Principles' were enunciated a few years later. His premise that only best quality or unadulterated goods should be sold and that a maximum of 5% interest should be paid on capital invested would both have appealed to the Pioneers.

Lowery's pamphlet was the product of the progress in establishing co-operative stores in the North East and also probably the catalyst for many new joint stock co-operative stores, also mostly in the North East. The progress related by Lowery of the Newcastle Joint Stock Provision Stores of which he was a member, which had sold three thousand shares and 'will open in a few days', had already resulted in a co-operative store being opened in St Peter's Quay, Newcastle, and societies had been or were being set up in Walker, Winlaton, South Shields, Sunderland and beyond. 'The Newcastle Directors have had letters from many parts of the kingdom for instructions how to proceed, stating that it is the unanimous wish of the people in their respective neighbourhoods to adopt the principle.'[466] Lowery's pamphlet was the response to these requests.

Robert Lowery did not mention his pamphlet on exclusive dealing and joint stock companies in his autobiography. There he made a few passing references to exclusive dealing but of the joint stock provision companies, and his own role in them, he said not a word, and his pamphlet remained almost forgotten and ignored for more than a century.[467]

In 1963 F W Leeman, a Director of the Nottingham Co-operative Society and the author of the Society's centenary history of that year, quoted the introductory words 'To the Men and Women of Great Britain, You who are the slave class, who have no part in the Constitution' from a pamphlet

---

[465] *Co-operation's Prophet: The life and Letters of Dr William King of Brighton with a Reprint of The Co-operator, 1828-1830*, T W Mercer, 1947.
[466] *Address to the Fathers and Mothers ...* , Robert Lowery, in Northern Liberator, 1839.
[467] Until it was reproduced by Brian Harrison and Patricia Hollis in *Robert Lowery, Radical and Chartist*, 1979.

held at the University of London's Senate Library whose author was 'a member of the Nottingham Co-operative Store'.[468] Leeman noted the similarity of the words to those used by James Sweet in a letter published by *Nottingham Review* a year later in December 1840 addressed to 'Fellow countrymen, – To you, the children of wretchedness – the enslaved and toil worn millions, who starve over your scanty pittance of *taxed crust* ...'[469] and concluded that the pamphlet he had seen was written by James Sweet.

James Sweet might well have instigated the publication seen by Leeman, and been the 'member of the Nottingham Co-operative Store' who appeared as the author on the cover of the pamphlet of early 1840, but most of the content had been extracted from Lowery's pamphlet written in late 1839. The Nottingham version omits the sections on the formation of joint stock provision stores, makes some changes to punctuation and capitalisation, and adds a final page: 'Rules of the Nottingham Co-operative Store.'[470] Those Rules set out on the back page of the Nottingham pamphlet do not correspond to 'THE PLANS' Lowery put forward in his pamphlet, all of which were removed in the Nottingham version. They both provide for the issue of an unlimited number of shares at 10s and both restrict voting rights to one vote per member regardless of the number of shares held, but that is about all that they do have in common.

In the Nottingham Rules there is no mention of selling for ready money only; selling only best quality or unadulterated goods; selling below market prices; or for a maximum of 5% interest on capital invested. Some of the rules, of a Committee filled by rotation of members and fines for refusing to serve or attend meetings, are reminiscent of those of earlier co-operatives which adopted the practices of friendly societies, and indeed of the system of appointment of constables by rotation among the ratepayers which can be traced back to the civil law of the Saxons, and which had recently been abandoned in England by the Police Acts of 1839. The Nottingham rules do, however, indicate that profits are to be distributed by a dividend on purchases rather than on shares, as rule 13 provides for

---

[468] *Co-operation in Nottingham*, F W Leeman, 1963.
[469] *Nottingham Review*, 25th December 1840 (original emphasis).
[470] *Address to the Working Classes on Exclusive Dealing – 1840*, by 'a member of the Nottingham Co-operative Store', University of London Senate Library.

'memorandum books' in which a member's purchases are recorded so that 'each may receive interest in proportion to the amount which may be expended.'[471]

James Sweet was certainly in touch with Chartists in the North East around this time. In January 1840 he received from Chartists in Sunderland 'a Chartist song', which he read to a meeting and then arranged for copies to be made.[472] Given the date of publication and the discussions which ensued soon after this, it would not be unreasonable to suppose that a copy of Lowery's pamphlet was received with the songsheet. At around this time Newcastle Chartist Thomas Devyr, who had been charged with sedition, jumped bail and set sail for the United States in January 1840 with John Rucastle who had been a friend of Lowery. According to the *Nottingham Mercury*, Rucastle would be 'recognised at the Fox and Hounds and the King George on Horseback, etc as the individual who visited Nottingham a week or two ago in the character of an agent for the *Northern Liberator*'.[473] Rucastle might have been the conduit through which Lowery's pamphlet reached Nottingham. But if Lowery's pamphlet and the provision stores in the North East were the inspiration for establishing the Nottingham Co-operative Store, the rules seem to have derived from other sources.

At the Nottingham Chartist meeting at the Democratic Chapel on Monday 27th January 1840 James Sweet 'announced his intention of establishing a Victualling Store or, in other words, a Provision Store; having fifteen determined fellows, with ten shillings each ...' and 'a plan for a co-operative society was submitted to the meeting, approved, and several persons indicated their intention of becoming members.'[474] The following week he reported to a crowded meeting at the Chapel that '35 shares were now taken up for the provision store.'[475] This was slow progress indeed, as the *Mercury* noted triumphantly a month later: 'Shares for Sweet's Chartist Store at a dead standstill – no buyers.'[476] Whether they opened a store is not clear, and there are no further reports

---

[471] Ibid.
[472] *Nottingham and Newark Mercury*, 7th February 1840.
[473] *Nottingham and Newark Mercury*, 14th February 1840.
[474] *Nottingham and Newark Mercury*, 24th January 1840; *Nottingham Review*, 24th January 1840.
[475] *Nottingham Review*, 31st January 1840.
[476] *Nottingham and Newark Mercury*, 28th February 1840.

of this venture in the local newspapers. Two years later another report appeared in the *Nottingham Review* of a meeting at the Rancliffe Arms to set up a co-operative store but there is no further news of this venture either.[477]

In 1847 the *Nottingham Review* reported that members of the 'Nottingham Co-operative Society' held their weekly meeting on Saturday evening, enrolled new members, and agreed to meet weekly at the King George on Horseback, but it is unlikely that there is any direct connection between this society and that of 1840.[478] It suggests that the idea lay dormant and was revived after a seven year gap, as a report in the *Review* in 1848 records that the 'Nottingham Co-operative Trading Association' was formed on the 25th October 1847 and began selling provisions at the end of November 1847, their store being open on three occasions each week for a total of eleven hours. The meeting also records thanks to Mr and Mrs Mellors, the landlord and landlady of the King George on Horseback, which suggests that the store might have been located on the premises of the public house. That it was established and held meetings regularly at the King George, a long established meeting place for Chartists; of the Three Counties Association of Framework Knitters; and the home of Operatives' Library No. 2, does provide a clear link between the Chartist co-operators of 1840 and the society of 1847.

There was no further news of another society which was, according to a footnote to the Nottingham Co-operative Store Rules in 1840, being formed at the Golden Fleece at Fisher Gate, but another society at Dob Park, Basford, apparently prospered as it was registered under the Friendly Societies Acts in 1845, although the date of its eventual demise is not recorded.[479]

A store was open for business in Hyson Green and was trading in February 1840 when the *Mercury* enquired whether the 'peace-law-and-order' loving Woodhouse would fancy the 'Moscowing' of the 'store at Hyson Green.'[480] In July the *Review* reported that an attempted burglary at the store had been thwarted by a passer-by, who had his teeth knocked out for his trouble by the three rascally intruders. The store keeper is

---

477 *Northern Star*, 19th February 1842.
478 *Nottingham Review*, 5th November 1847.
479 *The Basford Co-operative Friendly Trading Association*, FS1/571/223, National Archives.
480 *Nottingham and Newark Mercury*, 21st February 1840. 'Moscowing' refers to arson.

named as Mr Woodhouse.[481] As there is no reference to a Chartist store being established in this period in Hyson Green, this would appear to be the store founded in 1830 which had celebrated its ninth birthday in 1839.

James Woodhouse had been involved in the local Chartist movement since the calling of the first big public meeting in September 1838 when 2,000 working men and women gathered in Lees Close, Carlton Road, and approved a plan proposed by himself for a Nottingham Working Men's Association modelled on the London association.[482] He had been a signatory to the broadsheet which was placarded in Manchester in July 1839 calling for exclusive dealing, boycotting excisable goods, withdrawing money from the savings banks, converting paper money into gold, gathering the 'Arms of Freemen' and commencing a 'Sacred Month'.[483]

By August many of the Convention members had had second thoughts about the advisability of the 'sacred month' to enforce adoption by Parliament of the People's Charter. In the debates of that month Woodhouse was one of the delegates who expressed reluctance to commit to an immediate 'sacred month' unless sufficient preparations were made to feed people during the strike. Like many others from the midland and northern towns he was concerned that a strike embarked upon without sufficient preparation would be bound to end in disaster, as most working men and their families had no savings and would be unable to feed themselves for more than a week. They would be obliged to return to work, placing themselves at the mercy of triumphant and vindictive employers. This was also the view which had been put forward by Bronterre O'Brien speaking in the town in July.[484]

Shortly before the start of the 'sacred month' Feargus O'Connor and the Convention backed down and substituted a three day 'national holiday' in its place. On the day on which it was due to begin, Monday 12th August, people began to gather in Nottingham's Market Place and the Mayor issued a proclamation against the meeting. The crowd, now more than 500 in number, proceeded to march four abreast to the Forest where they were addressed by Jonathan Barber and James Woodhouse. Shortly after

---

[481] *Nottingham Review*, 10th July 1840.
[482] *Nottingham Review*, 7th September 1838.
[483] *The Early Chartists*, Dorothy Thompson, 1971.
[484] *Exclusive Dealing in the Chartist Movement*, Peter Gurney, in Labour History Review, April 2009.

this Thomas Nixon, magistrate, arrived on his horse, and was pelted with stones. Woodhouse called for order, General Napier arrived with his dragoons, and the crowd dispersed peacefully.

Two days later James Woodhouse was arrested at his home in Hyson Green and taken to the Magistrates Room at the Police Office in the afternoon where a large crowd had gathered. He was detained in the police cells for two days for further examination, and then charged with 'riotous and tumultuously assembly', before being committed for trial.[485] Defending himself in Court a week later he asserted that the demonstration had been a peaceful one, marked by the singing of hymns and the reading of prayers. He was committed for trial at the Lent Assizes the following March, where he was persuaded to plead guilty on the tacit understanding that he would not be sentenced for the offence.

James Woodhouse, despite his cautious approach to the 'national holiday', had found on his return from the Convention that he was unable to resume his work as a framework knitter because no frame holder would rent him a frame.[486] This was long before his conviction at the Assizes in 1840. He had been the subject of police observation and reports to the Home Office, and the local newspapers were inclined to cast him as a dangerous 'physical force' Chartist, hence the *Mercury*'s sarcastic reference to him as the ' "peace-law-and-order" loving Woodhouse'. The frame holders combined to teach him a lesson by depriving him of his livelihood. In recognition of his service to the Chartist movement, the Nottingham Working Men's Association paid him a guinea a week to do work for the Association, and it was from this situation that he came to be employed by the co-operative society at Hyson Green.

It was in April 1841 that the Chartists of Arnold opened a meeting hall to accommodate 400 people, set up a library and planned a Sunday school for children, associated with 'a co-operative store, which is working well, and in connection with [it] we have commenced a sick society, and there is also another co-operative store and sick club in connection with it in our village'.[487] One of these two societies was probably the Arnold Community Society which registered as a friendly society in 1840 and aimed to 'use

---

[485] *Nottingham Review*, 16th August 1839.
[486] *The Lion of Freedom: Feargus O'Connor and the Chartist Movement, 1832-1842*, James Epstein, 1982.
[487] *Northern Star*, 24th April 1841.

funds gained in Trade, in the purchase or cultivation of land, or in erecting suitable buildings for the benefit and convenience of the Members.'[488] Twenty two of its rules relate to friendly society functions, but the twenty fourth and final rule relates to the agent who buys for the store. The society met monthly at 'the Store House'.

The year 1840 was the time when enthusiasm for co-operative provision stores reached a peak. By 1841 the North of England Joint Stock Co-operative Society was being split by claims of fraud and incompetence, and in February 1842 a special meeting was requisitioned by members of the society to wind it up.[489] Holyoake claimed that 'it broke up by a distribution of salts and senna to each member, being probably the only unsold stock ... the oddest final dividend that is to be met with in the annals of co-operation.'[490] Nottinghamshire does not appear to have witnessed quite the same degree of enthusiasm for co-operative ventures that had been evident in some other parts of the country, nor the same degree of litigiousness, but some of those which had been formed continued for a while to trade, and occasionally there were reports of a new society being formed.

In January 1844 the co-operative store in Arnold was said by James Sweet to be doing well and the society at Carrington was 'prospering beyond their most sanguine expectations.'[491] In March 1844 the Chartists of Radford met at Mr Wildbore's at Bloomsgrove Street 'for the purpose of commencing a co-operative store'.[492] In 1845 Chartist Henry Dorman was elected to attend a conference on 'Land and Co-operative Questions' and the meeting agreed that he should support any plan to employ people upon the land 'and to induce them to become members in the co-operative stores.'[493] It was in that year that the *Mercury* reported that members of the 'Provident Co-operative Society' were meeting at Mr Dorman's Temperance Hotel at Clare Street, Lower Parliament street, the only reference in existence to that society.[494] In 1847 Chartists meeting in

---

[488] *Arnold Community Society*, FS1/571/235, National Archives.
[489] *Northern Star*, 12th February 1842.
[490] *The History of Co-operation*, G J Holyoake, 1908.
[491] *Northern Star*, 27th January 1844.
[492] *Northern Star*, 9th March 1844.
[493] *Northern Star*, 19th April 1845.
[494] *Nottingham Chartism*, Peter Wyncoll, 1966, quoting source: *Northern Star*, 22nd February 1845.

Arnold were urged to buy their shoes from 'the workmens' own shop' at 55 Glasshouse Street.

In May 1850 the *Northern Star* published a letter from an anonymous correspondent who had passed a shop in the town with 'Co-op Labour and Provision Store' above its door. Established, the author wrote, to provide themselves with good food and clothing, and sell to the public, their chief object was to 'carry on the Co-op Labour question by employing their own members at their own trades.'[495] With less than 30 members this small society might have been the 'workmens' own shop' in Glasshouse Street, but the size of its membership suggests that it was the premises of the Nottingham Co-operative Trading Association.[496]

The Carrington Co-operative Society which was enjoying trading success in 1844 appears to provide the only formal link between the Chartist co-operatives of the 1840s and the Lenton Industrial and Provident Society, founded in 1863 on the Rochdale model, which passed eventually into the present day Co-operative Group. This would place the earliest 'root' of the present Co-operative Group's 'tree' in Nottingham at Carrington in 1840, some twenty three years before the birth of the Lenton society which has traditionally been considered the fount of Co-operation in Nottingham.

In March 1874 the Carrington co-operative society was considering an amalgamation with the Lenton and Nottingham society but nothing appears to have resulted from the discussions at that time. Two years later in December 1876 the Carrington Co-operative Industrial Society called a special meeting of members to be held in the schoolroom in neighbouring King Street to consider winding up the society. Shortly before the closure meeting was held in January 1877 the Board of the Lenton and Nottingham Co-operative Society received a request for an amalgamation and responded by sending a sub-committee to the Carrington society to meet the directors. At that time the Lenton and Nottingham society was enjoying a period of rapid growth and trading success.[497] The Lenton and Nottingham Society committee inspected their property and made a successful offer of £1,230 for their shop at the

---

[495] *Northern Star*, 25th May 1850.
[496] It is possible that the 'workmens' own shop' and the Nottingham Co-operative Trading Association were the same society.
[497] The Society was renamed *Lenton and Nottingham* in April 1873.

183

junction of Market Place, Carrington.[498] Three months later the Lenton Society's quarterly report noted that 'The Carrington Society, also, has ceased to exist; your Society taking the place of it, where we trust to do a good business'.[499]

Some of the people who had been involved in Chartism in Nottingham continued to be involved in co-operative societies many years later. James Anthony, the framework knitter and 'uncompromising Chartist' who had chaired the meeting in Arnold in 1843 which resolved to put up a candidate for the post of assistant parish overseer and defeated the Anglican candidate, was a founder member of the Arnold Industrial & Manufacturing Society in 1868.[500] This society aimed to establish a co-operative hosiery factory at its premises in Church Street, Arnold, and also included among its founders Hermon Parkinson who was at that time also a member of the management committee of the Lenton Co-operative Society.

By 1874 James Anthony was managing a co-operative provision store, which had been opened in Church Street by the Lenton Co-operative Society in 1866 following a deputation from residents of Arnold. The Lenton Society had at first responded to the deputation 'with a view to the formation of a Co-operative Society in that village' but three weeks later resolved 'to open a Store at Arnold with all possible despatch'. Before and after that time *Wright's Directory* was still listing a Co-operative Store in Arnold operating under the name of 'Thomas Franks and Co', which suggests that an unregistered pre-Rochdale society, possibly with a closed membership, was still trading there under the name of its agent, perhaps one of the two Chartist co-operative societies in the village, lingering on from its formation more than twenty years earlier in 1840.[501]

---

[498] *Carrington Co-operative Industrial Society Ltd, Winding Up*, FS8/33/1634, National Archives; *Lenton and Nottingham Co-operative Society Ltd, Minute Book*, DD GN 1/1/2/2, Nottinghamshire Archives.

[499] *Lenton and Nottingham Co-operative Society Ltd, Quarterly Report*, March 1877, DD GN 1/1/2/3, Nottinghamshire Archives. 'Also' in this report refers to a previous note that the Nottingham Pioneer Co-operative Society had been recently absorbed by the Lenton and Nottingham Co-operative Society. The original Carrington store was demolished in the 1960s and a new store replaced it on Mansfield Road which is still trading.

[500] *The Arnold Industrial and Manufacturing Society, Rules*, FS8/26/1196, National Archives.

[501] *Wright's Directory*, 1864, 1868; *Lenton Co-operative Society Ltd, Minute Book*, DD GN 1/1/2/1, Nottinghamshire Archives.

In 1870 the man whose name represented Nottingham Chartism above all others, James Sweet, who had promoted the Nottingham Chartist co-operative society more than thirty years earlier in 1840, presented registration documents to the Registrar of Friendly Societies on behalf of the Nottingham Industrial Co-operative Manufacturing Hosiers Society from its address at the Mission Hall in Cross Street. It had been in existence for twenty years since 1854, and was dissolved one year after its rules were approved in 1871.[502]

Illustration 19: William Hemm.
Seconded Feargus O'Connor's candidature in 1847. Later a Committee man at Lenton Industrial & Provident Society, and School Board member.

William Hemm, born in 1820, was another active Chartist and co-operator whose activities spanned the decades. It was he who seconded O'Connor's nomination as parliamentary candidate for Nottingham in 1847. A mechanic and a member of the Amalgamated Society of Engineers, he left Nottingham for work in Manchester in 1852, returning via Derby where he worked for the Midland Railway Company and became involved in the Derby Co-operative Provident Society, being elected to its Committee in 1863. On arrival in Nottingham he joined the Lenton Co-operative Society, became involved with the society in 1867 and was elected to its Committee in 1868, on which he served for twenty years until his death in 1889. He was a highly respected member of the committee and at his funeral the Society closed all the stores at 4pm in

---

[502] *The Nottingham Industrial Co-operative Manufacturing Hosiers Society Ltd, Rules,* FS8/29/1372, National Archives.

tribute to him and paid for the funeral carriages. He had been an active member of the Primitive Methodists at Canaan Street chapel in Broad Marsh since his early years in Nottingham, and a teetotaller. His commitments to Chartism and politics, to temperance, education, and co-operation as a social and political tool, bridged the period from pre-Rochdale Chartist co-operation to the years of the rapid growth of consumer co-operation of the late nineteenth century.[503]

Henry Cope, framework knitter and member of the New Radford Chartist locality, and secretary of the Radford Operatives' Library No. 5, was a founder member and first secretary of the Radford Co-operative Trading Association established in 1857.[504] The Trustee of the society was James Saunders, one-time treasurer of the same Chartist locality, who had taken part in the campaign against Church rates with Cope in Radford in 1845. In 1862 Henry Cope appears again, as a Director of the Nottingham Bread and Flour Industrial Society.

Bread and flour societies had made their first appearance in the eighteenth century in the form of flour clubs set up by friendly societies to purchase wheat and have it ground for their members.[505] Larger societies moved on to rent or build their own windmills, and in 1796 the first steam powered mill was opened by the Birmingham Bread and Flour Company. Societies were established in other towns around this time as a result of the high prices being charged for flour due to the grain shortages arising from poor harvests. Societies were set up in Long Eaton, Newark and Mansfield and in 1816 a society was established in Nottingham by 16 friendly societies, although it did not trade. Some were so successful that the private millers considered ways of putting a stop to them. In 1814 private millers in Wolverhampton brought a Bill of Indictment against the Union Mill's chairman and committee, who were charged with working an illegal combination. Convictions could have resulted in the chairman being hanged and the transportation of the committee for seven years. After a 14 hour trial a not guilty verdict was returned and the church bells of the town were rung in celebration of the victory.[506]

---

[503] *Lenton Co-operative Society Ltd, Press Cuttings*, DD GN 1/13/1/1-35, Nottinghamshire Archives.
[504] *Radford Co-operative Trading Association, Rules*, FS8/5/141, National Archives.
[505] *Eighteenth and Nineteenth Century Consumer-Owned Community Flour and Bread Societies: Collective Response to Market Failure*, Joshua Bamfield, 1996.
[506] *Union Mill*, Wolverhampton History and Heritage.

Milling societies were formed again in 1846-47 during another period in which the price of corn had risen dramatically and the Hull Anti-Mill Society, formed during the first period of activity in 1795 and still trading successfully and undercutting the flour and bread prices of local millers and bakers, became the model for the Leeds District Flour Mill which began business in 1847. Besides aiming to reduce flour and bread prices they were also committed to providing pure food by baking unadulterated bread. Other mill societies, mostly in Yorkshire, were formed in this period and several of them included members of the Redemption Society, men who had been active in the Owenite socialist movement a few years earlier and had understanding and experience of co-operative organisation.

In July 1847 a *Nottingham Review* editorial quoted approvingly from the *Herald of Co-operation,* the mouthpiece of the Redemption Society in Leeds, which reported that the Leeds mill was being copied in 'Birkinshaw, Pudsey, Bradford, Lincoln and Nottingham.'[507] A week later the *Review* announced that 'a portion of the working classes are in earnest in this matter, and intend to hold their first meeting for the formation of a society, at the Pelican, New Radford, on Saturday evening at 8 o'clock.'[508] The Pelican public house at Alfreton Road was the second home of the Radford Operatives' Library after its move from the White Swan and its librarian was Henry Cope. There is no further news of this venture and no names of its participants but, given his later involvement in the Bread and Flour society, it may be that Henry Cope was the instigator of the meeting in 1847 which, even if it did not develop immediately as intended, foresaw the possibilities for a bread and flour society in the town.

The Nottingham Bread and Flour Industrial Society started in business in 1854 and appears to have initially enrolled under the Friendly Societies Acts in 1855, becoming registered as an Industrial and Provident Society in 1863. It would seem to have enjoyed the patronage of the Town Council, having numerous Councillors and Aldermen on its Board, used the Council's coat of arms on its rule book, and held its committee meetings in the Town Hall. The secretary was one Kemp Sanby, whose day job was clerk to the lunatic asylum, and one of its functions may have been to supply the lunatic asylum, house of correction and workhouse with

---

[507] *Nottingham Review,* 9th July, 1847; *Herald of Co-operation,* June 1847.
[508] *Nottingham Review,* 16th July, 1847.

wholesome bread and flour, its motto declaring that 'To labour is the lot of man; then his least reward should be – good food, cheap and unadulterated.'[509] With a limit of 5% interest on share capital and a maximum of one share per member, it paid a dividend on purchases, not in cash but in kind, in the form of flour or bread. Its main premises were at Parliament Row in Parliament Street, but it had other premises, including a shop in Ruddington and a mill in the Meadows.

Illustration 20: Nottingham Bread & Flour Society.
Mill at Cromford Street, Meadows.
Pictured here in 1973 before demolition.

The society was a successful trading concern with 600 members but in 1866 the mortgage holder died, the loan to the society was called in and the society ceased trading. The creditors were paid off, leaving nothing for the shareholders. The mill in Cromford Street changed hands and was eventually demolished during the redevelopment of the Meadows in the 1970s.[510]

Of all the pre-Rochdale trading societies so far recorded here the one which outlasted them all was what came to be known as the Hucknall Torkard Mill Sick Society.[511] Its origins lie in the first sick benefit society in

---

[509] *Nottingham Bread and Flour Industrial Society*, FS8/10/295, National Archives.
[510] Ibid.
[511] *Hucknall Torkard Mill Sick Society*, FS3/309, National Archives.

Hucknall founded by cotton spinners from Hucknall and Arnold in September 1770. Its founder members included William Hankin, the Hucknall parish clerk who became 'head man' of the society and Joseph Newbutt, clerk to the society, who later occupied a similar position with the Female Friendly Society at the Green Dragon.[512]

Ten years later the society divided and the Hucknall members continued alone from their meeting place at the Half Moon Hotel. William Stanley, the landlord of the Half Moon, assisted five years later in the purchase of a windmill at Broomhill and when the trees had grown tall and obstructed the passage of the wind, with the gratuitous help of local farmers they hauled it away in 1826 to a new site at Sandy Lane. The society had several members who gave long service to the society and members of the Franks family were appointed as millers for 62 years of the mill's existence.[513] In 1883 the mill was provided with a steam engine to ensure constant power to the grindstone and for most of the nineteenth century profits of the mill were added to the funds of the sick society. It was not until the mill became unprofitable and a burden to the sick fund that the mill was eventually closed in 1928 and demolished in 1930.

Illustration 21: Hucknall Torkard Sick Society Mill, Sandy Lane, Hucknall. The Mill, pictured c.1925 before demolition in 1930.

[512] *Female Friendly Society at the Green Dragon*, FS3/309, National Archives.
[513] *History of Hucknall Torkard*, J H Beardsmore, 1909.

This society clearly enjoyed the loyalty of some long serving and dedicated officials and this probably contributed much to its longevity. It seems also to have avoided financial scandals and disputes. It might appear surprising that the Leeds District Flour Mill should have been the inspiration for a new generation of intending co-operative millers in Nottingham in the 1840s when a successful mill had been operating so close to home for more than fifty years, but the Hucknall millers were not aiming to convince others of the rightness of their scheme whereas the Redemptionists and their converts in Yorkshire were experienced propagandists for a cause.

Other co-operative schemes during the first half of the nineteenth century included the construction of houses and workshops by and for stocking weavers and warp hands. Houses with weaving workshops on the upper floors and gardens in front in Pleasant Row, Lenton Street, Saville Row and Lindsay Street in Hyson Green were said to have been constructed by societies of working men around 1820 'who paid by instalments, it is said, £70 each, and used the upper rooms as workshops, and secured long gardens in front, being a great improvement upon the cribb'd, cabin'd, and confined courts and yards of New Radford', and a similar scheme named Club Row was built in Hucknall Road, Carrington around the same time.[514] Ambrose Williamson, lacemaker, Chartist, member of the Chartist Land Company, and a founder of the Carrington co-operative society was one of Club Row's residents in the 1840s.

The co-operative scheme which attracted most support from working men and women in Nottingham in the middle of the nineteenth century was not the bread and flour society, the provision society, or the house purchase club, but the Chartist Co-operative Land Society.

---

[514] *Old Nottingham Suburbs*, Robert Mellors, 1912; *The History of Carrington*, Terry Fry, 1999.

Chapter 13: The Chartist Co-operative Land Society

On the evening of Saturday 17th February 1844, when the members of the National Charter Association arrived at Elmer and Mary Ann Rollett's Temperance Hotel in Warser Gate, their main speaker for the evening was Philip McGrath, elected to the NCA's Executive Committee the previous year and one of Feargus O'Connor's strongest supporters in what would become the Chartist Co-operative Land Society.

Feargus O'Connor had first spoken of the importance of creating smallholdings upon which working men and women from the towns could live productively after the failure of the 'sacred month' in September 1839. To a large Chartist meeting in Glasgow he gave the reasons that a 'sacred month' was bound to fail as the dependence of industrial workers on weekly wages and their inability to save a sufficient part of the value they created. He drew upon shared legends of a golden past when 'they could test the value of labour by a month's or a year's holiday, until the rights they sought for were granted. (Loud cheers). And now if every man had his plot of land, his store house, and the key to his larder, no tyranny could last as long as their provisions held out. (Renewed cheering.)'[515] He did not need to develop a coherent historical basis for his claims as there was at that time a prevailing sense that wages had been falling for decades and that real incomes were continuing to decline, a belief that was not confined to Chartists. O'Connor went on to assert that:

> 'the land of the three countries is capable of supporting in affluence, comfort, and splendour, six times the amount of their present population (Loud cheers.) ... lots of five acres would open the field for every man's industry, would supply to every man a store of wholesome food, would furnish to every man the means of healthful and natural employment'.[516]

During his term in York jail in 1841 O'Connor wrote a series of *Letters to Irish Landlords*, that were published in the *Northern Star*, in which he advised Irish landowners to create small peasant holdings on their land to prevent the large estates being bought up by the new manufacturing class. A later historian of Chartism, who was not well disposed to O'Connor,

---

[515] *Northern Star*, 24th August 1839; *The Lion of Freedom*, James Epstein, 1982.
[516] *Northern Star*, 24th August 1839.

commented wryly that O'Connor was speaking as one country gentleman to another and that his words 'must have afforded strange reading to the operatives who devoured the *Northern Star*'.[517] Nevertheless, the prospect of leaving behind the poverty and insecurity of industrial life in favour of a secure plot of five acres, where healthy food could be grown and consumed, family life restored, and the man's place could be restored to the head of the table, had a long-standing appeal to many male operatives in the industrial towns and cities.[518] This was the period when the socialists were creating the predominantly agricultural Queenwood community in Hampshire, although Feargus O'Connor made it clear that his ideas had nothing in common with them. 'Already the heralds of bigotry have begun to bellow out "Socialism". Well ... I tell you that my plan has as much to do with Socialism as it has with the Comet', he told the readers of the *Northern Star*.[519]

In September 1842 Mr R T Morrison, who had been active in the campaigns against capital punishment and against the compulsory Church rates at St Mary's, began to make appearances in Chartist meetings. In September he wrote to the *Nottingham Review* a long and somewhat florid letter which concluded with the statement that 'Yes, gentlemen, to the land the people must return, as the only means of defeating a heartless and unfeeling aristocracy, who exact the last farthing from an oppressed and starving poor.'[520]

It would seem that informal discussion on the land was taking place at this time among Nottingham Chartists as well as among socialists. Part of the appeal of smallholdings was that it was a way of meeting the property qualification for enfranchisement, and in Rochdale a sustained campaign by John Bright and the Rochdale Freehold Land Society towards the end of the decade succeeded in doubling the Rochdale electorate by this means.[521]

It was in 1843 that the idea matured and began to make headway. Not all Chartists were enthusiastic. The *Northern Star* adopted a stance of disbelief that O'Connor's motives might be misunderstood:

---

[517] *The Chartist Movement*, Mark Hovell, 1917.
[518] *Land Reform and Working Class Experience in Britain and the United States, 1800-1862*, Jamie L Bronstein, 1999.
[519] *Chartism: A New History*, Malcolm Chase, 2007; *Northern Star*, 29th April 2007.
[520] *Nottingham Review*, 2nd September 1842.
[521] *Weavers of Dreams*, David J Thompson, 2012.

'We have been surprised to have received two or three communications from which it would appear that some Chartists look upon Mr O'Connor's proposition for the appropriation of the land to the legitimate purpose of supporting the people in comfort, as calculated to lead people away from the struggle after political right ... We are amazed to think how such an idea can have entered any body's head ... if duly understood and acted on, [it is] calculated to be the most powerful collateral aid to the enfranchisement of the whole people that has yet occupied the people's mind'.[522]

In the summer of 1843 William Hill, editor of the *Northern Star*, lectured at the Exchange Hall, which was reported to be full to capacity. Henry Dorman chaired and William Hill spoke for almost three hours. Hill spoke for the Charter but the Land Plan found its way into the speech. Having elaborated upon the state of the economy and the poverty in the towns 'he compared the position of our forefathers, who had each their own piece of land, and each sat under the branches of their own fig tree'.[523]

The Chartist Convention which met in Birmingham in September 1843 spent some time discussing a proposal from O'Connor to establish a National Charter Association for Mutual Benefit which would 'provide for the unemployed, and means and support for those who are desirous to locate upon the land.' Tidd Pratt, the Registrar of Friendly Societies, rejected this first attempt at enrolment on the grounds that the society's objects were neither religious nor charitable and consequently might be regarded as seditious.[524] This was among the reports given by Henry Dorman to a crowded meeting on the Land Plan in Nottingham in late September.[525]

The Land Plan was discussed by Chartists in Nottingham in detail on Monday 9th October 1843. At a public meeting in the Democratic Chapel chaired by James Sweet the divisions were initially apparent to all present. Mr R T Morrison had been the Nottingham delegate to the recent

---

[522] *Northern Star*, 20th May 1843.
[523] *Nottingham Review*, 21st July 1843.
[524] *Some Practices and Problems of Chartist Democracy*, Eileen Yeo, 1982.
[525] *Nottingham Review*, 23rd September 1843.

convention and had served on the committee to oversee the enrolment of the plan under the Friendly Societies Acts, and there was much criticism of the Registrar's response in obstructing the registration. Morrison proposed a motion asserting that Chartists be 'determined to use every legal means in our power to compel that functionary to perform his duty, and enrol the plan of organisation.'[526] Mr Dorman immediately saw that the meeting was being moved to take a stand against Tidd Pratt before the principle of the plan had been approved, and pointed out that passing the motion would imply support for the Land Plan. Mr William Lilley then moved an amendment 'That the land plan of organisation is incompatible with the Charter.' Opponents of the plan declared that people were too poor to be able to benefit from it and, if the plan were enrolled, it would destroy the agitation for the Charter. Mr Morrison in reply said that 'the whole of the speakers had argued as though the plan compelled men to contribute to the land fund, and that it was to take precedence ... neither did the loan fund take precedence, but was subsidiary to the Chartist agitation, and the impediments thrown in the way of enrolment proved its value.' On the basis of his emotional but shaky logic Jonathan Barber declared that he would now support it, and was followed by Henry Dorman who did the same 'as he now saw that the land question was to be made subsidiary to the Charter. (Cheers).' A vote was then taken 'and the original motion was carried by an immense majority – only sixteen hands out of the large meeting being held up for the amendment.'[527]

The *Northern Star* reported in its next edition that the Land Plan had been altered and on the Monday following another Chartist meeting was held. Henry Dorman asked Mr Morrison for an explanation of the 'altered plan'. The twists and turns in the process of attempting to register the Land Plan were now well under way. Morrison replied that the alteration entailed the removal of the principles of the Land Plan from the registration document in order to improve its chances of being accepted for registration. Morrison himself disagreed with this change being made without the approval of the convention delegates and the meeting proceeded to vote unanimously against the alteration.

At this point it would seem that there was a majority in favour of the Land Plan but disquiet about the methods being used to secure its

---

[526] *Nottingham Review*, 13th October 1843.
[527] Ibid.

legality, while those who opposed it believed it would undermine the campaign for the six points of the Charter and that it was too impractical to succeed. Both sides in this debate were not alone in underestimating the popularity that the Land Plan would engender. In the same month Christopher Doyle, a Chartist from Manchester and a member of the NCA Executive, spoke on the Land Plan at meetings in Hucknall, Radford and Carrington.[528] It was reported that at Carrington the members were keen to join as soon as it was enrolled.

Christopher Doyle and Philip McGrath were allies of O'Connor and were both active in promoting the Land Plan. McGrath was twice in Nottingham in January 1844, addressing meetings at the New Inn at Carrington, at the Democratic Chapel, and at Arnold, but although plans were made and remade at national level during the year, at local level the Land Plan was dormant while other matters took precedence. The Masters and Servants Bill was attracting the attention of Chartists in Radford; petitions were being circulated in support of Thomas Cooper, Leicester Chartist, who had been convicted of sedition and imprisoned in Stafford gaol; funds were being raised to pay off the expense of defending the victims of the Battle of Mapperley Hills; and plans were being considered for a working men's hall in the town.

Meanwhile, the Reverend James Orange was promoting another kind of allotment scheme. Speaking at a meeting of the Footpaths Protection Association in Nottingham in August 1844 he condemned local landowners for stopping up the footpaths. He wished, he said, 'not only to see the poor man open to himself a way across the fields, but he would like to see him permanently located on the land, with his cottage and his garden.'[529] Orange had been promoting the idea of allotments and land settlement since publishing 'A Plan for the Poor' in 1841 and registering the Nottingham and Midland Counties Artisans' and Labourers' Friendly Society, for which he became the travelling agent in 1842. The friendly society and the cottage garden scheme aimed to 'encourage industry, education, temperance and morality' and had the support of some of the middle class lace and hosiery manufacturers of the town.[530]

---

[528] *Nottingham Review*, 2st October 1843.
[529] *Nottingham Review*, 16th August 1844.
[530] *James Orange and the Allotment System*, R A Church, in Transactions of the Thoroton Society, 1964.

Despite his averred wish to see the poor resettled on smallholdings, his allotment plan was for quarter acre plots where 'instead of frequenting the pot house ... they work early and late in the gardens.'[531] Local landowners the Duke of Portland and Earl Manvers put aside land for allotments, and when the Earl of Chesterfield did so he was so impressed by the improvement in the morals of his tenants – evinced by the reduction in poaching on his land – that he turned an additional 25 acres of land into allotments. The socialists were not impressed. 'The question of allotments is now going the round of the counties. Its discussion appears to ease the conscience of the landowner, and cast a gleam of hope over the condition of the labourer', commented the *New Moral World*.[532]

James Orange and his allotment plans were not popular with local Chartists either. In response to questions on his attitude towards the New Poor Law, he had expressly stated that he had no comment to make on it.[533] He made his political motivations abundantly clear in 1845. 'Encouragement is better than fines to provide good order' he told the readers of the *Nottingham Review* in a letter recommending his allotment plan.[534] Pressed to explain his views on the Chartist Land Plan when it was attracting large numbers of members in the summer of 1846 he refused to pass any positive comment and responded irritably that he would 'never again attempt to answer any question respecting Mr O'Connor or his movement.' He was denounced by the few Chartists in his audience. 'The opinion here is that Mr Orange is sent out by the Whigs to bid for popularity at the next general election' was their verdict.[535] This was, however, an unintended acknowledgement that allotments and residential smallholdings were popular among the urban working classes, regardless of who sponsored them, and after the 1845 Enclosure Act the possibility of acquiring one increased considerably.

William Hill, editor of the *Northern Star* speaking in Arnold in 1843, had noticed the number of allotments bought with the money workers had withdrawn from savings banks and commented that 'Their money will always be used for their benefit and not for their oppression'.[536] He was

---

[531]   Ibid.
[532]   *New Moral World*, 24th December 1844.
[533]   *Nottingham Review*, 16th April 1841
[534]   *Nottingham Review*, 17th January 1845.
[535]   *Nottingham Review*, 8th August 1846.
[536]   *Nottingham Review*, 4th August 1843.

probably referring to those allotments which were created on land that was not the property of the landed gentry but which the workers themselves owned, through their membership of the Arnold Community Society.[537]

By 1845 the Chartist Land Plan had developed to the point at which it could be brought to the Chartist convention at Manchester in April. The Nottingham delegate, Henry Dorman, was given a unanimous *carte blanche* mandate to 'support any plan to employ people upon the land, and to induce them to become members in the co-operative stores.'[538] Connecting the Land Plan with provision store co-operatives before the Land Plan even had a co-operative title suggests that the Land Plan was expected to entail a degree of communal organisation and activity and was perhaps intended as a final riposte to the opponents, though seemingly few in Nottingham, who had decried the Land Plan as a return to private land ownership and peasant farming.

The Convention approved the Land Plan, the Chartist Co-operative Land Society was unveiled and a committee was set up in May 1845 to draw up the rules. By May the names of towns where land society branches had been set up began to appear in the *Northern Star*, and in June a list of inaugural meetings was published, including one in Carrington on the 6th July which would appear to have been the first in Nottinghamshire. In August the first meeting of town shareholders was held in the Democratic Chapel and a committee elected. James Sweet was elected branch treasurer, and Abraham Widdowson, a Chartist from Carrington who was also involved in the Operatives' Hall Society, was elected branch secretary. They resolved to meet weekly from 8pm to 9pm every Monday to provide information and enrol new members.

In November 1845 the opinion of Counsel engaged by the NCA was positive: 'The object of the Society, though new in character is undoubtedly legal ... [it] should be duly enrolled under the Friendly Societies Acts'.[539] A further conference on the Land Society was held in Manchester in December, and Radford Chartist James Saunders was the Nottingham delegate. Amended rules were agreed and an application as made to have it enrolled as a friendly society in January 1846.

---

[537] *Arnold Community Society*, FS1/571/235, National Archives.
[538] *Nottingham Review*, 19th April 1845.
[539] *Nottingham Review*, 1st November 1845.

The Registrar of Friendly Societies, Tidd Pratt, rejected the application and a new set of rules were submitted and again rejected in July. In September Jonathan Barber addressed a meeting in Carlton on 'the benefits of Co-operation' and James Sweet explained the workings of the Land Society. The next month O'Connor reported that the application for enrolment had been rejected and the society was now provisionally registered as a joint stock company under the new name of the Chartist Co-operative Land Company. The provisional registration allowed the company to enrol shareholders and collect deposits from them but did not permit any trading activity or land purchase, and to complete the registration it was necessary for the signatures of one quarter of the shareholders to be attached to the registration document. In December 1846 the name was changed again, to the National Co-operative Land Company, but an attempt to complete the registration was unsuccessful and its registration remained provisional.

The Chartist land branches in Nottingham had been busy for more than a year enrolling members to the Society and collecting subscriptions and, in April 1846 when the first land ballot was held, George Clarkson became the first member from Nottingham to be successful, drawing twentieth place in the ballot for a 4 acre plot, followed in August by Radford lacemaker Charles Tawes who was successful in acquiring a 2 acre plot on the first estate at Herringsgate which was purchased and settled in 1846 and renamed O'Connorville.[540] Feargus O'Connor saw Mr Tawes as a splendid advertisement for the success of the Land Plan. 'Charlie', he said, 'had been shut up in a Whig bastille, separated from his wife and children. Now he has been reunited with them and lived in independence. Now he has four pigs in his sty. Would he have ever got them by sticking in Radford workhouse?'[541] Tawes was later interviewed by an undercover reporter from the *Nottingham Mercury* who extracted some damning comments from Tawes on the size of the pigs and the potatoes at O'Connorville, which he claimed were smaller than those in Nottingham, but after another visit from O'Connor he was quoted in the *Nottingham Review* as repudiating the report and describing the reporter as a 'scandalising vagabond.'[542]

---

[540] *Northern Star*, 25th April 1846; *Nottingham Journal*, 24th April 1846.
[541] *The Chartist Land Company*, Alice Hadfield, 1970.
[542] *Nottingham Review*, 8th October 1847; *The Chartist Land Company*, Alice Hadfield, 1970.

That the Land Plan was being operated outside the law was not considered to be a matter of great importance to many of its supporters, and when it was granted provisional registration as a company in October 1846 many felt that it was only a matter of time before full registration and legality were achieved. Co-operative and friendly societies, albeit on a much smaller scale than the Land Company, had operated outside the law as unregistered bodies for decades and many continued to do so, including some in which Nottingham Chartists had been engaged in promoting and running for several years. Their experience was that the protection for their funds arising from friendly society enrolment was minimal, and lack of registration implied no illegality and imposed no penalties, and the Land Company, despite its name, was still a 'Co-operative' organisation, it's title proclaimed it to be so, at least until March 1847 when it was again renamed and became the National Land Company.

The influx of subscriptions to the Land Society and Land Company during 1845 and 1846 had been so great and immediate that the sponsors had felt they had no alternative but to proceed with the plan in order to maintain morale, regardless of the legal situation. O'Connor told the Select Committee of the House of Commons in 1848 that 'The people [however] were, so fascinated, that the receipts went on at a speed which I had no reason to contemplate. As soon as they reached £4,000 I was determined to carry on the plan into instant operation.'[543]

Success bred more success. Land company branches were operating in Nottinghamshire in 1847 in Radford, Carrington, Nottingham, Mansfield, Mansfield Woodhouse, Sutton in Ashfield, Skegby, Worksop and Retford.[544] More local names appeared among those successful in the ballots for land and cottages: John Dennis from New Radford at Snigs End estate and Arthur Shaw from Nottingham for two acres at Lowbands in 1846; George Copp for three acres and Frances Wright and Nathaniel Lee from Nottingham for two acres in 1847 also at Lowbands; J Holmes and J Hoe from Nottingham for four acres at Charterville, G Close from Nottingham and John Lawton from Retford for three acres at Snigs End in 1848; and John Cogill from Newark for four acres at Great Dodford in 1848.[545]

---

[543] *Nottingham Review*, 21st July 1848.
[544] *Nottingham Review*, 15th October 1847.
[545] *The Chartist Land Company*, Alice Hadfield, 1970.

In the summer of 1847 an estate known as Heywood Oaks, south of Blidworth in Nottinghamshire, was put up for sale by auction and Feargus O'Connor put in the highest bid of £20,000 on behalf of the Land Company, but it was £4,000 below the reserve price and the bid failed.[546] Had it been successful it might have become the only Land Company estate outside of the cluster of estates located in the present counties of Oxfordshire and Gloucestershire.

In August a party of Nottinghamshire members of the Land Company went to the opening of the Lowbands estate, where there appeared 'some banners which had recently seen service at the Nottingham election, and many people with northern accents.'[547]

Illustration 22: A Chartist cottage at Charterville (Minster Lovell). Pictured in 2007.

In Carrington it was Benjamin Douse, active in the Chartist co-operative provision society in Carrington, who chaired meetings of the Land Company branch at the New Inn and he was elected to represent the Nottingham area at the Land Company Conference. By now the Company was reaching its peak with 600 branches in England, Scotland and Wales and its membership was said to be approaching 70,000.[548] The conference took place in September 1847 at a critical time. The provisional company

---

[546] *Nottingham Review*, 25th June 1847.
[547] *Land Reform and Working Class Experience in Britain and the United States, 1800-1862*, Jamie L Bronstein, 1999.
[548] *The Chartist Land Company*, Alice Hadfield, 1970.

registration would expire at the end of October and there was no prospect of complete registration being achieved within this time limit. The requirement to obtain the signatures of a quarter of all shareholders was proceeding, but at a cost of £3 15s for every hundred names the expense of registering them would have been prohibitive, and the attempt was eventually abandoned.[549] Company law was not designed for a mass membership organisation such as the Land Company had become and it was many years before legislation was achieved that would give a measure of recognition and protection to working class organisations engaged in trading activities, acquiring land or engaging in banking.

In October a well attended meeting of Nottingham members of the Land Company was held at the Seven Stars at Barker Gate, with William Hemm in the chair. The growing tide of press denigration of O'Connor was condemned and a committee, including veteran radical Thomas Roper, was elected to raise funds to support O'Connor against those who were attempting to unseat him from Parliament.[550] The following week another meeting was held, at the Guildhall. Despite the size of the meeting room, it was almost full to capacity and the meeting was constantly interrupted by latecomers trying to get in. Henry Dorman spoke on the Land Plan and 'the advantages to be derived from going upon the land, physically, morally, intellectually, socially and politically.'[551] Subscriptions to the Land Company continued to flow in.

The year 1848 began with near record levels of subscriptions being received for the Land Plan in Nottinghamshire. In the single week ending 8th January national receipts totalled £2,432 and from Nottingham £44 12s 6d.[552] Two months later another attempt was made to gain registration of the Land Plan as a friendly society. A report appeared in the *Northern Star* in March: 'Mr O'Connor has just concluded a splendid speech of an hour and a half's duration, and has obtained leave to bring in a bill to extend the law of Friendly Societies to embrace the National Land Company and the Oddfellows.' It continued in highly optimistic vein. 'Sir George Grey treated the subject in a fair and dignified manner, assuring the Honourable Member for Nottingham that he was in error, if he supposed

---

[549] *Some Practices and Problems of Chartist Democracy*, Eileen Yeo, 1982.
[550] *Nottingham Review*, 22nd October 1847.
[551] *Nottingham Review*, 29th October 1847.
[552] *Nottingham Review*, 14th January 1848.

that there was any intention on the part of the government or the House to refuse legal protection to the savings of the poor.'[553]

The Bill was presented to Parliament by Feargus O'Connor and Thomas Wakley, surgeon and radical MP for Finsbury. It was supported by petitions, including one from Nottingham written by James Sweet with 104 signatures in which the petitioners declared themselves 'friends to Peace, Law, Order' but added that 'our social condition must be improved', a statement that has been interpreted as subtly invoking violence in retribution should Parliament reject the bill – which it did.[554]

By the autumn of 1848 the subscriptions had declined to a trickle. In the week ending 8th July they were a mere £89 15s 1d, and that was the total for the whole of England, Wales and Scotland. Nottingham's contribution accounted for £4 13s 3d. In August, after the government made it clear that changes to the Friendly Societies Acts would not embrace the Land Company, and that the Land Plan as operated was an 'illegal scheme', national receipts fell to £38 18s 4d, and Nottingham's contribution to £1 5s 4d. By October the national receipts were £17 3s 3d and Nottingham's part of it a mere 2s 6d.[555] Apart from the New Radford branch no other branch in the Midlands had made a contribution since August. After October the *Review* stopped printing the reports.

Nottingham members of the Land Company had been amongst the most loyal and were still contributing small amounts when almost every other branch had abandoned the field. Even as late as August 1848 when the fortunes of the Land Plan were in what must have been recognised as terminal decline it was resolved 'That the best thanks of this meeting of members of the National Land Company are hereby given to the directors, for the faithful discharge of their duties, and for the determination evinced by them in repelling the attacks of a base, brutal, and corrupt press.'[556]

The Commons debates on O'Connor's bill resulted in the setting up of a Select Committee to investigate the Land Company. In July 1850 O'Connor petitioned Parliament to wind up the company and this was eventually

---

[553] *Northern Star*, 18th March 1847.
[554] *Land Reform and Working Class Experience in Britain and the United States, 1800-1862*, Jamie L Bronstein, 1999.
[555] *Nottingham Review*, 14th July; 25th August; 27th October.
[556] *Nottingham Review*, 25th August 1848.

carried out in 1851. The following year the first Industrial and Provident Societies Act recognised the existence of co-operatives in law for the first time, though without naming them as such.[557] Even so, they were still not protected against fraud, were not granted limited liability until another Act in 1862, and had to wait even longer before being able to carry out banking operations legally (the Co-operative Wholesale Society did so illegally until the law was changed). The Chartist Land Plan was by then long gone and memories of it fading. It was many years since O'Connor had been admitted to the lunatic asylum in Chiswick and his death in 1855.

For James Sweet the work incurred in connection with the Land Plan did not come to an end in 1848. He presided at the last Land Conference at the Snigs End estate in 1849, visited O'Connor in Chiswick lunatic asylum, and gave evidence on his mental health to the Lunacy Commission in 1853.[558] When William Goodchap, the man appointed to wind up the Land Company, arrived in Nottingham in 1856 to receive, over a period of three weeks, the claims made by company members for repayment of what was left of their investments, it was James Sweet who received or visited many of the company members in the town and presented on their behalf up to 400 members' claims totalling £1,400. He was, as always, methodical and not one of his claims was rejected, attracting a compliment from the barrister on the 'honourable and businesslike manner in which he brought forward his claims.'[559]

How far active Chartists were themselves involved in the Land Society as members has been the subject of some debate among historians. Regrettably the records of the Land Society and Company are incomplete but those which do exist include the names of 1,368 residents of Nottinghamshire and among them are some who are manifestly identifiable by their names, addresses and occupations as prominent Chartists: James Sweet, Martha Sweet, Benjamin Humphreys, Henry Mott from the Peacock Inn locality and James Saunders from Radford; James Anthony from Arnold; George Kendall from Sutton in Ashfield, among thirteen likely matches. Another eighteen appear to be known Chartists

---

[557] *Land Reform and Working Class Experience in Britain and the United States*, 1800-1862, Jamie L Bronstein, 1999.
[558] *James Sweet*, John Rowley, Dictionary of Labour Biography, 1977.
[559] *Nottingham Review*, 24th October 1856.

based upon their place of residence or occupation.[560] The absence of some can be satisfactorily explained by the loss of parts of the Land Company registers. The presence of many of the most active members in the surviving registers suggests that active Nottinghamshire Chartists were well represented among the company membership, and this reflects the broad support which the Land Plan enjoyed among active members in the town.

The registers of Land Company members make interesting reading. By gender, 8% of the Nottinghamshire members of the Land Company for whom records exist were women, a large proportion of whom worked in the lace trade. Of an estimated total Nottinghamshire membership of around 2,500 people that would equate to around 200 women members.[561] This is still a small proportion of the whole membership but double the rate of female membership calculated elsewhere.[562]

By occupation, 52% of all members for whom records exist were framework knitters or lacemakers. With shoemakers these three occupations accounted for 58.3% of the Land Company members.[563] This is identical to those which have been calculated for National Charter Association membership in Nottingham.[564] According to another source these occupations were even more significant at the level of Chartist leadership.[565]

By residence, 83% of Land Company members for whom records exist lived within the boundaries of the present day City of Nottingham, and 41% within the 1848 boundaries of the Town of Nottingham, with Basford and Radford contributing an additional 21% of the names.[566] Membership in Mansfield was almost non-existent, compared with the substantial numbers in Kirkby and Sutton in Ashfield where the membership consisted almost entirely of framework knitters.

---

[560] See Appendix 1 for 31 names in the Land Company registers identified as definite or likely active Chartists.
[561] See Appendix 2 for an analysis of women members of the Land Company.
[562] *Women's Politics in Britain 1780-1870: Claiming Citizenship*, Jane Rendall.
[563] See Appendix 3 for the analysis of occupations of members of the Land Company.
[564] See the sample of NCA members used by James Epstein in *Some Organisational and Cultural Aspects of the Chartist Movement in Nottingham*, 1982.
[565] A survey of the Chartist leadership in Nottingham increases the ratio of these occupations to 71.7%: see *1848: Chartism in Derby and Nottingham in the Year of Revolution*, Matthew Roberts, unpublished paper, 2011.
[566] See Appendix 3 for places of residence of members of the Land Company.

The full total of Land Company members in Nottinghamshire, estimated at around 2,500, is a reflection of the continuing appeal of an independent life of toil on the land that so many were prepared to make financial sacrifices to achieve. The fact that the company was the brainchild of a man derided by much of the press as egotistical and preposterous, and managed locally by men and women known to be Chartists, frequently marked down by the local press as dangerous scoundrels, is also a mark of the respect and trust in which they and their movement were held by those members. There are few enough opportunities to gauge the opinions of 'the people', voteless and voiceless, in contrast to those of 'the class' who governed their lives, but the Land Company is one, and it points to a conclusion different to that of most observers, contemporary and current alike. The evidence points to a close affinity between the members and the activists and the working population of Nottinghamshire in general.

Despite the failure of the Land Plan and the financial losses which members sustained from it, the appeal of allotments and smallholdings did not lessen, even if the appeal of rural living among town dwellers did not outlast the hungry forties. The Calverton Chartist George Harrison, speaking at the Labour Parliament in 1854, claimed that at least 300 land societies had emerged since the winding up of the Land Company, including 'half a dozen' in Nottingham.[567] William Wylie in his history of Nottingham published in 1853 said that 'Some years ago, according to William Howitt, there were seven thousand gardens in and around Nottingham, and the number has considerably increased. The taste for these gardens is general, and is a pleasing feature almost peculiar to the lace metropolis.'[568]

---

[567] Quoted in *We Only Wish to Work for Ourselves: the Chartist Land Plan*, Malcolm Chase, 1996.

[568] *Old and New Nottingham*, William Wylie, 1853.

Conclusion

By all recorded accounts, support for the Land Plan had been solid among Chartists in the lace metropolis almost from its inception. After initial doubts the critics, such as Henry Dorman and Jonathan Barber, were won over and remained committed and loyal to the end. This was not the case in every part of Britain, and there had been some prominent and vocal opponents of the plan, like Bronterre O'Brien, who remained consistently opposed to it.

For some historians, as for some Chartists, it was a diversion from political activity, a retrogressive move from collective urban industrial struggle to the individualism of the rural peasantry, promising no more than a return to the idiocy of rural life, a deviation from the class struggle.[569] For those who have hoped to find in Feargus O'Connor a nascent revolutionary leader, an Irish Robespierre or a Kossuth, his Land Plan was an embarrassment. Consequently the Land Plan has been ignored or understated in many histories of Chartism despite reputedly having at its peak some 70,000 subscribers.[570]

Even today there are few published accounts of the Chartist Land Plan and, in spite of the abundance of local and national reports in the *Northern* Star and other journals, the popularity of the plan has seldom been conceded. In Nottingham 'the Land Plan did not generate very much in the way of enthusiasm,' a local historian commented, and 'the romantic and quixotic desire to return to the land never succeeded in generating much more than a limited support amongst the workpeople of Nottingham.'[571] However, inspection of the Land Company registers shows evidence of Land Company membership in parts of Britain where there was no Chartist organisation at all. Where Chartism was active, and support for the Land Plan was organised, large numbers of members were recruited. This was the case in Nottingham, where the occupational profile of the membership closely reflected the local economy, and where

---

[569] I am aware that 'idiocy' should now be re-translated as 'isolation', but as Marx was referring to the conditions of rural life and not to the peasants, the original seems perfectly apt.

[570] Withering attacks on the land plan – 'the next great folly' – were made by the Chartist and contemporary historian of Chartism, Robert Gammage in *A History of the Chartist Movement*, 1894.

[571] *Nottingham Chartism*, Peter Wyncoll, 1966.

active Chartists were intimately involved both as individual members and as active organisers of the scheme. This is a conclusion which challenges the orthodox view of the Land Plan.

Owenite socialism has met with a similar fate from contemporary observers and historians. Robert Owen, despite Engels' eulogy – 'Every social movement, every real advance in England on behalf of the workers links itself on to the name of Robert Owen'[572] – has been written off as a benevolent autocrat, a weaver of fanciful dreams, and the socialist movement which grew from his ideas derided as impractical, based on ideas which 'the more completely they were worked out in detail, the more they could not avoid drifting off into pure phantasies.'[573] In short, 'Utopian.'

The association between socialism and the infidelism of prominent socialists who lectured in Nottingham, such as Emma Martin, Margaret Chappellsmith and Robert Cooper, probably helped to ensure that many supporters would keep a low profile, the movement would gain notoriety and ridicule in press reports or, worse still for historians as well as for propagandists in their time, there would be a complete embargo on reporting. Yet the socialists had as good an analysis of the ills of society as the Chartists, and a clearer image of the kind of society they wanted to construct and, as James Rigby, social missionary from Salford, added during a debate with Chartists in Leicester in 1842, 'even if the Charter became the law of the land ... the people would have to begin new agitation for the reconstruction of society.'[574]

Co-operation, from the time of the Rochdale Pioneers especially, has also suffered at the hands of past and present historians. Original records of societies which had no long term ambitions, no world-making agendas, have not survived, the Blue Ball Club in Blidworth being a rare exception. Co-operative activity, after the collapse of the first movement after 1834, was disparate activity hidden from recorded history, ridiculed by newspapers such as the *Nottingham Mercury*, tainted by its association with failed socialist utopianism on the one hand, to being regarded as another irrelevant, diversionary, short lived activity among Chartists on the other.

---

[572] *Socialism: Utopian and Scientific*, Friedrich Engels, 1880.
[573] Ibid.
[574] *Leicester Chronicle*, 9th July 1842.

When Holyoake wrote *Self Help: History of the Rochdale Pioneers* he penned a tale that inaugurated the legend of the Pioneers. In so doing he perpetuated a myth that Chartists and co-operators were at daggers drawn. It was the socialists alone, he maintained, who originated co-operation. 'The fact is, the Chartists were impediments in the way of it. They were the most troublesome opponents the co-operators had to contend with. The Chartists were opposed to co-operation' he claimed.[575]

This may have been the case in Rochdale (although his own accounts are unconvincing) but it was not the case in Nottingham. There the socialists were few in number and, in comparison with their strength in Lancashire and London, ill-equipped to engage in rivalry with the Chartists had they motive to do so. In Nottingham the evidence credits the Chartists for espousing co-operation, not the socialists from whence that movement had originally sprung. Chartists were active in founding numerous co-operatives, including the society in Carrington whose shop and members were taken over by the Lenton and Nottingham Co-operative Society in 1877, and several Chartists – but most notably William Hemm – served that society almost into the last decade of the century. There is no evidence to suggest that the socialists in Nottingham in the 1840s were at all interested in co-operatives as a tool of social reconstruction.

The reasons for the continuing involvement of Chartists in co-operative societies would be something of a puzzle if their movement really had been a single issue campaign for the six points of the Charter, but it was not, as their participation in numerous political and social activities in Nottingham has established. What is perhaps puzzling is the role they chose for co-operatives in their campaign for the charter.

Exclusive dealing had been a very practical reaction to that section of the enfranchised middle class that working class men and women encountered daily, and whose overbearing manner towards them was remarked upon by the Nottingham Female Political Union. Exclusive dealing sought to combine the spending power of the working classes, as both a threat and an inducement to the 'shopocrats' to modify their hostility to the Chartist movement and vote for Chartist candidates. This campaign was a practical one at a time when most working men did not

[575] *Self Help by the People: A History of the Rochdale Pioneers*, G J Holyoake, 1858. For a modern interpretation see: *The Meaning of Rochdale; the Rochdale Pioneers and Co-operative Principles*, Brett Fairbairn, 1994.

have the vote, and as long as the ballot was not secret, but open and recorded, those who did have the vote could be subjected to persuasion by those who did not.

Co-operative societies, however, were a potential threat to all shopkeepers, whether supportive of Chartism or not, and could offer them no inducement, apart from winding-up their societies. There is no evidence that they even provided much in the way of financial support for Chartist campaigns, being joint stock companies in which most of the profit, if there was any, was distributed to shareholders. That so many co-operative societies were set up by Chartists indicates that their motives for doing so went beyond the electoral tactics which inspired exclusive dealing. For some Chartists this was a diversion from the immediate task. Ernest Jones, a Chartist and friend of both O'Connor and George Julian Harney, said 'No one can appreciate the value of Co-operation more than I do. It is what we must carry out when we have the political power – that is, the Charter; but if you think to get the Charter by means of commercial co-operation, you are bad coachmen, for you are putting the cart before the horse.'[576] It was a view that was not shared by Chartists in Nottingham.

The first successful Rochdale-model co-operative society in Nottingham – with open membership, low and fixed interest on capital invested, profits distributed as dividend on purchases not shares – was founded in Lenton many years after the Rochdale Pioneers had set up their society in 1844. Its originators were to be found, not from the socialist movement, nor from Chartism, but from non-conformism and temperance. Nevertheless, strands of almost every movement and campaign discussed in these chapters were carried forward by the new society for many decades to come, and it is through the early history of the Lenton Industrial & Provident Society that some of these strands will be brought together and this book concluded.

In the summer of 1858 the establishment of a Lenton Temperance Society was proposed. With the support of local leather manufacturer and Scotch Baptist, John Bayley, it took root almost immediately and soon had a Reading Room, in which evening lectures and meetings were held. Mutuality seemed to have a particular interest for them and in 1861 they discussed the rules of a Lenton Temperance Savings Bank, and in 1862

---

[576] *A History of the Chartist Movement*, Robert Gammage, 1894.

showed interest in the Nottingham Permanent Benefit Building Society.[577]

In March 1863 John Bayley, the son of Thomas, and Benjamin Walker, a local lace manufacturer, introduced Co-operation into the discussions at the Temperance Society. The following month Walker read some correspondence he had exchanged on Co-operation with gentlemen in Todmorden, Lancashire, and Islington, London. A week later a proposal to set up a co-operative society was agreed at a meeting in Bayley's factory in Leen Gate, Lenton, and the first 25 members were enrolled. A rule book was drawn up and approved by the Registrar and on 12th May 1863 the members elected a committee to run the 'Lenton Industrial and Provident Society Ltd'.

Illustration 23: Lenton Industrial & Provident Society, Branch No. 1, Abbey Street. The first branch from 1863 as it appeared a century later.

The new society's first registered address was at the Reading Room of the Lenton Temperance Society and there it remained for eleven years until their purpose built central premises in Greyfriar Gate were opened in 1874. The commitment to temperance among the founders of the co-operative society remained in effect for ninety years. It was not until 1952

---

[577] *Lenton Co-operative Society Ltd, Minute Book*, DD GN 1/1/2/1, Nottinghamshire Archives. The minute books and quarterly reports are the main sources for details of the society in this chapter.

that the Nottingham Co-operative Society, as it was now known, bought a private shop with a wines and spirits licence in Beeston and began to develop a licensed trade, a move which even then aroused dissension within the membership.

Owenite socialism had been thoroughly committed to sobriety, but the association of socialism with infidelity had put it beyond the bounds of acceptability by the religious temperance and teetotal reformers. Despite the number of activities and distractions they promoted as alternatives to alcoholic liquor, 'Secularism was one of the few reforming causes from which the teetotal leaders abstained.'[578] The rancour between religious and secular advocates of temperance which had persisted throughout the 1830s and 1840s did not dissipate until the rift had been made explicit.

The secretary of the new Nottingham Christian Temperance Society, set up in 1851, said that 'the old Temperance society was conducted in a measure by men professing Infidel principles, with the religious classes this became a stumbling block.'[579] David Heath, a solicitor's clerk in the Borough Coroner's office, and a recent adherent to Chartism, left the society after it refused to allow atheists, such as himself, to stand for office. Secularists responded, following a lecture in the Assembly Rooms by Robert Cooper, the former socialist missionary, in 1852, by setting up a Secular Society, which thenceforth met regularly at the Queen Adelaide in North Street, Sneinton. After that, the two movements went their separate ways.

When the Lenton and Nottingham Co-operative Society, as it was now styled, moved into their spacious new central premises at Greyfriar Gate in July 1874, the first organisation to book their fourth floor meeting hall for a course of lectures was the Secular Society, and they continued to meet there during the seven years in which the society had possession of the premises, before financial misfortunes led to its sale.[580] There they could meet in a welcoming environment and without the presence of alcoholic drink, and it was in the Co-operative Hall that Charles Bradlaugh, one of the founders of the National Secular Society, made his first appearance in the town, speaking on taxation reform in August 1874.

---

578 *Drink and the Victorians*, Brian Harrison, 1970.
579 *Drink and Temperance in Nottingham 1830-1860*, J J Rowley, 1974.
580 *Lenton Co-operative Society Ltd, Minute Book*, DD GN 1/1/2/1, Nottinghamshire Archives.

Unlike many other meeting room proprietors in the town in past decades, the co-operative society put freedom of association into practice and did not discriminate on the grounds of religion or non-religion: the second organisation to use the new hall was the Bible Defence Association. Richard Carlile, Emma Martin, all those radicals and reformers who had been refused hall bookings, and the proponents of an operatives' hall, would have applauded them.

The co-operative society had been founded on the initiatives of two major employers in the area, Thomas Bayley, who served as the first President, and Benjamin Walker, who was elected as the first Secretary and remained on the committee for sixteen years. Both men were active non-conformists with a strong interest in education. As dissenters they were not favourable to the local domination of children's education by the Anglican Church in Lenton and in 1871 they opened an non-sectarian school in a disused factory. In the first week of opening 194 children were enrolled and within three years school attendance had exceeded 400, by which time the buildings had become inadequate for their purpose. With other benefactors, plans were made for a new school to be built. The newly-established Lenton School Board, finding the plans would 'not interfere with the rates,' supported their project and the foundations were laid in 1873 by Benjamin Walker and A J Mundella, another man with co-operative connections, and the Lenton Unsectarian School opened in 1874 at its new location at the junction of Lenton Boulevard and Sherwin Road.[581]

The Lenton Co-operative Society made its first grant to an external organisation at the quarterly meeting of members in December 1867. It was for £10 and was made to the unsectarian British School, run on the Lancasterian monitorial system, in Arnold, where the society had recently opened a branch shop. This was the beginning of the society's commitment to education. In May 1871 they agreed that 'the crockery be lent to the Lenton Unsectarian School for their school treat, they to make all damages good,' and the December quarterly meeting in 1873 agreed that £50 be given to the Lenton Unsectarian School committee 'in

---

[581] *The History of the Parish and Priory of Lenton*, John Godfrey, 1884; *Old Nottingham Suburbs: then and now*, R Mellors, 1914. A J Mundella, Liberal MP for Sheffield and later a minister in Gladstone's cabinets, was a partner in a Nottingham hosiery company, living in The Park. He had been the President on day two of the Co-operative Congress in 1869, the first such Congress since the days of Robert Owen.

consideration of Lenton being the birthplace of this Co-operative Society.' In 1877 the Nottingham School Board took over the responsibilities of the Lenton School Board. The following year Mr William Hemm, former Chartist and now in his sixth year as a member of the co-operative society committee, was elected to the Nottingham School Board as a working men's candidate.

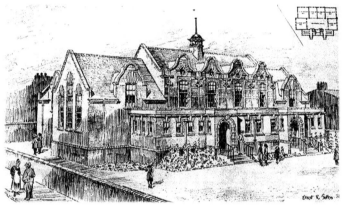

Illustration 24: Lenton Unsectarian School, Lenton Boulevard.
Pictured c. 1875.

William Hemm had been a founder member of the Nottingham Pioneer Co-operative Society, founded in 1874 to manufacture textiles and act as 'general dealers' at its premises at Woolpack Lane.[582] In conjunction with Matthias Mather, a colleague in that society, he had also made the first proposal to the Lenton and Nottingham Co-operative Society that a proportion of its profits be put aside quarterly for an educational committee of its own in 1877.[583] The subject was considered important enough for a Special General Meeting to be held on the subject. The proposal was very modest: that 0.25% of the profits be put aside for an educational department and a committee be elected to manage it, but it set the society on a path that led, not without some backward steps, to a substantial involvement in numerous educational, political and social activities in the years to come.

The forerunner of these activities were the tea meetings which the

---

[582] *Nottingham Pioneer Co-operative Society Ltd, Rules*, FS8/35/1761, National Archives; *Morris and Co., Directory*, 1877, Nottinghamshire Archives.
[583] *Lenton Co-operative Society Ltd, Minute Book*, 1/1/2/3, Nottinghamshire Archives.

society held whenever an occasion merited it. No doubt tea had been served at the Temperance Society meetings, as it had been at socialist meetings several decades earlier, and was considered suitable for an event where women as well as men were present. The first co-operative tea meeting was held in October 1863 in the month before the first store in Old Lenton was opened for business. Arrangements were made for 100 members to be seated, and white and brown bread, plum cake and seed cake, were provided for refreshment. Four months later another was held and this time 300 sat down to tea and heard the guest speaker, William Cooper, one of the Rochdale Pioneers, speaking on Co-operation. Soon after this the society began to subscribe to *The Co-operator*, and subsequently to the *Co-operative News*, and offered copies to local reading rooms. So began a corresponding commitment to blending social and propagandist activity, similar to that of the Chartists at the Democratic Chapel and the peripatetic socialists at various meeting places in the town.

The co-operative society began making donations to the General Hospital, starting with five guineas in 1869 and a two more of the same amount in 1871, and in 1872 they cast a vote in the election of an Honorary Surgeon, a practice repeated on many occasions in the years thereafter. The hospital had been founded in 1782 as a charitable institution and it was here that people infected by cholera had been brought in 1832, and where the dying and injured were brought from Garners Hill in 1844 after the execution of William Saville. Hospitals such as the General, 'open to the Sick and Lame poor of any County', were considered part of the community and were not accorded the opprobrium accorded to the 'Physicians, who produce no wealth, and little knowledge', in the words of the *New Moral World* in 1835.

The co-operative society also contributed to that holistic approach to health, in which illness and disease would be banished 'when the people were taught to live in accordance with natural laws', as James Sweet put it.[584] They did so by providing unadulterated foods, their committee resolving from the opening of their own bakery in 1864 that they would 'buy only such flour as is free from adulteration'; by prohibiting smoking in all their premises in 1870; by being among the first traders in the town to introduce an 'early closing day' for their staff; and by providing houses

---

[584] *Nottingham Review*, 5th January 1850.

for members, which they started to do in 1876.[585]

When the Women's Co-operative Guild was formed much later in the century, the society supported the establishment of Guild branches, initially in Nottingham and Arnold. By 1914 the Guild had around 30,000 members nationally, and was becoming a force to be reckoned with, having made their mark when they became the only working class women's organisation to submit evidence to the Royal Commission on Divorce law Reform. Refusing to submit to demands initiated by the Manchester and Salford Catholic Federation to stop campaigning for reform of the divorce laws, the Guild lost its annual grant from the Co-operative Union, which had taken a decision to appease the Catholic Church. The Guild branches in Nottingham were among the overwhelming majority which refused to be blackmailed by the Catholic Church or the Co-operative Union and maintained their stance until the grant was renewed. Robert Owen, Emma Martin, Margaret Chappelsmith and the infidels of 1844 would have been proud of them.

In 1926 when the Guild opened a birth control clinic in Market Street, believed to be only the third such clinic in Britain, it was an occasion which Susannah Wright and Richard Carlile would have looked upon with approval, even if it had taken a century since their presence in Nottingham to achieve.[586]

The co-operative movement was not the only working class movement in the latter part of the nineteenth century to promote social and political objectives such as those described here. Many other organisations and movements did so too, but the co-operative movement embraced a wider range of them than most, impelled as it was by the need to expand its retail, productive, social and educational services to a growing membership, and influenced in turn by the growing confidence of organised women and men in its membership.

When the Reform League resurrected the campaign for universal suffrage in the 1860s it did so without the social activities that had been part of Chartism in Nottingham, and it might be argued that it was all the more successful for doing so. Unlike Chartism it was indisputably a single issue campaign, which did not aim to remodel society or to create new

---

[585] *Lenton Co-operative Society Ltd, Minute Books*, DD GN 1/1/2/2/ and 1/1/2/3, Nottinghamshire Archives.
[586] *Women of Nottingham*, Nottingham Women's History Group, 2011.

forms of social ownership in the process. The Co-operative movement, from its inception, and increasingly from the latter part of the nineteenth century onwards, sought to do both.

Not every campaign waged by the socialists and the Chartists has been won. Chartists like James Sweet would be puzzled by the continuing failure to recognise the importance of equal sized districts in the electoral system, and the gerrymandering that is still employed at times of boundary revisions to disadvantage the dominant party's opponents.

Emma Martin and R T Morrison would be dumbstruck to find that the death penalty for murder remained in force until 1965, that it was challenged by Parliamentary vote every year for another 30 years, and was not finally abolished, for crimes such as espionage and mutiny in the armed forces, until 1998.

Susannah Wright and William Howitt would be astonished to learn that laws on blasphemy were not abolished until the twenty first century; that the Church of England has still not been dis-established; that the House of Lords still exists and Bishops still sit in it.

Robert Owen, Mary Ann and Jane Abbott, C H Clarke and William Hemm would have applauded the creation of four hundred and fifty Co-operative schools in Britain during the second decade of the twenty first century but would have difficulty in believing, after more than a century of almost universal, secular, education, that 'faith' schools would be encouraged as a matter of public policy, with all the potential to restore the religious discord of their own time two centuries ago.

And what would the campaigners who succeeded in thwarting the imposition of an Anglican chaplain on the Nottingham workhouse at the expense of the ratepayers in 1836 and 1838 have to say about the £29m being spent annually on chaplains in the NHS at the end of the first decade of the twenty first century? Messrs Kennedy, Burbage and Woodhouse must be turning in their graves.

In the twentieth and twenty first century histories of British social and political history, Co-operation has often been ignored, or reduced to the role of a worthy grocer. The role of the Co-operative movement in challenging the values and practices of a capitalist society have generally been ignored. More frequently the movement has been used as an indication that 'many workers no longer saw themselves as complete "outsiders": they had gained a stake, however tenuous and ambiguous, in the "system" '.[587] In this version of events, Co-operation then becomes part of that state of affairs, earnestly sought after by the founders of the Mechanics' Institute and the Artizans' Library many years earlier, in which the working classes would come to respect the rights of property, and would seek and gain for themselves 'respectability.'

At the end of the film *Men of Rochdale*, made by the Co-operative Wholesale Society in 1944, some of the founding Pioneers, most of them veteran Chartists and socialists, appear through the clouds with a series of questions and answers for their mortal audience below. Resplendent in suits and waistcoats, sporting compendious whiskers, with watches and seals that would be sure to have excited Mr Fagin, they are the epitome of respectability.[588] But their exchange with the narrator belies their appearance and is a challenging and a fitting place to close this narrative:

> Miles Ashworth: 'I was a Chartist. I believed that when men and women got the vote, the ballot box, and payment for MPs, they would use that power to create a co-operative social order. Have they done that yet?'

> Narrator: 'They have the vote, but they have not used it as you hoped they would.'

> William Cooper: 'I were a socialist. We socialists wanted to make a city of brotherhood, a city of light on a hill for all to see, free from poverty and crime and meanness. Is there such a city yet?'

> Narrator: 'Not yet, William Cooper.'

> William Cooper: 'Then there is still work to be done.'

---

[587] *The Growth of Working Class Reformism in Mid-Victorian England*, Neville Kirk, 1985.
[588] *History of Co-operation*, G J Holyoake, 1908: the compendious whiskers and the watch and seals are borrowed from Holyoake's description of Jack Tellall, the 'well-behaved co-operator' who originally appeared in the *Co-operative Mirror*, 1830.

Appendix 1: National Land Company Members identified as Chartists

There was no obligation upon members of the Land Company to be members of the National Charter Association or even to be supporters of Chartism, although few would have joined had they been opposed to it. This table represents an attempt to match the names of Nottinghamshire members of the Land Company contained in the surviving registers from 1847 and 1848, now stored in the National Archives, with the names of active Chartists whose names appear in newspaper reports and other sources. The NCA membership records for Nottinghamshire, from which direct matches might have been made, have not survived.

List A represents those Land Company members for whom there is a strong positive match with known local Chartists. List B represents those for whom the match is less certain. Addresses and occupations are as given in the registers. As some occupations e.g. 'framework knitter' were very common, and addresses are often abbreviated, for example 'Radford', it is possible that some of the matches in both lists, but especially List B, may be inaccurate.

Table A:

Land Company member:	Place of residence:	Occupation:
William Anderson	Independent St, Carrington	Lacemaker
James Anthony	Arnold	Framework knitter
John Blatherwick	New Sneinton	Framework knitter
John Higgins	Garden Place, Carrington	Labourer
George Kendall	Sutton in Ashfield	Stocking weaver
Benjamin Humphreys	Lees Yard, Nott'm	Framework knitter
Henry Mott	Goosegate, Nott'm	Currier
John Smitham	Carlton	Stockinger
James Saunders	Denman St, Radford	Druggist
Joseph Souter	Browney St, Nott'm	Stockinger
James Sweet	Goosegate, Nott'm	Bookseller
Martha Sweet	Goosegate, Nott'm	Wife of James
Ambrose Williamson	Club Row, Carrington	Lacemaker

Table B:

Land Company member:	Place of residence:	Occupation:
William Andrews	Arnold	Framework knitter
Alfred Anthony	Arnold	Framework knitter
Joseph Anthony	Arnold	Framework knitter
Jacob Bostock	New Lenton	Stockinger
William Dexter	Kyme St, Nott'm	Joiner
Samuel Etches	Pleasant Row, Hyson Green	Lacemaker
William Ginever	Drake St, Nott'm	Stockinger
Charles Hall	Crossland St, Nott'm	Stockinger
Charles Oates	Sherwood	Stockinger
Thomas Oldknow	Sneinton Elements	Stockinger
William Oxley	Reform St, Sutton in Ashfield	Stockinger
Charles Poyser	Malt Court, Nott'm	Pattern ring maker
James Proctor	Cambridge St, Nott'm	Shoemaker
Joseph Saunders	Market Place, Carrington	Parish officer
John Sharp	Old St, Nott'm	Stockinger
William Sheppard	Orchard St, Radford	Machine builder
Joseph Simons	Wakefield Buildings, Radford	Shoemaker
Samuel Taylor	Chilwell	Stockinger

Appendix 2: Nottinghamshire Women Members of the National Land Company

The surviving registers of the Land Company contain the names of 113 women resident in Nottinghamshire, which is 8.3% of all Nottinghamshire members:

Place of residence:		Occupations:	
Town of Nottingham	52	Lace trades	32
Old and New Radford	13	Framework knitters	5
Old and New Lenton	10	Other lace/woollen/cotton	12
Old and New Basford	6	Servant	13
Hyson Green	4	Housekeeper	5
Bulwell	3	Dressmaker, seamstress	11
Sneinton	3	Milliner, bonnet maker	7
Lambley	3	Laundress	2
Sherwood	2	Other occupations (1 of each)	18
East Retford	2	Widows	5
Newark	2	Spinster	3
Stapleford	2		
St Anns	1		
Arnold	1		
Carlton	1		
Stapleford	1		
Wilford	1		
Oxton	1		
Beeston	1		
East Leake	1		
Kimberley	1		
Kirkby in Ashfield	1		
West Retford	1		
TOTAL	**113**	**TOTAL**	**113**

Addresses within the present day City boundaries account for 84% of the names of women members, which is the same as for all names in the registers, and 46% are from within the 1848 boundaries of the Town of Nottingham, compared with a similar figure of 41% for all names.

The only direct evidence of the number of single women is the 9 who gave their occupations as widows or spinsters, approximately 10% of the total. Thirteen were entered in the registers alongside men of the same surname and address, which suggests that they were mothers, sisters, wives or daughters of the male members. In a very few cases there appear to have been entire families in membership of the Land Company, such as the 4 male shoemakers and 2 female servants named Jackson living in New Lenton.

The Land Company registers survive in three ledgers compiled in alphabetical order. Two of these contain 826 Nottinghamshire members with surnames beginning with the letters A to G and G to J. The third contains 542 Nottinghamshire members from A to Z, of which A to J members account for 43% of the total. If the 826 members with A to J surnames in the first two registers also accounted for 43% of the total, the missing 57% of the names K to Z would have added another 1,094 names, raising the true total of Nottinghamshire members of the Land Company by 80% from 1,368 to 2,462 (quoted in the text as 'around 2,500').

Applying the same calculation to the number of women members in Nottinghamshire, the true total of Nottinghamshire members would rise from 113 to 204.

Appendix 3: Addresses and Occupations of Nottinghamshire Members of the Land Company

Place of residence:	Numbers	%
Town of Nottingham	558	40.7
Old and New Basford	152	11.1
Old and New Radford	135	9.9
Old and New Lenton	73	5.3
Sneinton	67	4.9
Hyson Green	44	3.2
Carrington	46	3.3
Sherwood	11	0.8
Bulwell	39	2.9
Cinderhill	5	0.4
Bobbers Mill	5	0.4
St Anns	1	0.1
Sub-total City of Nottingham [2013]	**1,136**	**83.0**
Other Nottinghamshire addresses	218	16.0
Not given	14	1.0
Total Nottinghamshire	**1,368**	**100.0**

The Land Company registers survive in three ledgers compiled in alphabetical order. The table above has been compiled from these ledgers. See Appendix 2 for the method used to arrive at an approximate figure for the true membership of the Land Company. Applying this to the number of addresses in the 1848 Town of Nottingham, the true total of Town members rises from 558 to 1,005 members.

A total Land Company membership in Nottingham of 1,005 is close to the 900 claims from Nottingham presented to the winding-up manager William Goodchap in 1856.[589] This would represent about 2% of the Town population or about 10% of Town households.

Although 151 different occupations were given by members in the registers of the Land Company, almost half are accounted for by framework knitters and lacemakers and three quarters by the 10 occupations shown below. The figure of 91 shoemakers compares with 80

---

[589] *Nottingham Review*, 24th October 1856.

in membership of the NCA in 1842, confirming a similarity between the composition of Chartist membership and that of the Land Company. Shoemakers were a significant group in Nottingham Chartism, parading with their own 'Nottingham Association of Chartist Shoemakers' banner in the demonstration which welcomed O'Connor to Nottingham in February 1842.[590]

Occupations	Numbers	%
Framework knitter/stockinger	395	28.9
Lacemaker	313	22.8
Labourer	104	7.7
Shoemaker/cordwainer	91	6.6
Miner	27	2.0
Smith	24	1.7
Tailor	23	1.7
Joiner	16	1.2
Framesmith	13	0.9
Servant	12	0.9
Other occupations	350	25.6
Total	**1,368**	**100.0**

[590] *Nottingham Review*, 15th October 1842; 16th February 1842.

Appendix 4: Co-operative Societies identified in Nottingham and Nottinghamshire

This list includes all the societies discovered in Nottingham prior to 1850 and all those mentioned in the narrative. Many other societies were formed in Nottinghamshire after 1850.

1767   Blue Ball Club established in Blidworth, Nottinghamshire.

1770   Hucknall Torkard Mill Sick Society established.

1771   The Blue Ball Club at Blidworth began mutual trading.

1820   Houses at Hyson Green and Carrington built by societies of weavers.

1827   Owenite co-operators in Nottingham set up a community society.

1828   A co-operative society set up in Balls Yard, Hucknall.

1829   First Hucknall Torkard Co-operative Trading Association set up at Half Moon Yard, Hucknall.

1830   Hyson Green Co-operative Trading Association established at 1 Union Row.

1830   A co-operative society set up in Mansfield at Westgate.

1830   A co-operative society set up Mansfield at Ratcliff Gate.

1831   A co-operative society trading in Newark.

1832   A co-operative society trading in Milton St, Nottingham.

1840   Formation of the first society to be named Nottingham Co-operative Society.

1840   A co-operative society established at the Golden Fleece, Fisher Gate, Nottingham.

1840   Basford Co-operative Friendly Trading Association established at Dob Park, Nottingham.

1840   James Woodhouse managing co-op society at Hyson Green.

1840   Arnold Community Society established.

1841   Nottingham, Carrington & Sherwood Number 1 Co-operative Trading Association set up.

1841   Two co-operative societies trading in Arnold.

1842   Meeting at the Rancliffe Arms to establish a co-operative society.

1844   Meeting in Bloomsgrove Street, Radford establish a co-operative society.

1845   Provident Co-operative Society meeting at Dorman's Temperance Hotel, Nottingham.

1845   The first Chartist Co-operative Land Society branch set up in Carrington, Nottingham.

1847   Land Society branches functioning in Radford, Carrington, Nottingham, Mansfield, Mansfield Woodhouse, Sutton in Ashfield, Skegby, Worksop and Retford.

1847   Nottingham Co-operative Trading Association established at the King George on Horseback.

1847   'Workmens' own shop' trading in Glasshouse Street, Nottingham.

1847   Meeting at the Pelican, Radford to set up a flour mill society.

1850   'Co-op Labour and Provision Store' trading in Nottingham.

1854   Nottingham Bread and Flour Industrial Society established.

1857   Radford Co-operative Trading Association established.

1863   Lenton Industrial and Provident Society Ltd established.

1864   Hucknall Co-operative Society Ltd established.

1868   Arnold Industrial & Manufacturing Society Ltd established.

1869   Winding up of the co-operative society established in Balls Yard, Hucknall in 1828.

1872   Nottingham Co-operative Machine Building Society Ltd established.

1874   Nottingham Pioneer Co-operative Society established.

1874   Nottingham Industrial Co-operative Manufacturing Hosiers Society established.

1877   Carrington Co-operative Industrial Society wound up, Lenton and Nottingham Co-operative Society buys their shop.

Appendix 5: Map of Nottingham Libraries and various locations

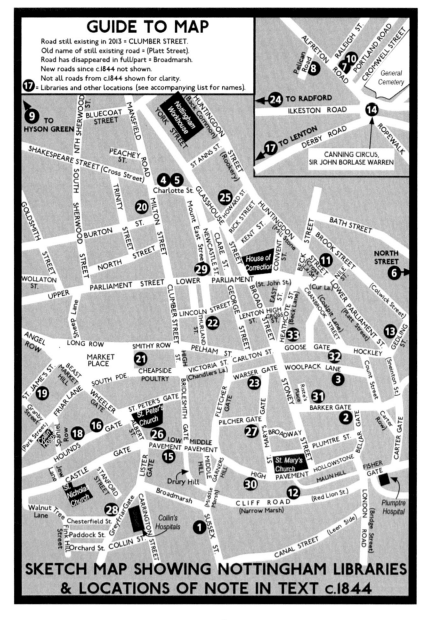

Guide to numbered locations:

Operatives' Libraries:
1. Operatives' Library No. 1, Rancliffe Arms, Turn Calf Alley, Sussex Street
2. Operatives' Library No. 2, Seven Stars, Barker Gate (moved to ...)
3. Operatives' Library No. 2, King George on Horseback, Woolpack Lane
4. Operatives' Library No. 3, Queen Caroline, Charlotte Street (moved to ...)
5. Operatives' Library No. 3, Pheasant, Charlotte Street
6. Operatives' Library No. 4, Queen Adelaide, North Street, Sneinton (off map)
7. Operatives' Library No. 5, White Swan, Alfreton Road (moved to ...)
8. Operatives' Library No. 5, Pelican, Pelican Road, Alfreton Road
9. Operatives' Library No. 6, Cricket Players, Hyson Green (off map)
10. Operatives' Library No. 7, White Swan, Alfreton Road
11. Castle Inn, Cross Street
12. Philomathean Book Divan, Loggerheads, Red Lion Street
13. Rancliffe Tavern, Gedling Street
14. Sir John Borlase Warren, Canning Circus
15. Temperance Operatives' Library, Low Pavement (moved to ...)
16. Temperance Operatives' Library, Houndsgate
17. Lenton Operatives' Library, Smith's Arms, Willoughby Street

Other Libraries:
18. Library for Females, Houndsgate
19. Mechanics' Institution, St. James Street (moved to...)
20. Mechanics' Institution, Milton Street
21. Artizans' Library, Exchange Hall (moved to...)
22. Artizans' Library, Thurland Street
23. Oddfellows, Barnsdall's Yard, Warser Gate
24. Radford Artisans' Library, Radford (off map)

Other Locations:
25. Sir Isaac Newton Inn, Howard Street
26. Assembly Rooms
27. The Theatre
28. Lenton Industrial & Provident Society buildings
29. Tradesmen's Mart
30. County Gaol
31. Democratic Chapel
32. Susannah Wright's bookshop

Bibliography

Primary sources – newspapers and journals:

The Crisis
The Charter
Chartist Circular
The Co-operative Magazine and Monthly Record
The Gauntlet
Herald of Co-operation
Leicester Chronicle
The Lion
London Dispatch and People's Police Register
Midland Counties Illuminator
The Movement
National Reformer
New Moral World
Nottingham Journal
Nottingham and Newark Mercury
Nottingham Review
Nottinghamshire Guardian
Northern Liberator
Northern Star
The Pilot
Poor Man's Advocate
The Poor Man's Guardian
The Prompter
The Reasoner
The Republican
Trades Newspaper and Mechanics' Weekly Journal

Primary sources – directories:

DEARDEN W, *Directory of Nottingham* (1834)
GLOVER, *Directory of Nottingham* (1844)
KELLY'S *Post Office Directory*, Nottingham (1855, 1876)
LASCELLE AND HAGAR, *Directory of Nottingham* (1848)
MORRIS AND CO, *Directory of Nottingham* (1869)
ORANGE, *Directory of Nottingham* (1840)
PIGOTT, *Directory of Nottingham* (1819, 1822, 1828, 1831, 1835, 1842)
PIGOTT, *Directory of Manchester* (1832, 1836, 1838)
SUTTON, *Directory of Nottingham* (1818)
WHITE, *Directory of Nottingham* (1832, 1844, 1853, 1864)
WRIGHT, *Directory of Nottingham* (1854, 1864, 1866, 1868, 1874)

Other primary sources:

Address to the Working Classes on Exclusive Dealing-1840, A Member of the Nottingham Co-operative Store, (GL 1840) University of London Senate Library

The Annual Register, or, A View of the History, Politics and Literature for the Year 1819 (Baldwin, Craddock and Joy 1820)

Borough Records (Nottingham) Volume 8, 1800-1835, Nottingham Local Studies Collection

Catalogue and Rules of the Operatives' Library No 1, 1843, Nottingham Local Studies Collection

Transcript of the Charter, (http://thefenwickweavers.coop/fenwick-and-the-co-operative-movement/transcript-of-the-charter/2013)

Greater Nottingham Co-operative Society, Reports, Minute Books, DD GN, Nottinghamshire Archives

Poll Book, Town of Nottingham, 1825, Nottingham Local Studies Collection

'Principles, Objects and Laws of the First Salford Co-operative Society', 1829, *British Labour Struggles: Contemporary Pamphlets 1727-1850* (Arno Press reprint 1972)

Robert Owen Correspondence Collection, Co-operative College Archive

Rules and Catalogue of the Artisans' Library, Radford, near Nottingham, 1839, Nottingham Local Studies Collection

To The Friends of Education, Scholars and Teachers of the Salford Co-operative School, 1833, University of London Senate Library

Unemployment in Nottingham (1837-38), Parliamentary papers, 1837, XXXI (http://www.victorianweb.org/history/poorlaw/nottingh.html)

Secondary sources:

ADAMS W E, *Memoirs of a Social Atom*, Volume 1 (Hutchinson 1903)

ASCHENBRENNER Caralee, *Please Don't Quote Me* (http://www.pacc-news.com/7-2-08/pdq7_2_08.html)

AUSTIN Michael, 'George Wilkins 1785-1865, Cleric and Polemicist', eds. CHAPMAN S and WALKER D, *Minster People* (Southwell Local History Society 2009)

BAILEY Thomas, *Annals of Nottinghamshire*, Volume 4 (Simpkin Marshall and Co 1852)

BAMFIELD Joshua, *Eighteenth and Nineteenth Century Consumer-Owned Community Flour and Bread Societies: Collective Response to Market Failure* (unpublished paper 1996)

BEARDSMORE J H, *History of Hucknall Torkard* (J Linney 1909)

BURKE E, *The Annual Register 1819* (Longmans 1819)

BELCHEM J, *Industrialisation and the Working Class* (Scolar Press 1991)

BELLAMY Joyce and SAVILLE John, 'Lloyd Jones', *Dictionary of Labour Biography*, Volume 1 (Macmillan 1972)

BELLAMY Joyce and SAVILLE John, 'Robert Cooper', *Dictionary of Labour Biography*, Volume 2 (Macmillan 1972)

BERGIN Tom, SHAW Stanley and PEARCE Dorothy, *Salford: A City and its Past* (City of Salford 1975)

BLACKNER John, *The History of Nottingham* (Charles Sutton 1815)

BLOCK Brian P and HOSTETLLER John, *Hanging in the Balance: A History of the Abolition of Capital Punishment in Britain* (Waterside Press 1997)

BOWEN Mary, *The Anglican Church in the Industrialised Town, St Mary's Parish, Nottingham, 1779-1884*, unpublished M Phil thesis (University of Nottingham 1997)

BRAKE Laurel and DEMOOR Marysa, *Dictionary of Nineteenth Century Journalism in Great Britain and Ireland* (Academia Press 2009)

BRINDLEY James, *The Marriage System of Socialism* (T Thomas 1840)

BRONSTEIN Jamie L, *Land Reform and Working Class Experience in Britain and the United States, 1800-1862* (Stanford University Press 1999)

BROWN W H, 'James Rigby' and 'Emma Martin', *Pathfinders* (Co-operative Union 1925)

BUSH M L, *What Is Love? Richard Carlile's Philosophy of Sex* (Verso 1998)

CAPLAN Maurice, 'The Poor Law in Nottinghamshire 1836-1871', *Transactions of the Thoroton Society*, (Thoroton Society 1970)

CAPLAN Maurice, *In the Shadow of the Workhouse: Implementation of the New Poor Law Throughout Nottinghamshire, 1836-1846* (University of Nottingham 1984)

CARLILE Richard, *Report of the Trial of Mrs Susannah Wright* (Carlile 1822)

CAUDELL Wini and others, *Early Settlers* (http://illinoisancestors.org/stephenson/ridott/earlysettlers.html)

CHAPMAN BROTHERS, *Portrait and Biographical Album of Stephenson County, Illinois*, Volume 2 (Chapman Brothers 1888) (http://genealogytrails.com/ill/stephenson/biohunt.html)

CHASE Malcolm, 'We Only Wish to Work for Ourselves: the Chartist Land Plan', eds. CHASE Malcolm and DYCK Ian, *Living and Learning: Essays in Honour of JFC Harrison* (Scolar Press 1996)

CHASE Malcolm, *Chartism: A New History* (Manchester University Press 2007)

CHURCH R A, 'James Orange and the Allotment System', *Transactions of the Thoroton Society* (Thoroton Society 1964)

CHURCH OF ENGLAND, *Nottingham St Mary*, (http://southwellchurches.nottingham.ac.uk/nottingham-st-mary/hhistory.php 2007)

CLAEYS Gregory, *Machinery, Money and the Millennium: from Moral Economy to Socialism 1815-1860* (Princeton University Press 1987)

CLAEYS Gregory, *Citizens and Saints: Politics and Anti-politics in Early British Socialism* (Cambridge University Press 1989)

COLLETT C D, *History of the Taxes on Knowledge* (T Fisher Unwin 1899)

COOK Alan, *History of Colwick*, (1970) (http://www.nottshistory.org.uk/books/colwick/colwick7.htm)

COOPE Rosalys and CORBETT Jane, *Bromley House 1752-1991* (Nottingham Subscription Library 1991)

COWIE Grace G and ROYLE Edward, 'Emma Martin', *Dictionary of Labour Biography* (Macmillan 1982)

CROSS Ira B, *Frank Roney Irish Rebel and Labour Leader* (University of California Press 1931)

CROSS Ira B, *A History of the Labour Movement in California* (University of California Press 1935)

DARLEY Gillian, *Villages of Vision* (Five Leaves 2007)

DONACHIE Ian, 'Orbiston: The First British Owenite Community 1825-29', *Spaces of Utopia: An Electronic Journal*, No 2, Summer 2006

THE EBENEZER FOUNDRY OF RESEARCH, *Ebenezer Elliott* (http://www.judandk. force9.co.uk/HatedEE.html)

ENGELS Friedrich, *Description of Recently Founded Communist Colonies Still in Existence* (Deutsches Bürgerbuch 1845) (http://www.marxists.org/archive/marx/ works/ 1844/10/15.html)

ENGELS Friedrich, *Socialism: Utopian and Scientific* (Lawrence and Wishart 1962)

ENGLISH ASMODEUS, *Revelations of Life In Nottingham* (1860)

EPSTEIN James, 'Some Organisational and Cultural Aspects of the Chartist Movement in Nottingham', eds. THOMPSON Dorothy and EPSTEIN James, *The Chartist Experience: Studies in Working Class Radicalism and Culture, 1830-60* (Macmillan 1982)

EPSTEIN James, *The Lion of Freedom: Feargus O'Connor and the Chartist Movement, 1832-1842* (Croom Helm 1982)

FAIRBAIRN Brett, *The Meaning of Rochdale: the Rochdale Pioneers and Co-operative Principles* (Centre for the Study of Co-operatives, University of Saskatchewan 1994)

FOSTER Peter, 'The Press and the Nottingham Cholera Outbreak of 1832', *Nottinghamshire Historian*, Autumn/winter 1989 (Nottinghamshire Local History Association 1989)

FRASER D, 'The Nottingham Press', *Transactions of the Thoroton Society* (Thoroton Society 1963)

FRASER D, 'Nottingham and the Corn Laws', *Transactions of the Thoroton Society* (Thoroton Society 1966)

FROW Edmund, *The New Moral World: Robert Owen and Owenism in Manchester and Salford* (Working Class Library 1986)

FULWIDER Addison L, *History of Stephenson County, Illinois* (S J Clarke, Chicago 1910) (http://archive.org/stream/historyofstephenv1fulw#page/n5/mode/2up)

FRY Terry, *The History of Carrington* (1999)

GAFFIN Jean and THOMS David, *Caring and Sharing: The Centenary History of the Co-operative Women's Guild* (Co-operative Union 1983)

GAMMAGE R, *A History of the Chartist Movement* (Browne & Browne 1894)

GENEALOGY TRAILS, *Ridott Township, Stephenson County, Illinois,* (http://www.genealogytrails.com/ill/stephenson/cityridottwp.html)

GLEADLE Katherine, 'Margaret Chappellsmith', *Dictionary of National Biography* (Oxford University Press 2004)

GODFREY John, *The History of the Parish and Priory of Lenton* (1884)

GORDON Peter, 'Robert Owen', *Prospects: the quarterly review of education*, Volume 24 (UNESCO: International Bureau of Education 1994) (http://www.ibe.unesco. org/fileadmin/user_upload/archive/publications/ThinkersPdf/owene.PDF)

GOSDEN P H J, *The Friendly Societies in England, 1815-1875* (Manchester University Press 1963)

GOSDEN P H J, *Self Help: Voluntary Associations in 19th Century Britain* (Batsford 1973)

GOULD F J, *The History of the Leicester Secular Society* (Leicester Secular Society 1900)

GRAVELROOTS, *Richard Cobden* (http://www.gravelroots.net/history/cobden.html 2006)

GREEN John A H, *History of the Nottingham Mechanics' Institution 1837-1887* (Stephenson, Bailey and Smith 1887)

GRIFFIN Colin, 'Chartism and Opposition to the New Poor Law in Nottinghamshire: the Basford Union Workhouse Affair of 1844', *Midland History*, Volume 4 (Maney 1974)

GURNEY Peter, 'Exclusive Dealing in the Chartist Movement', *Labour History Review*, Volume 74 (Society for the Study of Labour History 2009)

HADFIELD Alice, *The Chartist Land Company* (David and Charles 1970)

HALL Robert G, 'Hearts and Minds: The Politics of everyday Life and Chartism, 1832-1840', *Labour History Review*, Volume 74 (Society for the Study of Labour History 2009)

HANSARD, *House of Commons*, 25 March 1819, Volume 39, (http://hansard.millbank systems.com/commons/1819/mar/25/friendly-and-parochial-benefit-societies)

HARRISON Brian, *Drink and the Victorians* (Faber and Faber 1971)

HARRISON F M, 'The Nottingham Baptists: The Political Scene', *The Baptist Quarterly*, 1978 (Baptist Historical Society 1978)

HARRISON J F C, *Robert Owen and the Owenites in Britain and America* (Routledge & Kegan Paul 1969)

HILLQUIT Morris, *History of Socialism in the United States* (Russell and Russell 1903)

HOARE Peter, 'The Operatives' Libraries of Nottingham: a Radical Community's Own Initiative', *Library History*, Volume 19, No 3 (Maney Publishing 2003)

HOARE Peter, 'The Library World of Nottinghamshire in the 18th and Early 19th Century', *Transactions of the Thoroton Society* (Thoroton Society 2010)

HOLLIS Patricia, *The Pauper Press* (Oxford University Press 1970)

HOLYOAKE G J, *History of Co-operation* (T Fisher Unwin 1908)

HOLYOAKE G J, *The Last Days of Mrs Emma Martin, Advocate of Freethought* (Watson 1851)

HOLYOAKE G J, *The Social Means of Promoting Temperance* (University Press 1860)

HOLYOAKE G J, *A Visit to Harmony Hall, 1844* (Arno Press 1972)

HOLYOAKE G J, *Self Help by the People: The History of the Rochdale Pioneers* (Allen and Unwin 1893)

HOVELL Mark, *The Chartist Movement* (University Press 1918)

ILIFFE R and BAGULEY W, *The Mechanics' Institute: A Story in Pictures*, Volume 14 (Nottingham Historical Film Unit 1975)

JANES D, 'Emma Martin and the manhandled womb in early Victorian England', MANGHAM A and DEPLEDGE G *The Female Body in Medicine and Literature* (Liverpool University Press 2011). (http://eprints.bbk.ac.uk/4240/3/4240.pdf)

JONES Lloyd, *The Life, Times, and Labours of Robert Owen*, Volume 2 (Labour Association 1889)

KIRK Neville, *The Growth of Working Class Reformism in Mid-Victorian England* (Croom Helm 1985)

KNIGHT Frances, *Nineteenth Century Church and English Society* (Cambridge University Press 1996)

KOLMERTON Carol A, *Women in Utopia* (Indiana University Press 1990)

LAMBOURNE D, *Slaney's Act and the Christian Socialists* (Boston 2008)

LEEMAN F W, *Co-operation in Nottingham* (Nottingham Co-operative Society 1963)

LEES Frederick R, *The Book of True Temperance* (Trubner 1871)

LONGMATE Norman, *The Water Drinkers: a History of Temperance* (Hamish Hamilton 1968)

LOWERY Andrew, 'Address to the Fathers and Mothers, Sons and Daughters, of the Working Classes, on the System of Exclusive Dealing, and the Formation of Joint Stock Provision Companies, Shewing How the People May Free Themselves from Oppression', HARRISON Brian and HOLLIS Patricia, *Robert Lowery: Radical and Chartist* (Europa 1979)

McFADZEAN John and SMITH John, *A History of the Fenwick Weavers* (East Ayrshire Communities Federation 2008)

McCALMAN Iain, *Popular Radicalism and Freethought in Early Nineteenth Century England*, unpublished MA thesis (University of Nottingham 1996)

MARTIN Emma, *A Few Reasons for Renouncing Christianity and Disseminating Infidel Opinions* (Watson 1850)

MARTIN Emma, *The Missionary Jubilee Panic and the Hypocrites Prayer addressed to the Supporters of Christian Missions* (Hetherington 1844)

MARTIN Emma, *Religion Superseded* (Watson 1850)

MARTIN Emma, *The Punishment of Death* (Watson 1849)

MELLORS Robert, *Old Nottingham Suburbs: then and now* (J & H Bell 1914)

MERCER T W, *Co-operation's Prophet* (Co-operative Union 1947)

MINISTRY OF HEALTH, *Basford Board of Guardians*, MH/12/9234/41, National Archives.

MOGG Edward, *New Picture of London and Visitor's Guide to its Sights.* (E Mogg 1844) (http://www.victorianlondon.org/entertainment/colosseum.htm)

MORRELL Robert, 'Freethought in Nineteenth Century Nottingham', *Journal of Freethought History*, Volume 1, No 8 (Freethought History Research Group 2010)

MORRIS George, 'Primitive Methodism in Nottinghamshire', *Transactions of the Thoroton Society* (Thoroton Society 1968)

MORRISON R T, 'Class Legislation Exposed: or Practical Atheism Identified with the Advocates of Property Qualification for Legislative Enfranchisement' (1841), CLAEYS Gregory, *Chartist Movement in Britain 1838-52*, Volume 2 (Pickering and Chatto 2001)

NASH David, ed. *Blasphemy in Britain and America 1800-1930*, Volume 2 (Pickering and Chatto 2011)

NOTTINGHAM WOMEN'S HISTORY GROUP, *Women of Nottingham* (http://www.nottinghamwomenshistory.org.uk/Woman's%20History%20Group%20Booklet.pdf 2011)

ORANGE James, *History and Antiquities of Nottingham* (Hamilton Adams 1840)

O'NEILL Julie, 'Friendly Societies in Nottinghamshire', *Nottinghamshire Historian*, No 41, autumn/winter 1988 (Nottinghamshire Local History Association 1988)

O'NEILL Julie, *In the Club: Female Friendly Societies in Nottinghamshire 1792-1913* (Trent Valley Local Group 2001)

OWEN Robert, *A New View of Society*, 1813 (Penguin 1969)

PAROLIN Christina, 'The She-Champion of Impiety: A Case Study of Female Radicalism', eds. DAVIES Michael T and PICKERING Paul A, *Unrespectable Radicals?* (Ashgate 2007)

PARSONS A V, *Education in the Salford District 1780-1870* (Manchester University Press 1963)

PORTER Roy, *Disease, Medicine and Society in England 1550 1860* (Macmillan 1987)

PORTER Roy, *The Popularization of Medicine 1650-1850*, (Routledge 1992)

PURVIS M, 'Co-operative retailing in England 1835-1850: developments beyond Rochdale', *Northern History* (Northern History 1986)

RENDALL Jane, *Women's Politics in Britain 1780-1870: Claiming Citizenship* (http://www.keele.ac.uk/history/currentundergraduates/tltp/WOMEN/RENDELL /CORE1.HTM)

RICHARDS Will, *Blidworth at Work and Play* (1993)

RICHARDSON Ruth, *Death, Dissection and the Destitute* (Phoenix 1988)

ROBERTS Matthew, *1848: Chartism in Derby and Nottingham in the Year of Revolution*, (unpublished paper 2011)

ROWARTH W, *Observations on the Administration of the Poor Law in Nottingham* (1840)

ROWLEY J J, *Drink and Temperance in Nottingham 1830-1860*, unpublished MA dissertation (Leicester University 1974)

ROWLEY J J, 'James Sweet', *Dictionary of Labour Biography* (Macmillan 1977)

ROWLEY J J, 'Drink and the Public House', *Transactions of the Thoroton Society* (Thoroton Society 1975)

ROYLE Edward, *Radical Politics 1790-1900: Religion and Unbelief* (Seminar Studies in History 1971)

ROYLE Edward, *Robert Owen and the Commencement of the Millennium* (Manchester University Press 1998)

ROYLE Edward, *Victorian Infidels* (Manchester University Press 1974)

SAXTON Alexander, *The Indispensable Enemy: Labor and the anti-Chinese Movement in California* (University of California Press 1971)

SHELLEY Percy Bysshe, *The Mask of Anarchy* (1819)

SHEPPERSON W, British Emigration to North America (Basil Blackwell 1957)

SILVER Harold, *Concept of Popular Education* (McGibbon and Kee 1965)

SMITH Adam, *An Enquiry into the Nature and Causes of the Wealth of Nations* (1776)

SMYLES John, *Emigration to the United States* (Watson 1842)

STEWART W A C and McCANN W P, *The Educational Innovators 1750-1880* (Stewart 1967)

SUTTON Richard, *Nottingham Date Book 1750-1850* (R Sutton 1852)

TAYLOR Barbara, 'Emma Martin', *The Oxford Dictionary of National Biography* (Oxford University Press 2004)

TAYLOR Barbara, *Eve and the New Jerusalem* (Harvard University Press 1993)

THOLFSEN Trygve, *Working Class Radicalism* (Croom Helm 1976)

THOMAS Adam W, *A History of the Nottingham High School 1513-1953* (J & H Bell 1957)

THOMIS M I, *Politics and Society in Nottingham* (Blackwell 1969)

THOMIS M I and GRIMMETT J, *Women in Protest* (St Martin's Press 1982)

THOMPSON David J, *Weavers of Dreams* (Twin Pines Press 2012)

THOMPSON Dorothy, *The Early Chartists* (Macmillan 1971)

THOMPSON Dorothy, *The Chartists, Popular Politics in the Industrial Revolution* (Pantheon Books 1984)

TSUZUKI C, 'Robert Owen and Revolutionary Politics', eds. POLLARD S and SALT J, *Robert Owen, Prophet of the Poor* (Macmillan 1971)

TYLECOTE M, *Mechanics' Institutes of Lancashire and Yorkshire* (Manchester University Press 1957)

VINCENT David, *Bread, Knowledge and Freedom* (Methuen 1982)

WALKER J H, 'The Salem Chapel', *Transactions of the Thoroton* Society (Thoroton Society 1927)

WALKER Martyn A, 'The Nottingham Cholera Epidemic of 1832', *Transactions of the Thoroton* Society (Thoroton Society 1991)

WARDLE David, *Education and Society in Nineteenth Century Nottingham* (Cambridge University Press 1971)

WARREN J C, 'The Life of John Blackner', *Transactions of the Thoroton Society,* Volume 30 (Thoroton Society 1926)

WATTS M R, *Religion in Victorian Nottinghamshire: the Religious Census of 1851* (University of Nottingham, Adult Education Dept. 1998)

WEST Julius, *A History of the Chartist Movement* (Constable 1920)

WHEELER J M, *Biographical Dictionary of Freethinkers* (Progressive Publishers 1889)

WHITWORTH J C, *Blidworth: The History of a Forest Town* (Nottingham 1973)

WICKWAR William, *The Struggle for the Freedom of the Press 1819-1832* (Allen and Unwin 1928)

WIENER Joel, *The War of the Unstamped* (Ithaca 1969)

WOLVERHAMPTON HISTORY AND HERITAGE, *Union Mill* (http://www.historywebsite.co.uk/Museum/OtherTrades/BCN/UnionMill.htm)

WOOD A C, 'An Episode in the History of St Mary's Church, Nottingham', *Transactions of the Thoroton* Society (Thoroton Society 1952)

WYLIE William, *Old and New Nottingham* (Longmans 1853)

WYNCOLL Peter, *Nottingham Chartism* (Nottingham and District Trades Council 1966)

YEO Eileen, 'Robert Owen and Radical Culture', eds. POLLARD S and SALT J, *Robert Owen, Prophet of the Poor* (Macmillan 1971)

YEO Eileen, 'Some Practices and Problems of Chartist Democracy', eds. EPSTEIN James and THOMPSON Dorothy, *The Chartist Experience: Studies in Working-Class Radicalism and Culture, 1830-1860* (Macmillan 1982)

Index